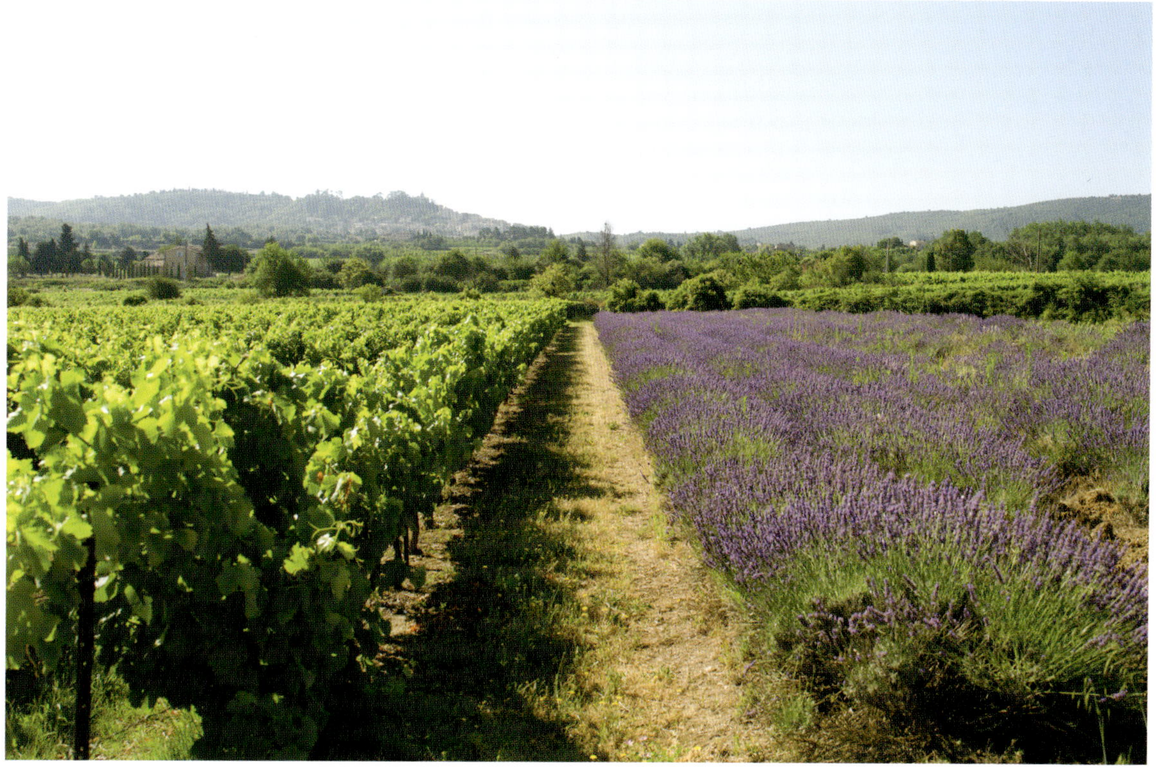

WINTER

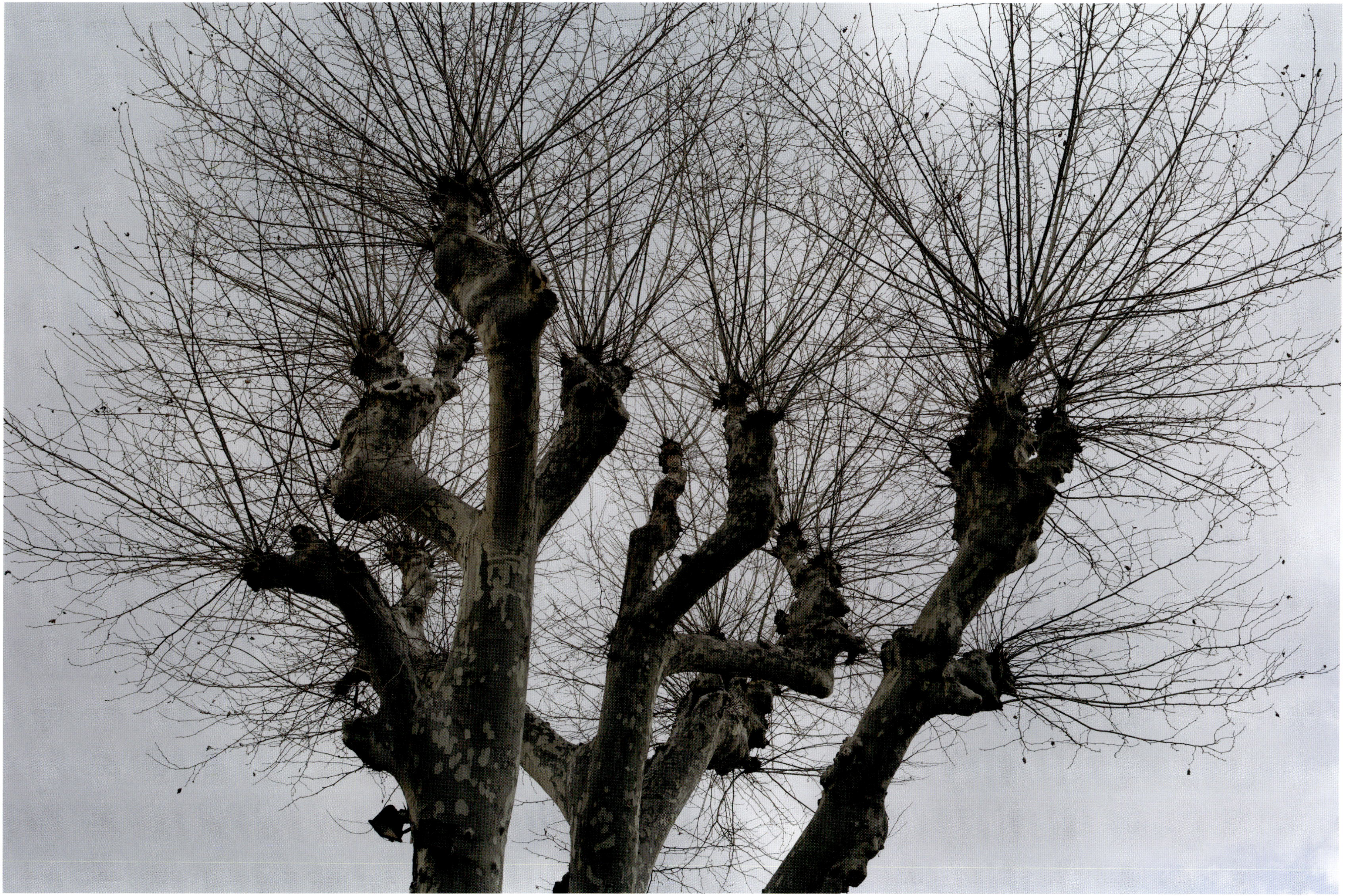

PLATE 1

SPRING

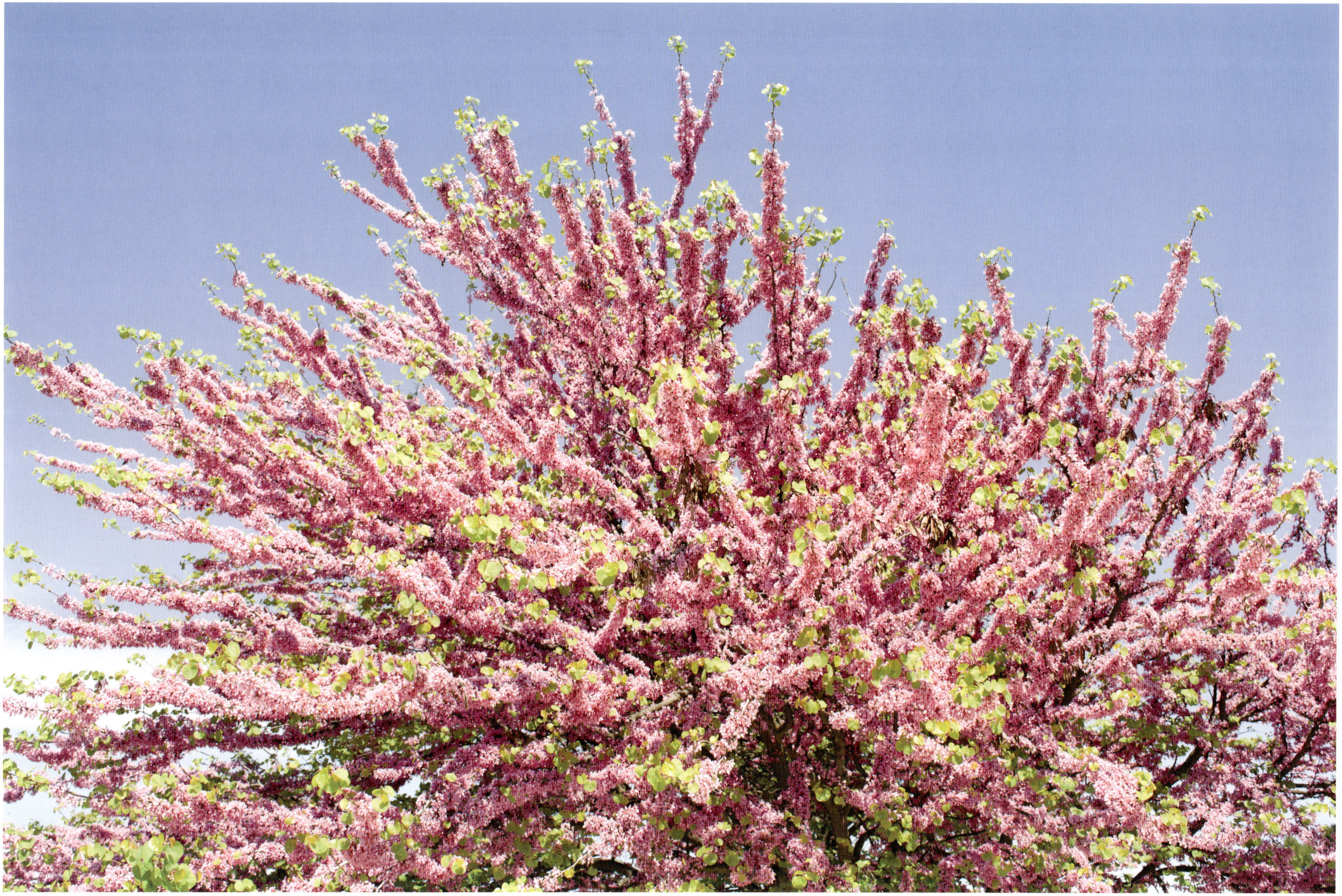

PLATE 2

SUMMER

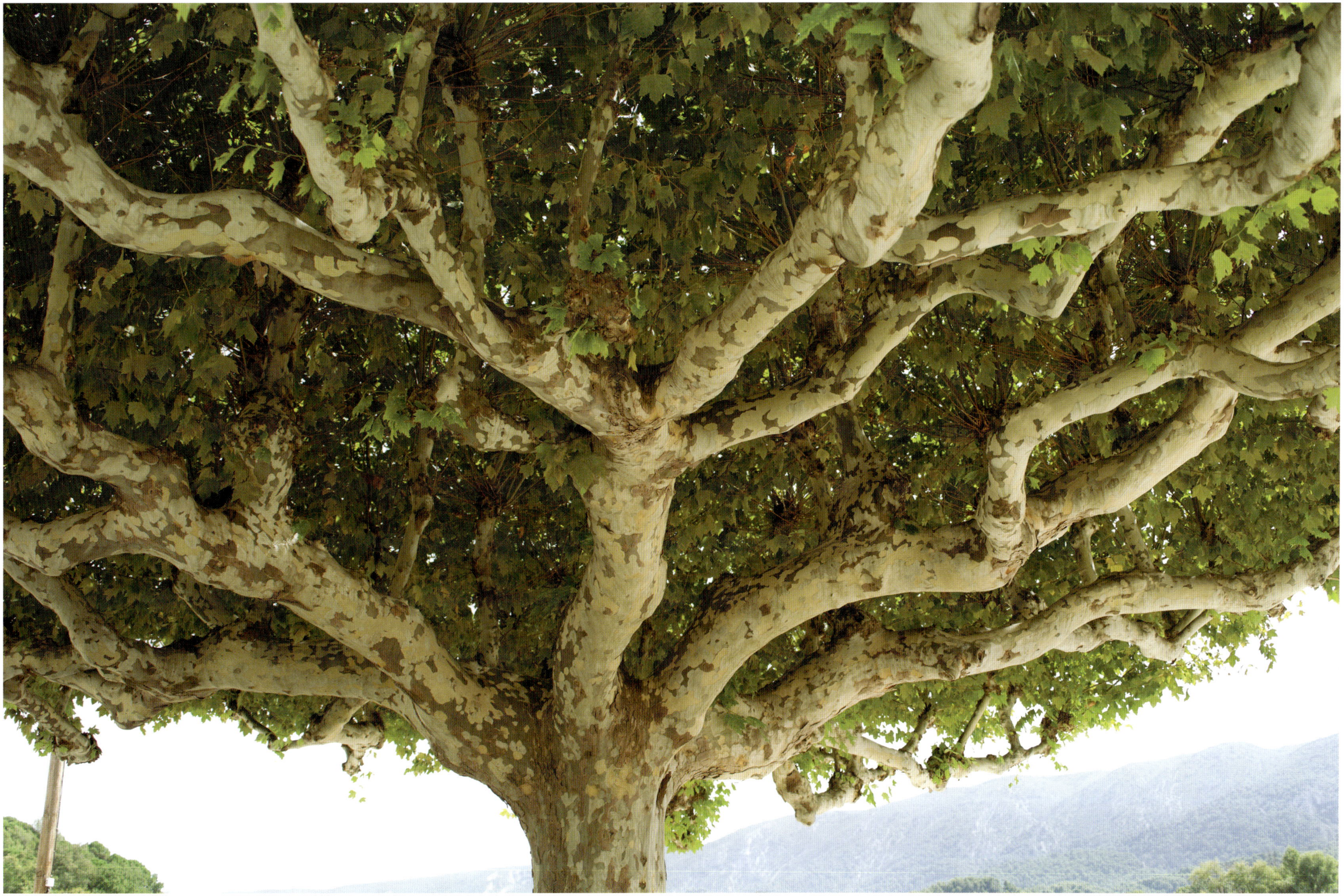

PLATE 3

AUTUMN

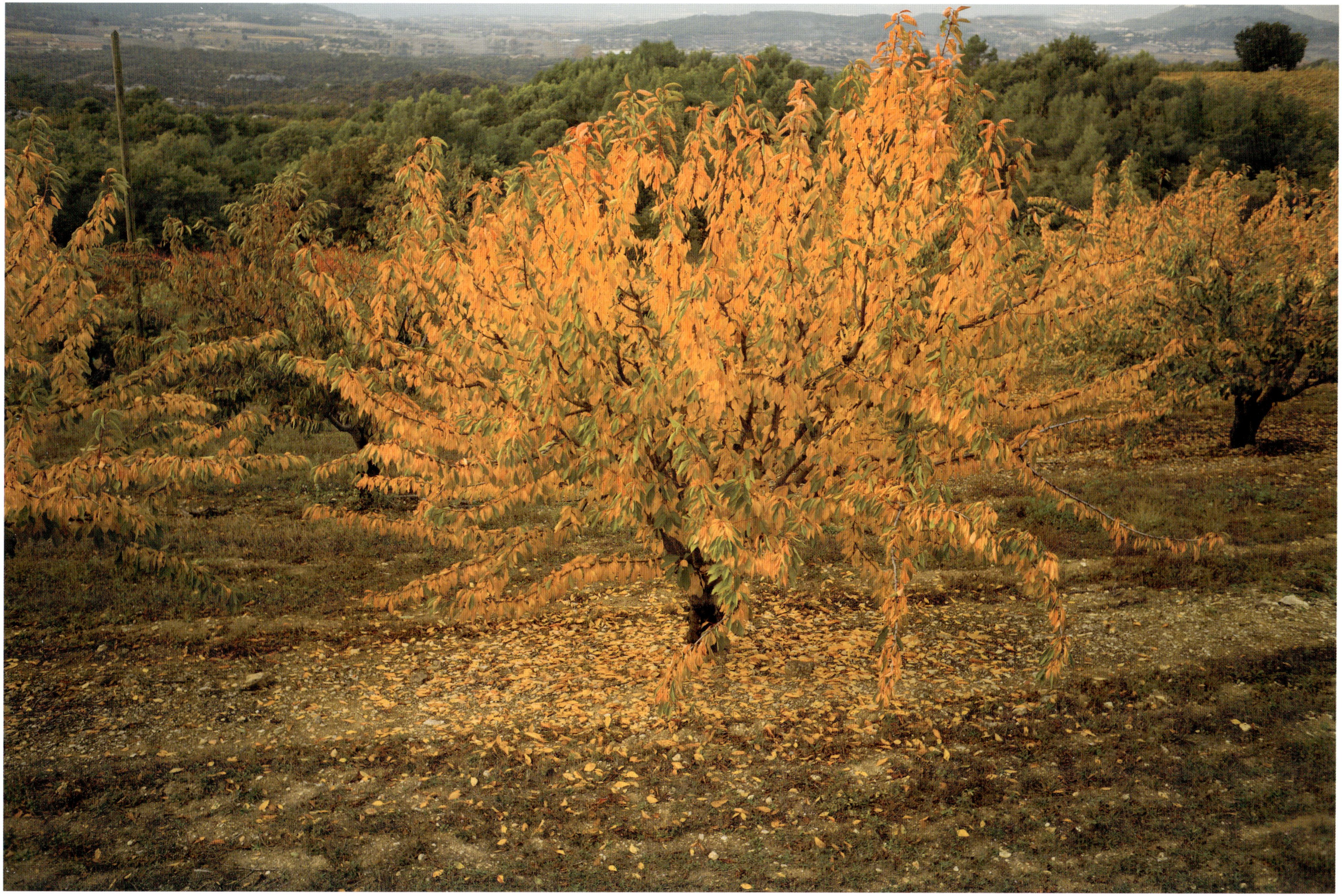

PLATE 4

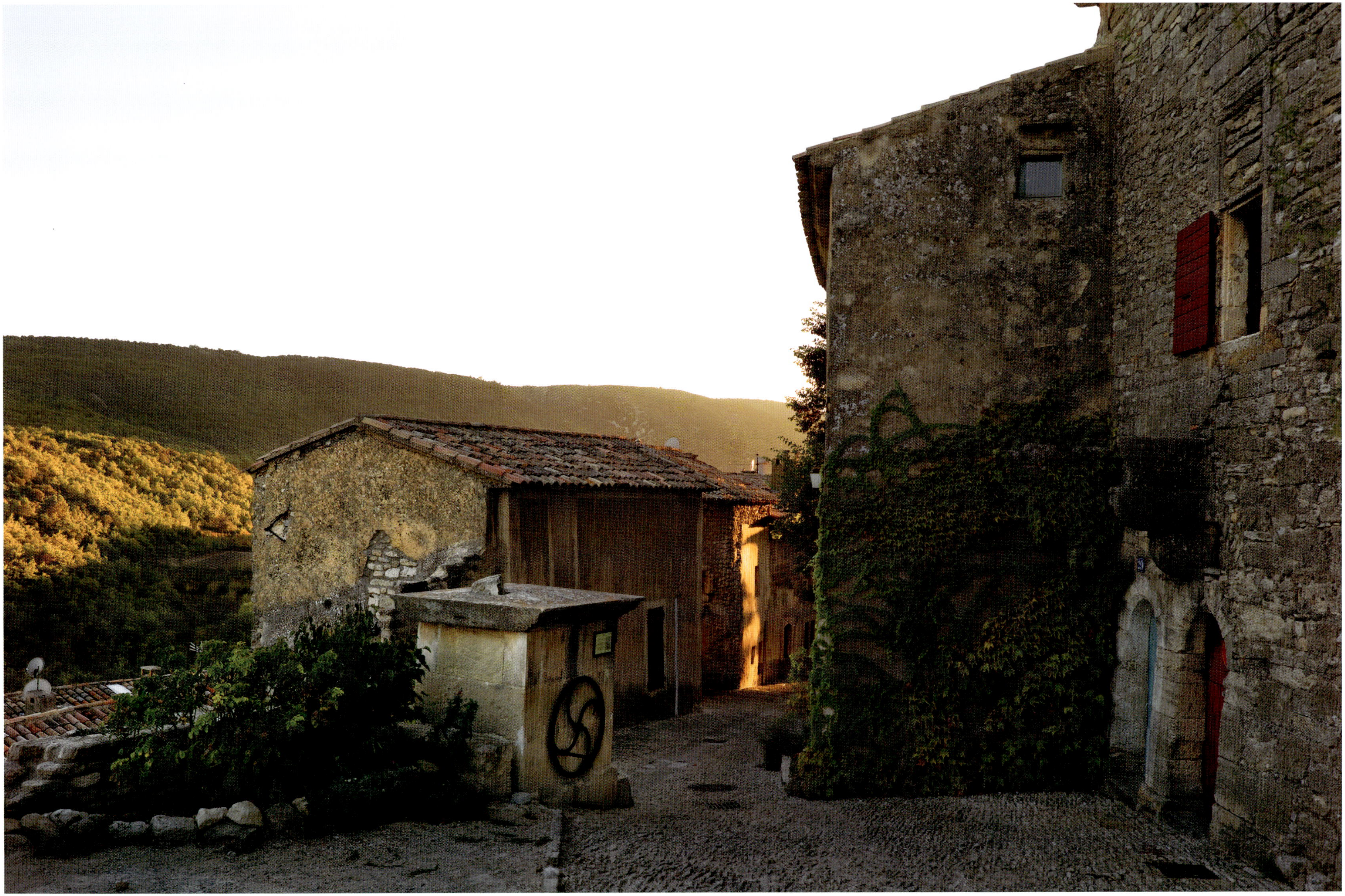

PROVENCE

LASTING IMPRESSIONS

JOEL MEYEROWITZ MAGGIE BARRETT

Sterling Signature
NEW YORK

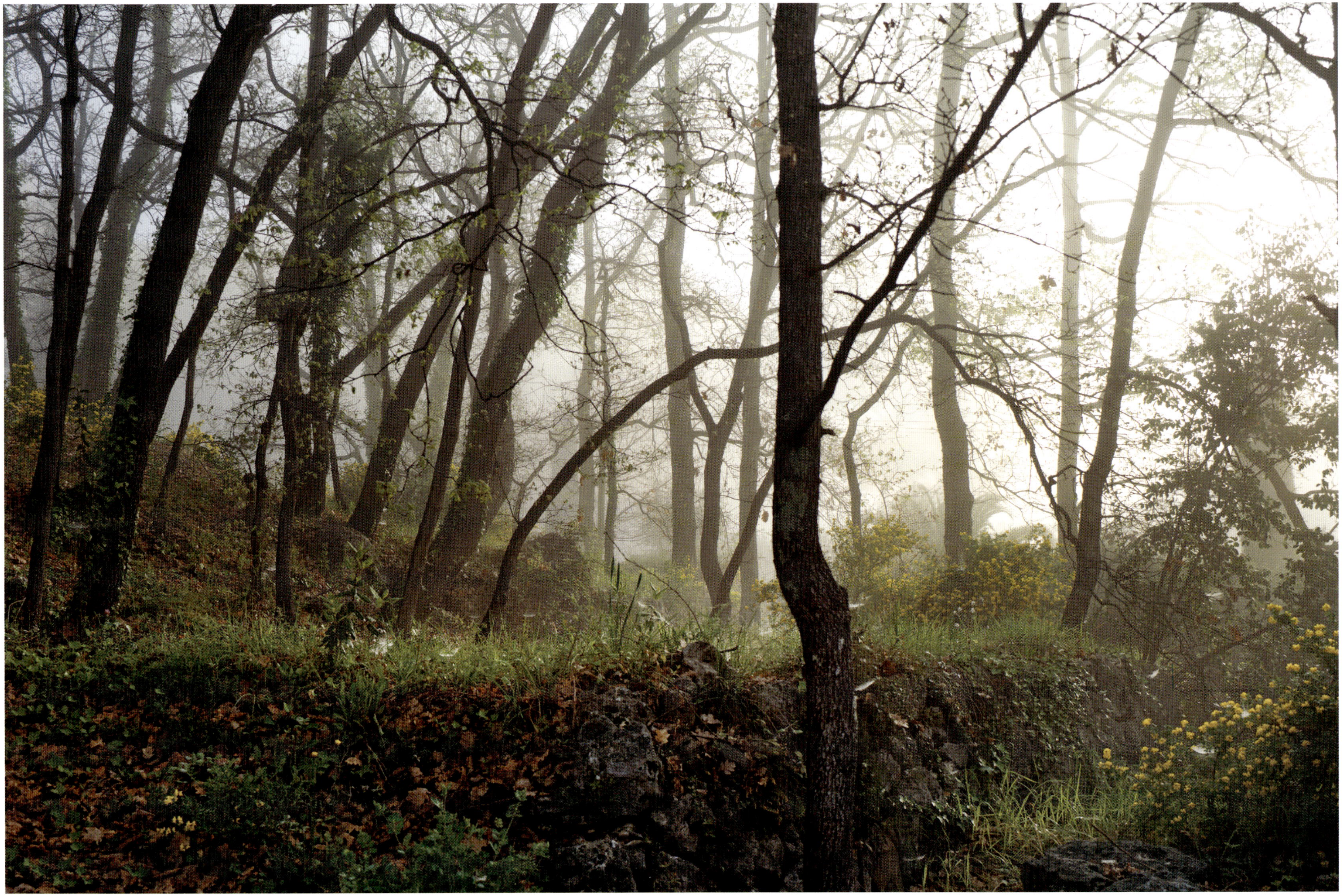

PLATE 5

INTRODUCTION

WE WERE OFFERED THE COMMISSION TO MAKE A BOOK ON PROVENCE AT AN EXTRAORDINARY MOMENT IN our lives. A moment when we had just, perhaps two weeks earlier, decided to sell our cottage on the water's edge on Cape Cod. It was a huge decision, to let go of a place where we had met, and a cottage that we had restored together nestled in an English garden by the sea.

It was there, for twenty-one years, that we put down roots, spent time with family and friends, swam at dawn, and kayaked up the moonbeam. It was the place where we always thought our ashes would be scattered at low tide. But like many things to which we humans become attached, it had become the thing that imprisoned us, both financially and emotionally.

With the recent loss of a close friend, we became highly conscious of our mortality and decided that we did not want to put off the things we kept saying we wanted to do: to spend more time together and to take a leap out into the world while we still have enough gray cells and working limbs to navigate the unknown.

Provence had not been on our list of places to explore and, in all honesty, when Sterling Publishing suggested it our initial response was "Provence? Why? Hasn't it already been done?" The answer was yes, but not by us. And anyway, who in their right minds would turn down an offer like that? Amazing how easily we can get in our own way. So we said yes. And we will be eternally grateful to Michael Fragnito and Barbara Berger for their vision and generosity.

And so it was that at the tail end of winter we set off on our adventure. Oh, Provence, you might say, what's such a big adventure about that? But does one have to travel to the wilds of Borneo or some such place in order to adventure? In fact, if it's a challenge you want, then going to a destination that's already well-documented will

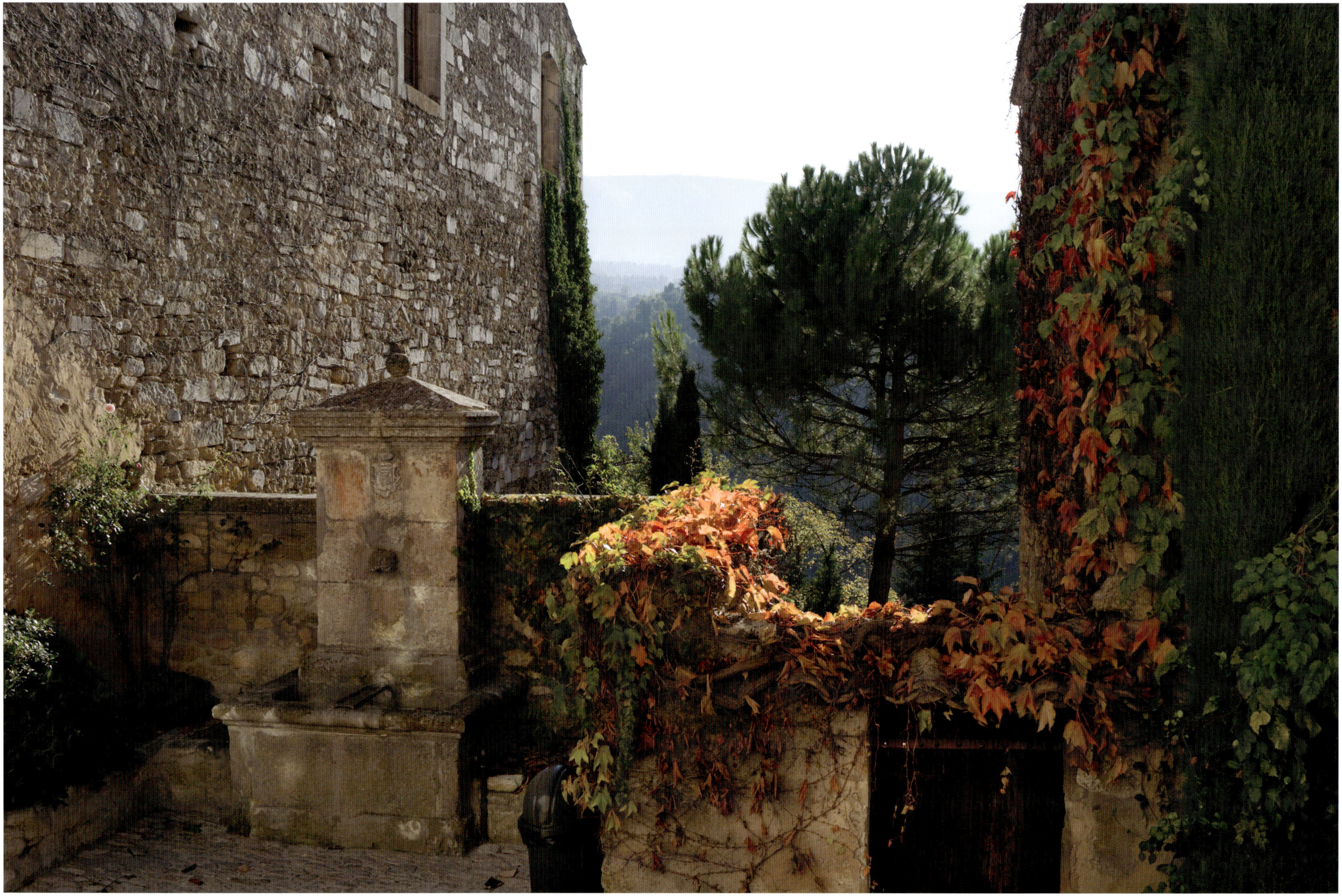

PLATE 6

force you to see beyond that which you "think" you know about such a place . . . if you are willing to let go of preconceived ideas and idealistic expectations.

Provence did that: it opened our eyes and our hearts. It challenged us with its almost secretive nature, both beckoning us on through its winding back roads and villages and hiding from us in the places where globalization has, like everywhere, made its soulless mark. Time and time again we would find ourselves searching for "our" Provence, and while we were sometimes thwarted, we were always eventually rewarded: the land, the light, the architecture, the markets, the food—all unique, all seductive. And the people, whom we came to greatly admire for their values, their aesthetic, their hard work, and their nonchalant attitude. They're not easily impressed, the Provençals, but they impressed us, not least with their patience while we tried to make ourselves understood in the most atrocious French.

In the four months we spent in Provence, we journeyed from east to west, traveling the gorges and the coast from Nice to Marseille. We climbed hillsides and picnicked in fields. We ate everything, all the time. When we first arrived our hearts belonged to Tuscany. What Provence taught us is that our hearts are as expansive as we allow them to be.

As I write this introduction I am sitting in our Manhattan apartment looking out to the Hudson River, and superimposed on this reality are the lasting impressions of Provence. They are with us daily and they remind us that when we mortals allow ourselves to open up to wherever we find ourselves, the world is a continual mystery waiting to be explored and experienced, each in our own way.

We hope that you, dear reader, will enjoy the adventure of this storybook and be encouraged to take a leap of your own.

WINTER/SPRING

March

IT IS WINTER HERE IN THE CÔTE D'AZUR VILLAGE OF TOURETTES-SUR-LOUP, AND WE'RE GLAD OF IT, AS WE had wanted to be introduced to Provence sans frills. We've just breakfasted in the lovely rustic kitchen of a house we've rented for the next eight weeks, just outside the village, and we're raring to begin our Provence adventure. In the morning, we take the road from the house, driving down, and around the many twists and turns until we come to the Loup at the bottom of the Gorge du Loup. The river is its own tsunami today, swollen beyond itself by a week of torrential rains, the trees along its banks naked and hard-bitten, the water rushing to the Mediterranean as if it can hardly wait to get there. When you look upriver, the water reflects the gray of the mountains, whereas down river, toward the sea, the water is tinged with a hint of the turquoise to come. The sun comes out for the second time today and we are surrounded by a million illuminated beads of rain clinging to branches, twigs, and moss—the moss a strident green that pulses with the urgency of spring.

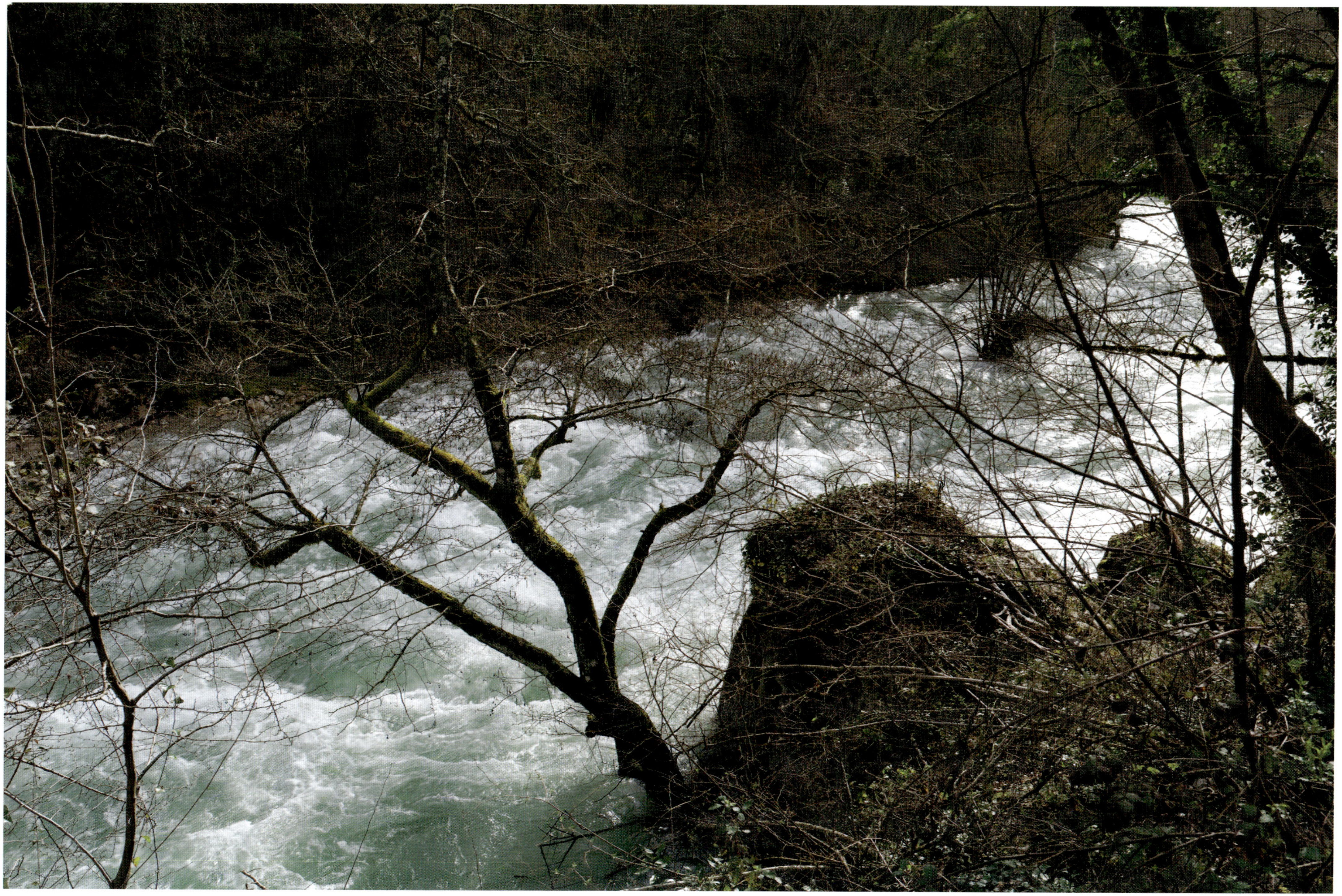

PLATE 7

PLATE 8

PLATE 9

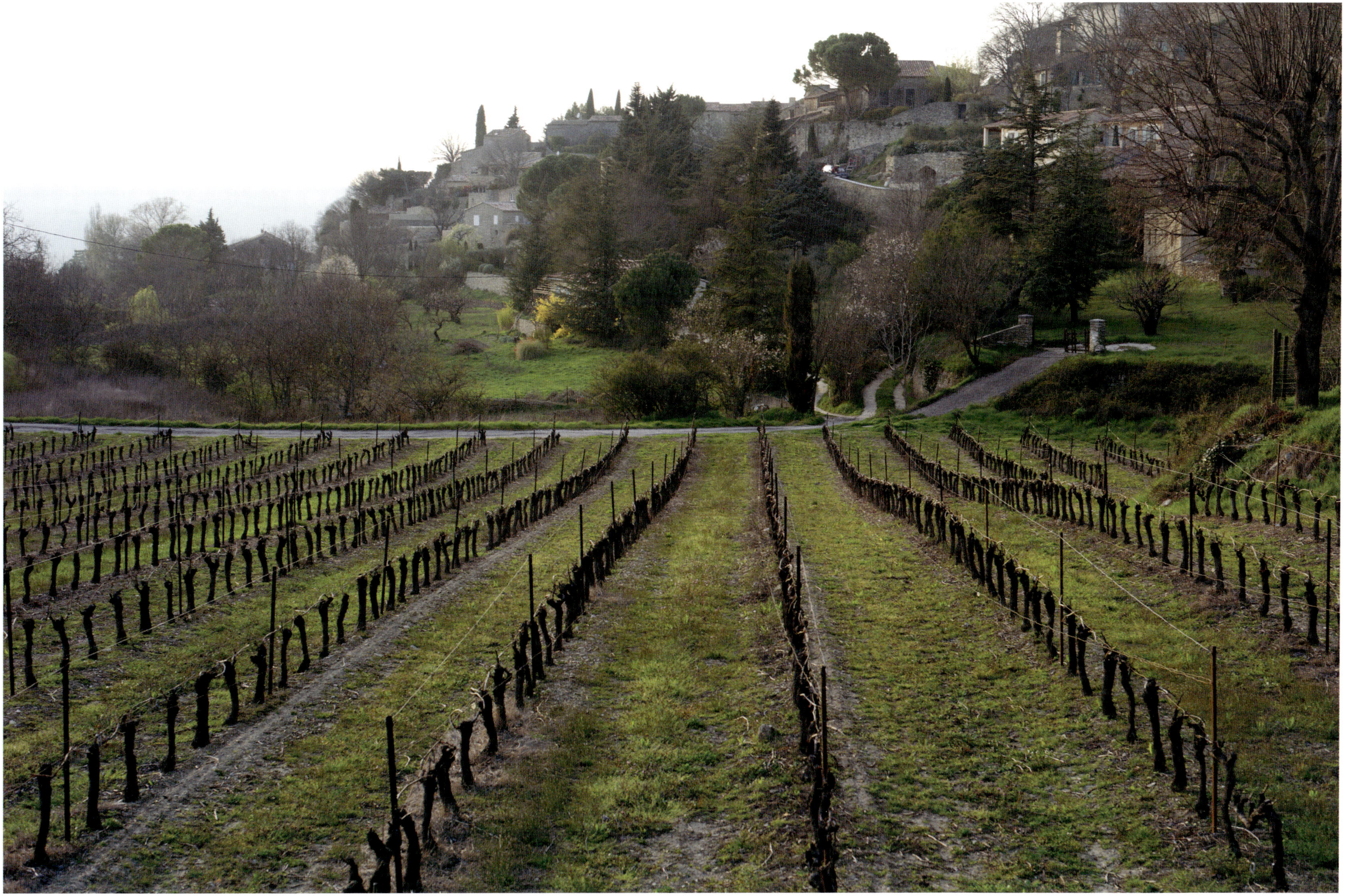

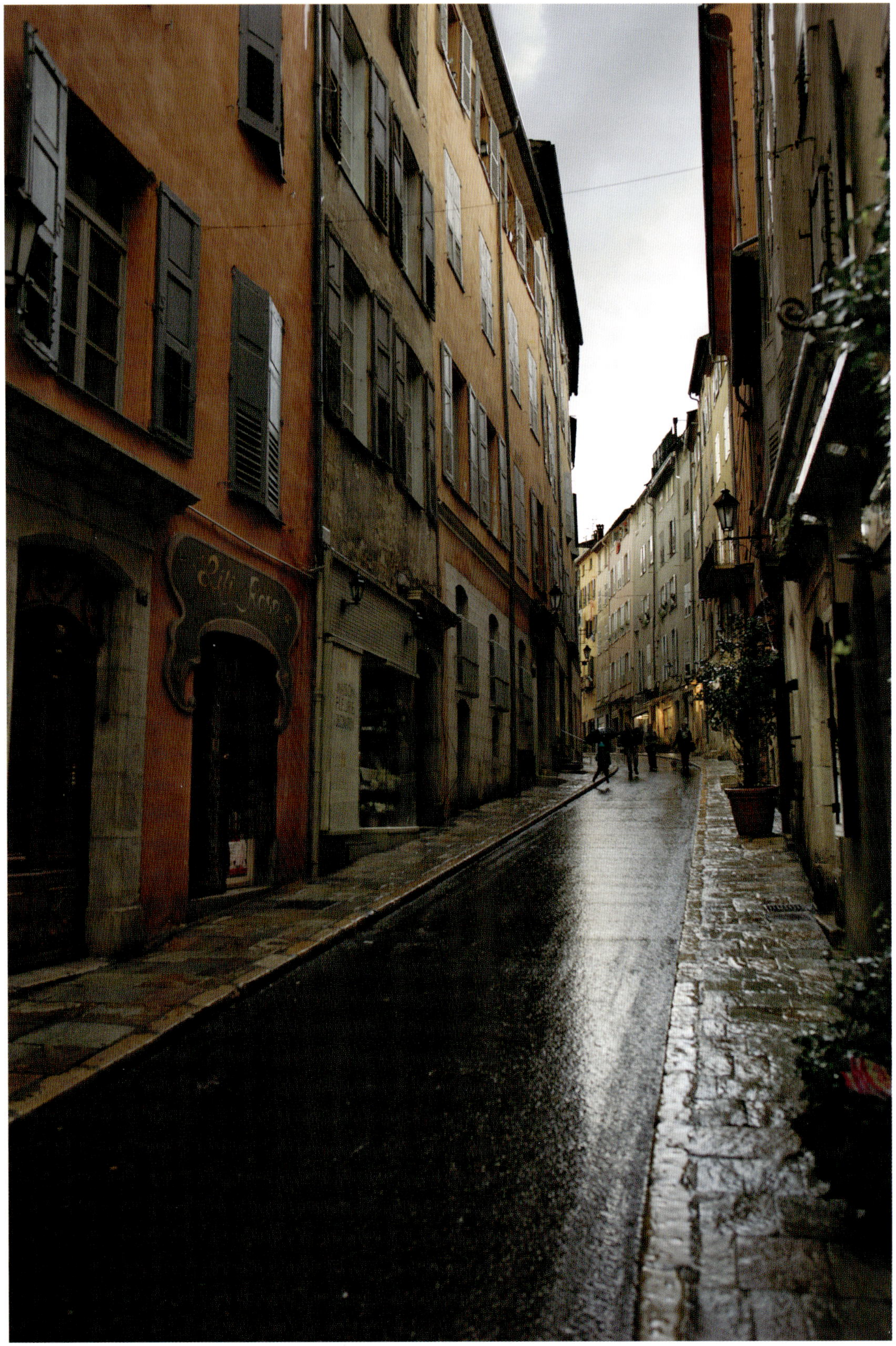

PLATE 10

PLATE 11 (OVERLEAF)

WE'RE HAVING A HARD TIME FINDING PROVENCE, AND FIND THAT WE MUST KEEP LETTING GO OF comparisons to Tuscany, where the land constantly revealed itself in its open, rolling nature. It's not like that here. This is tough terrain. Mountains and gorges. There is no horizon it seems, and isn't it the horizon that gives us that sense of expansiveness and possibility? So how do we find our way in here? What is it we are not willing to see?

Suddenly a break in the clouds allows the last of the daylight to pour down on the land and we catch a glimpse of its mystery, of its enormity, its juxtapositions between primal beauty and its modern urbanity. In that moment we come to understand that we must be willing to see the all of it in order to eventually reduce it to its essence.

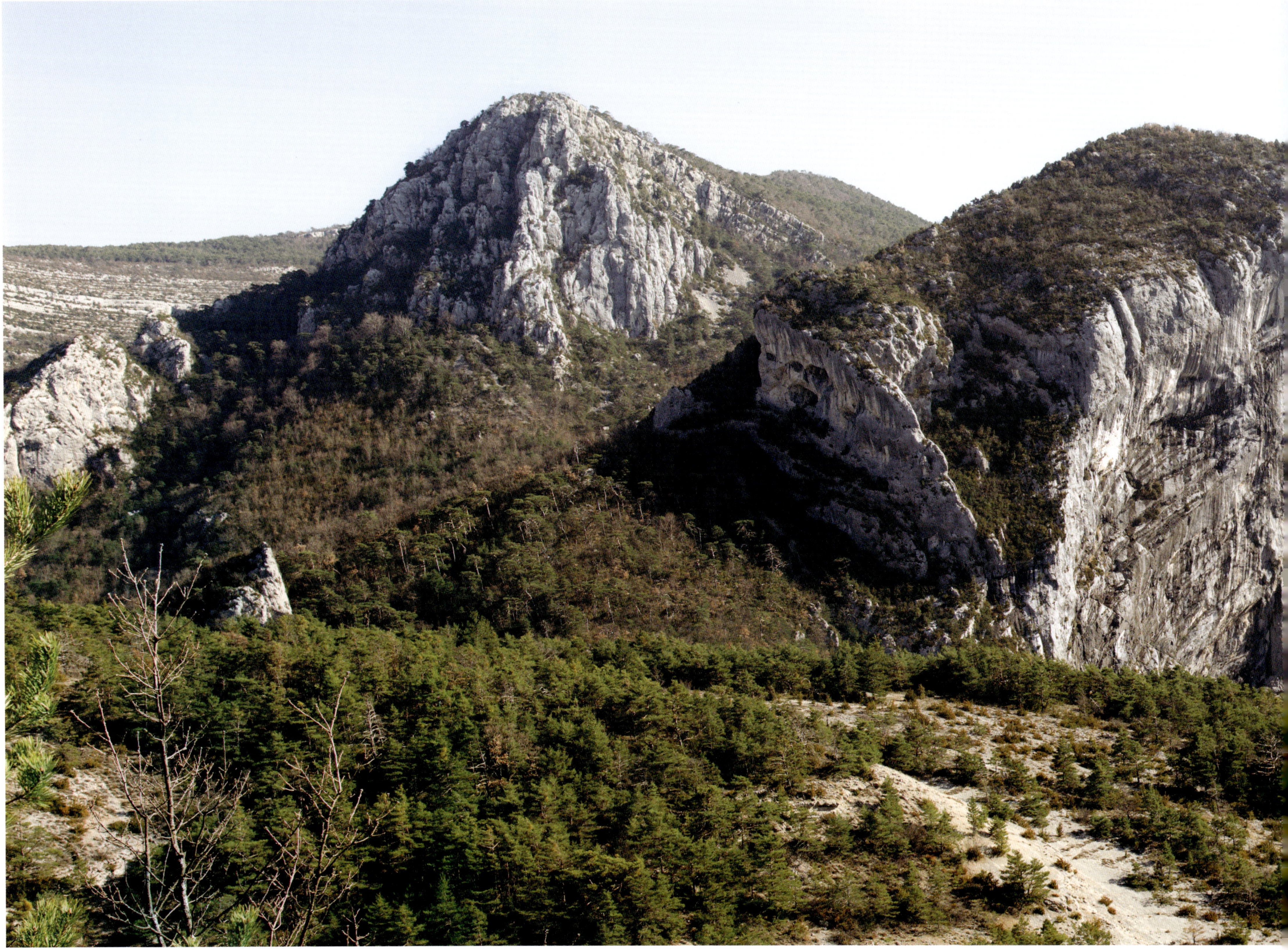

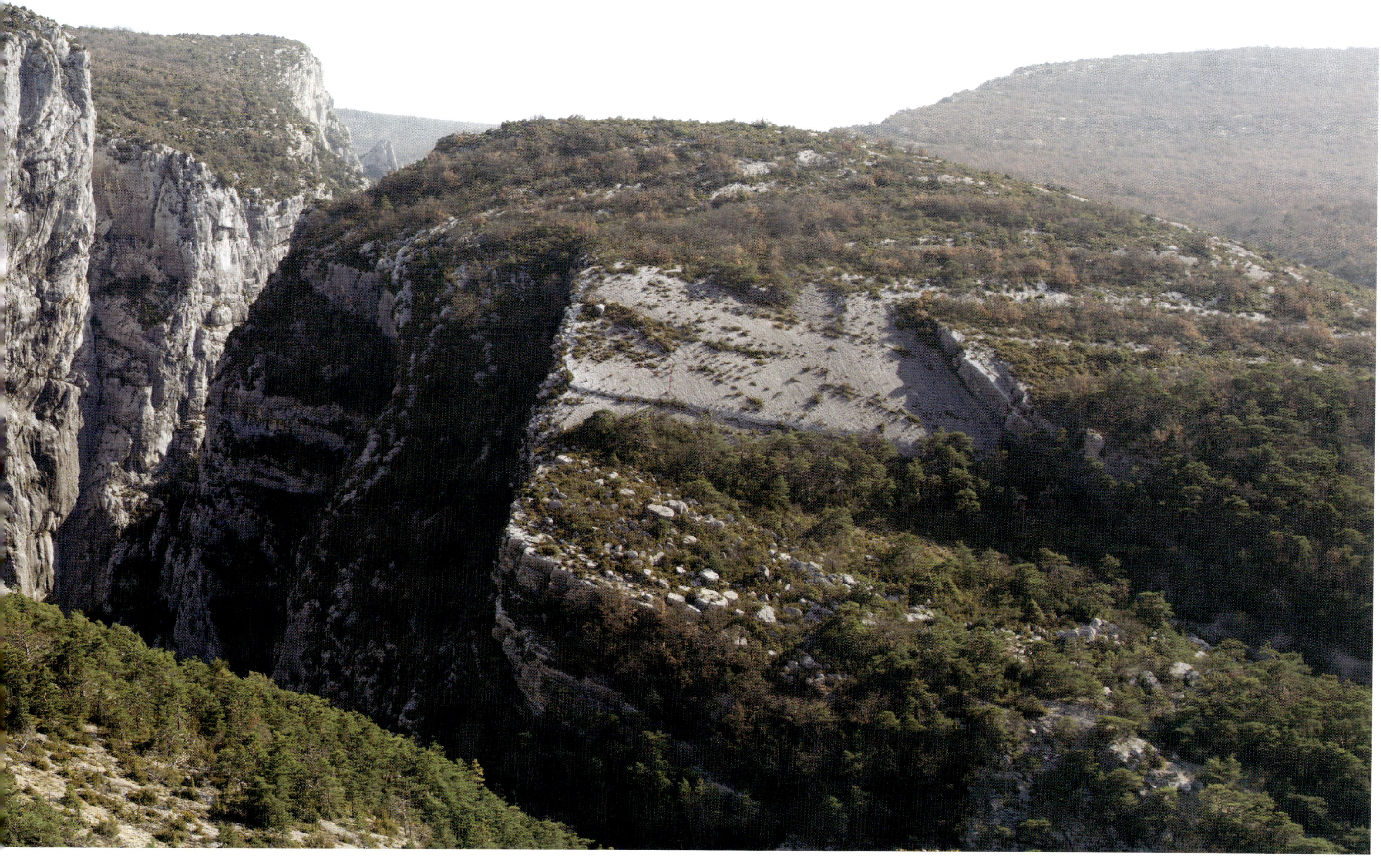

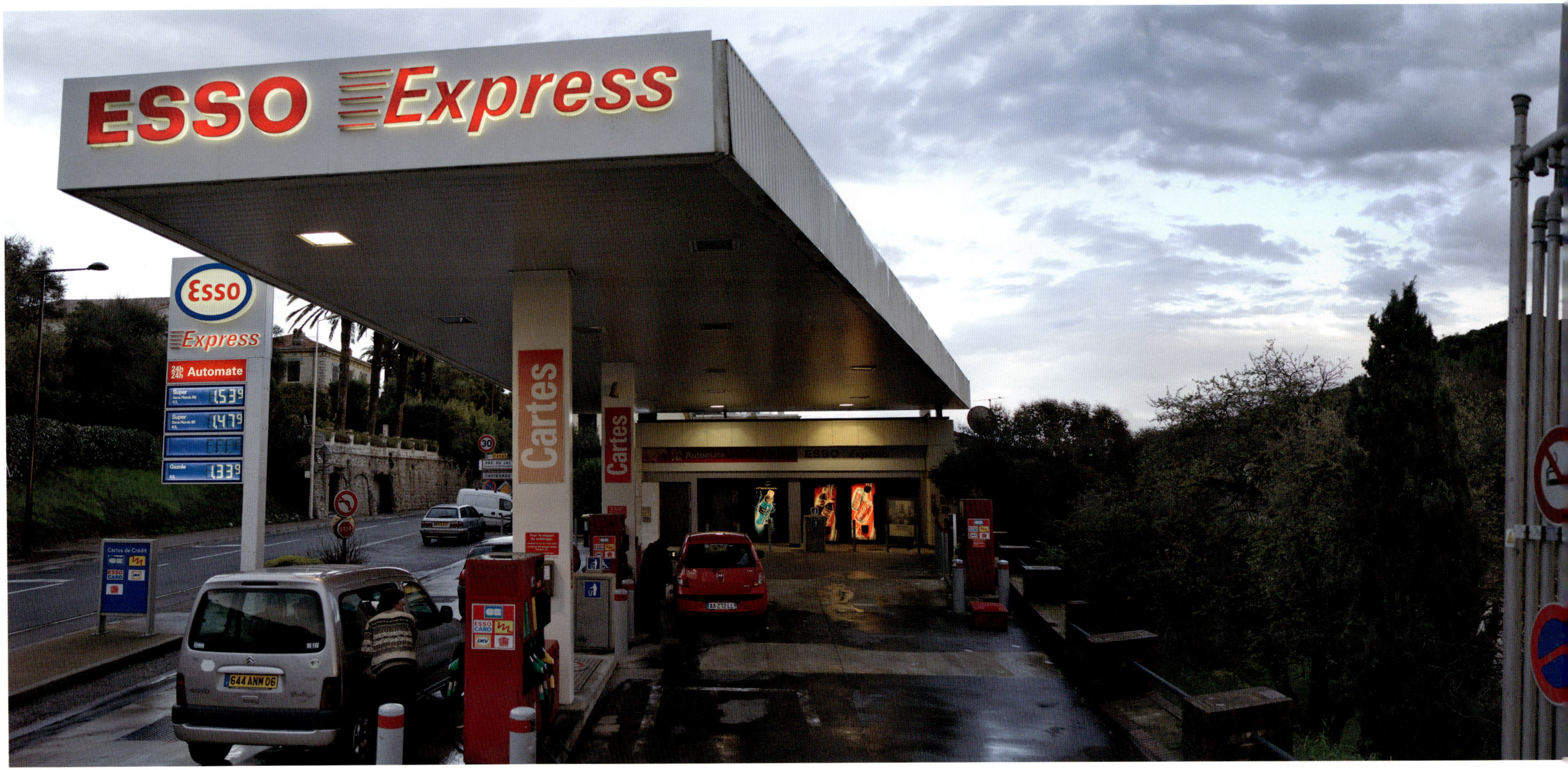
ESSO
Express
Esso
Express
24h 24h Automate
Cartes
Cartes
644 ANM 06

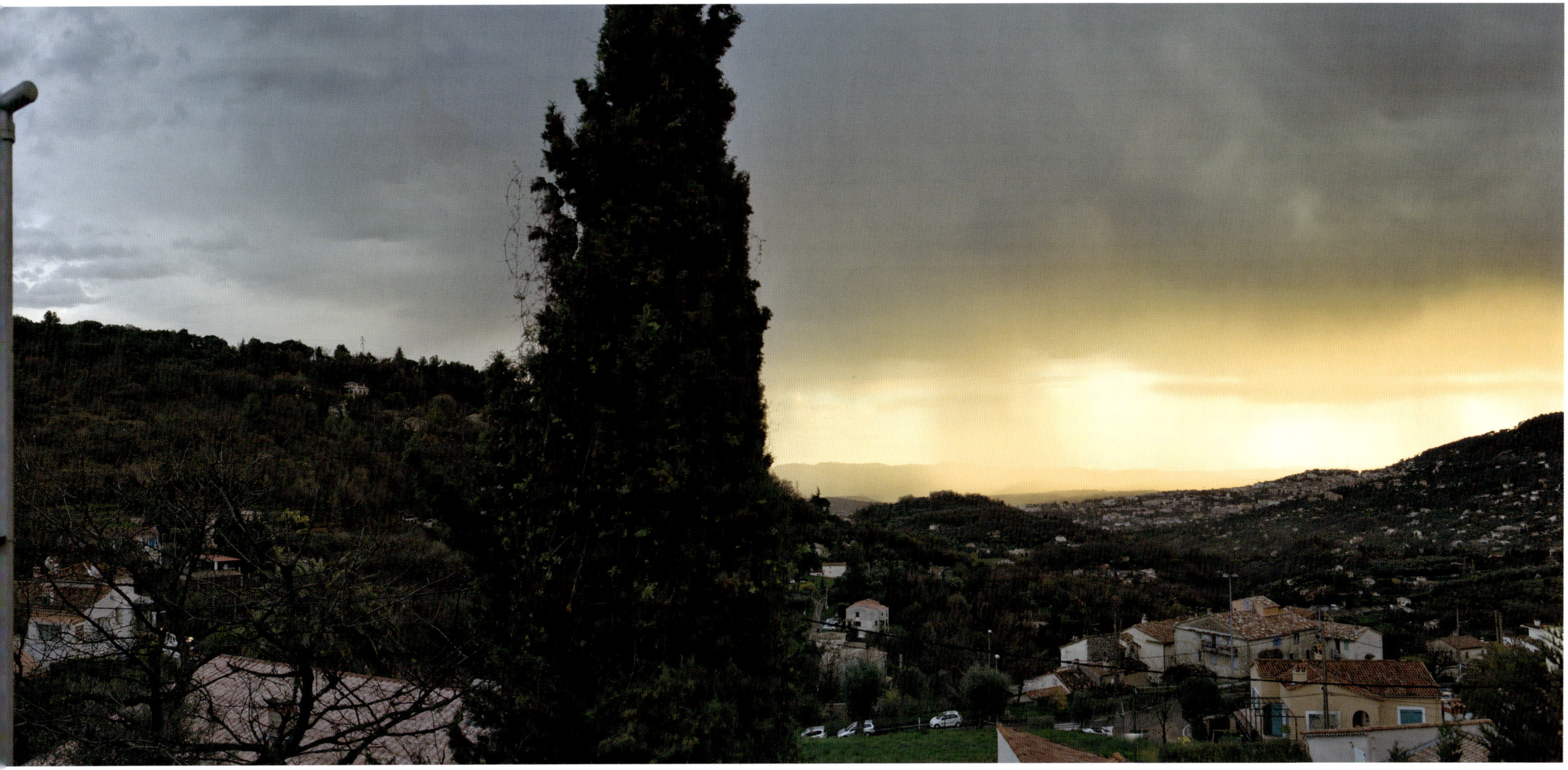

PLATE 13

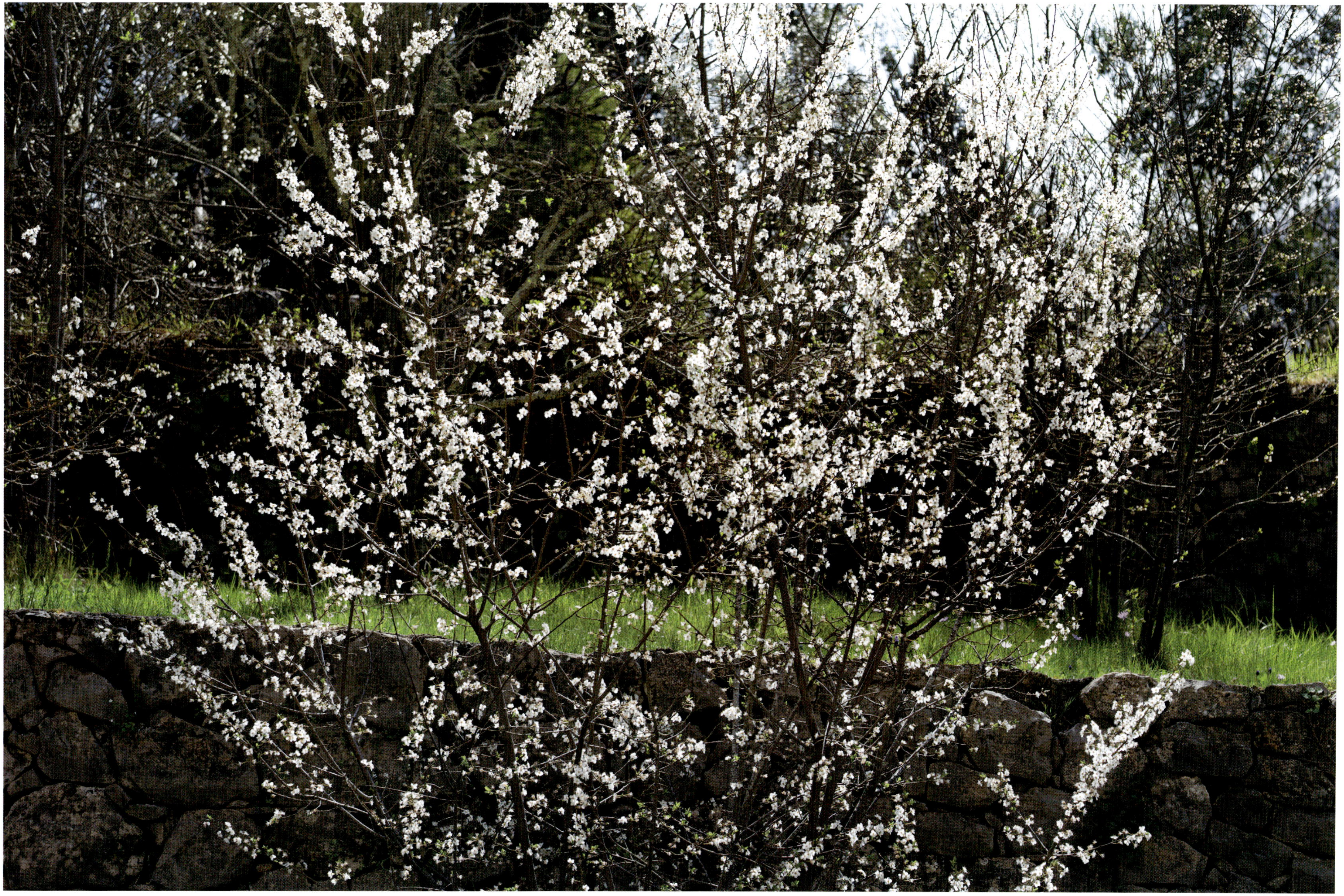

WE TAKE A WALK DOWN OUR ROAD, AND AS ALWAYS WHEN ON FOOT, WE ARE RIGHT-SIZED IN RELATION TO nature. This pedestrian pace allows us to see so much more than we have on our previous trips down here by car. Although there was something I saw from the car window the other day that made me gasp, and I am anxious to see, from this lowly perspective, what I was instinctively responding to.

We turn a corner and there it is: a patch of daisy-like flowers, the midmorning sun illuminating their petals so that the flowers appear to hover above the grass. The grass itself is soft and sweet, the handful of olive trees rooted there like wise old uncles. Four stone steps lead up to this little patch of heaven. It's so intimate and yet open to all. I pick my tree and lie beneath it. It's good to be reminded that one doesn't have to own something to enjoy it.

Back on foot, we round a bend in the road and are caught by surprise at a glimpse of the Mediterranean. The sea is just over there, always—yet we completely forget about it because we are living in the mountains. Mountains, sea. Winter, spring. Verdant grass, leafless trees. These juxtapositions are revealed to us in glimpses—or *aperçus*, as the French would say. And indeed, we are just getting an *aperçu* of the true terrain of Provence: it is a Land of Glimpses.

We feel enormous relief; this is what we had not been willing to see before because our expectations preceded us. These expectations we have of life become demands if we don't let go of them. The less we get what we want, the more we demand it, and the demand blinds us so that we are unable to glimpse the glimpse. Yet to take in that which reveals itself in a moment is to experience the vista of the moment: the immeasurable expanse of now.

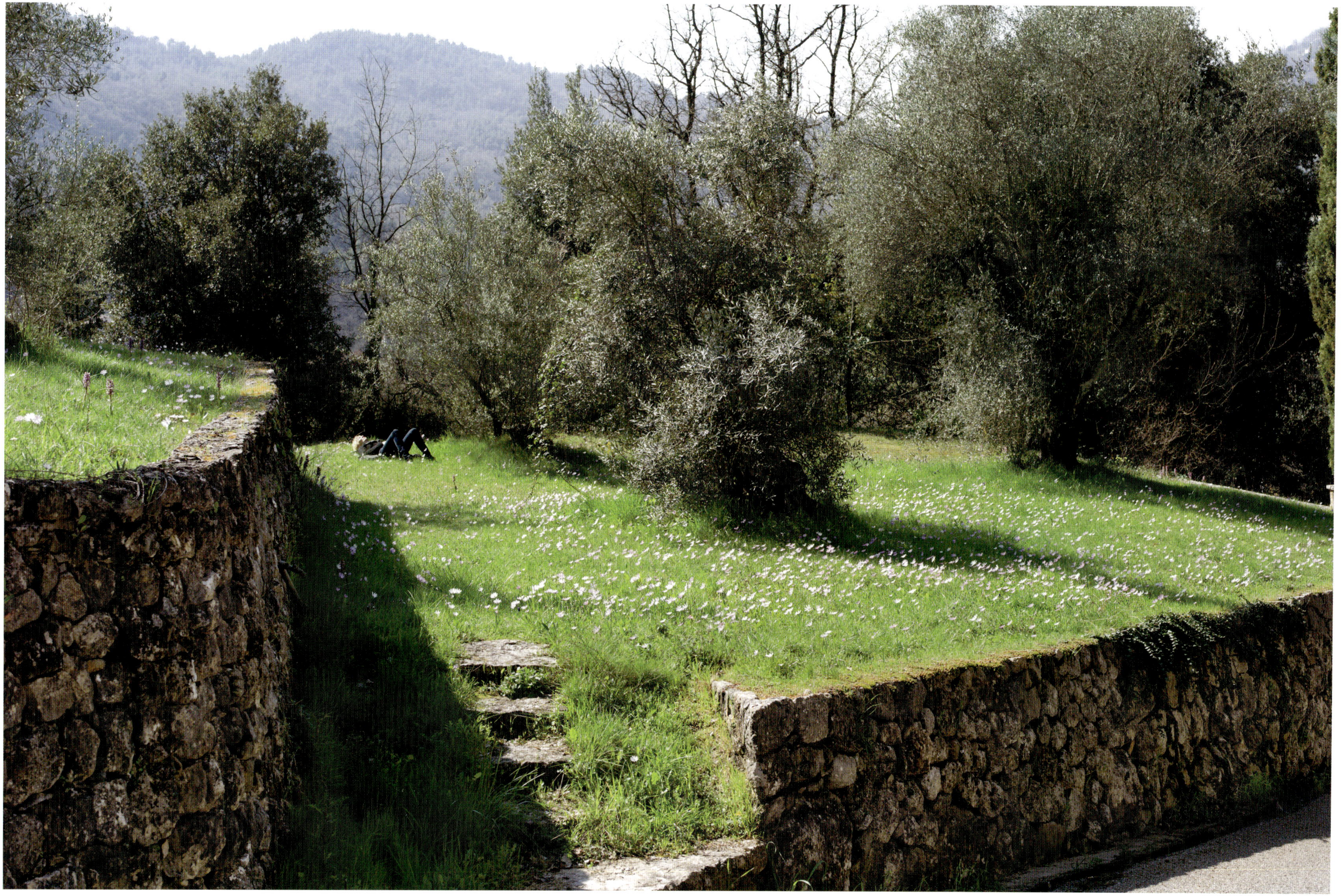

PLATE 14

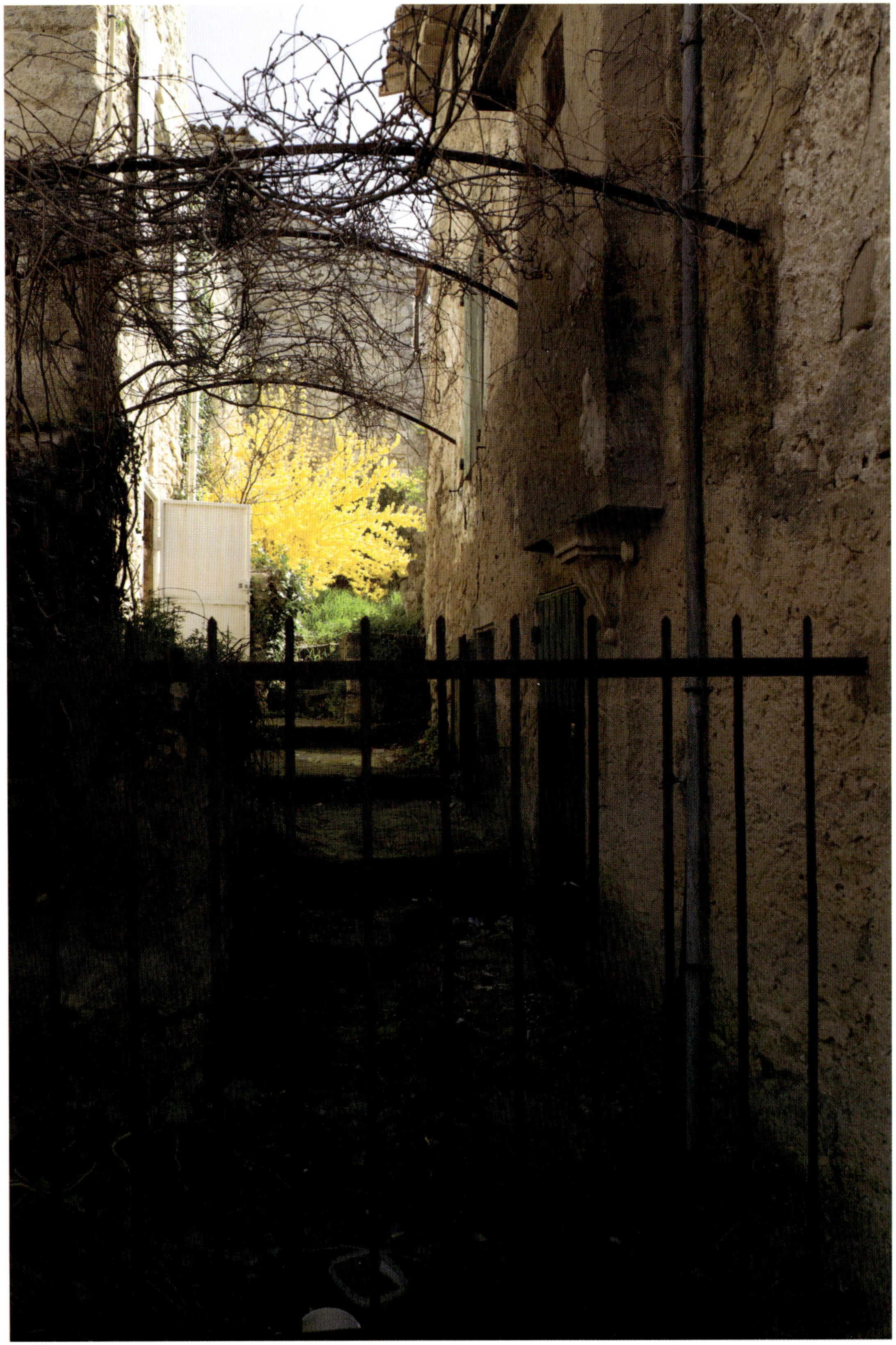

PLATE 15

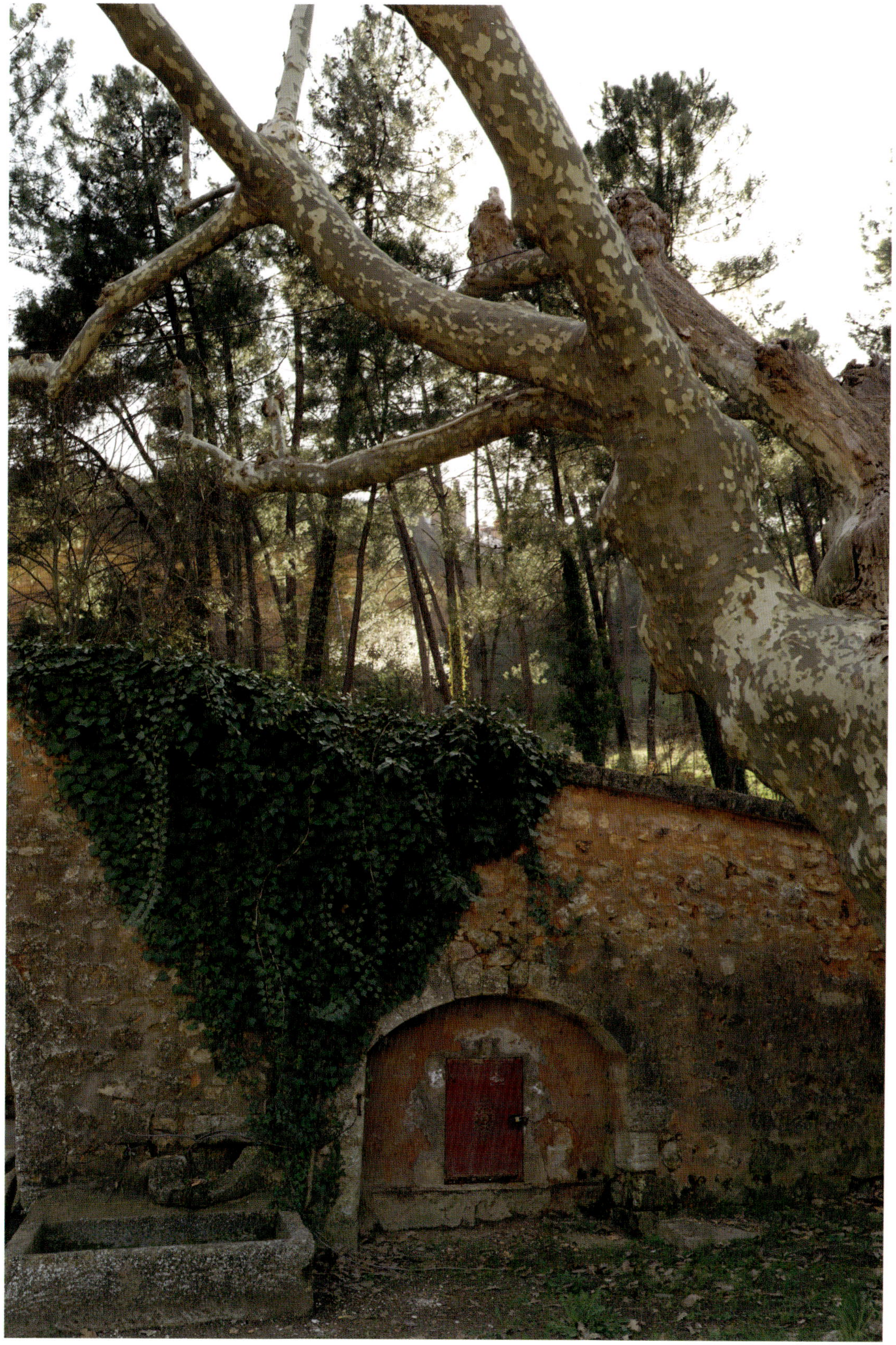

PLATE 16

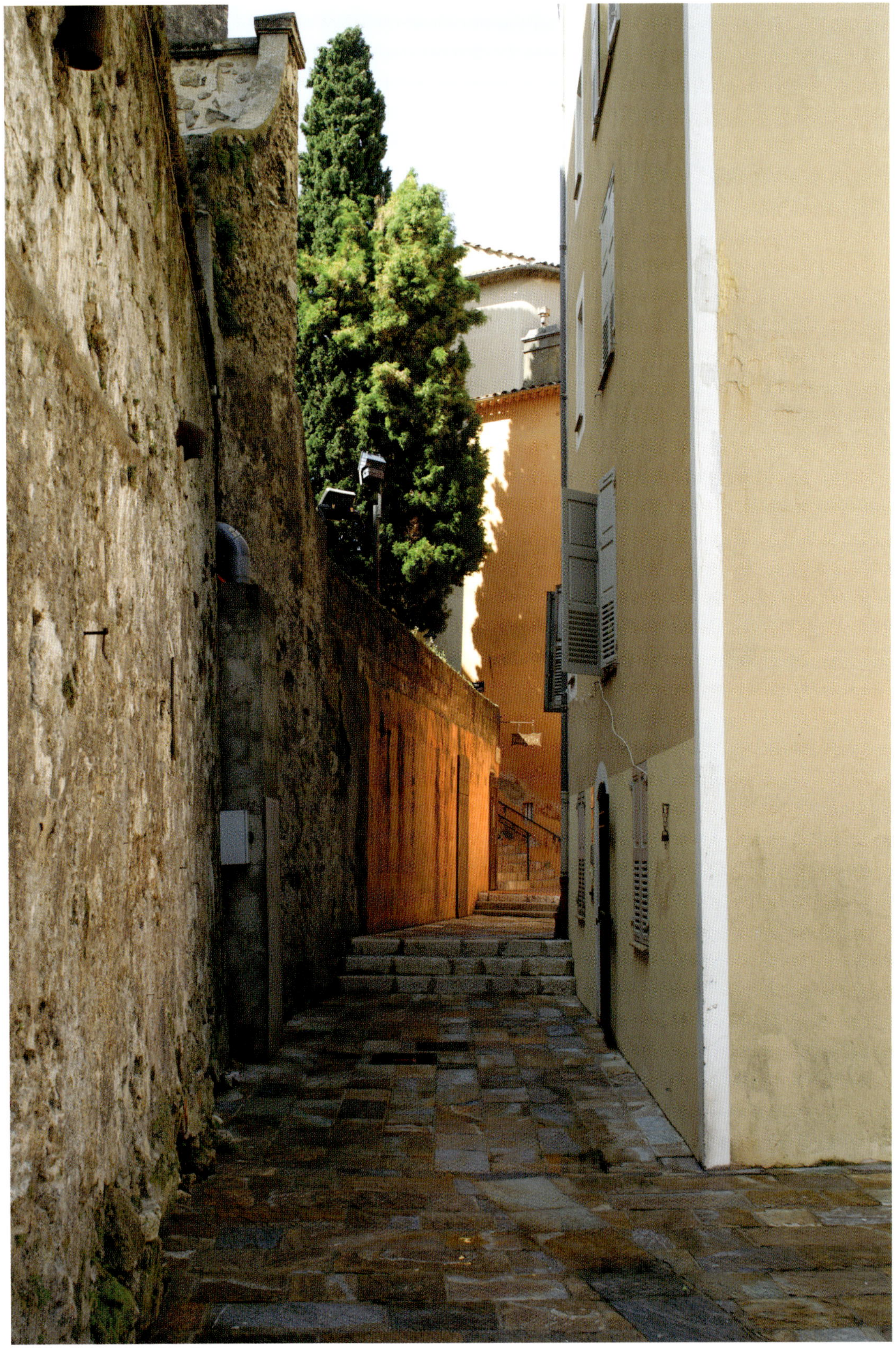

PLATE 17

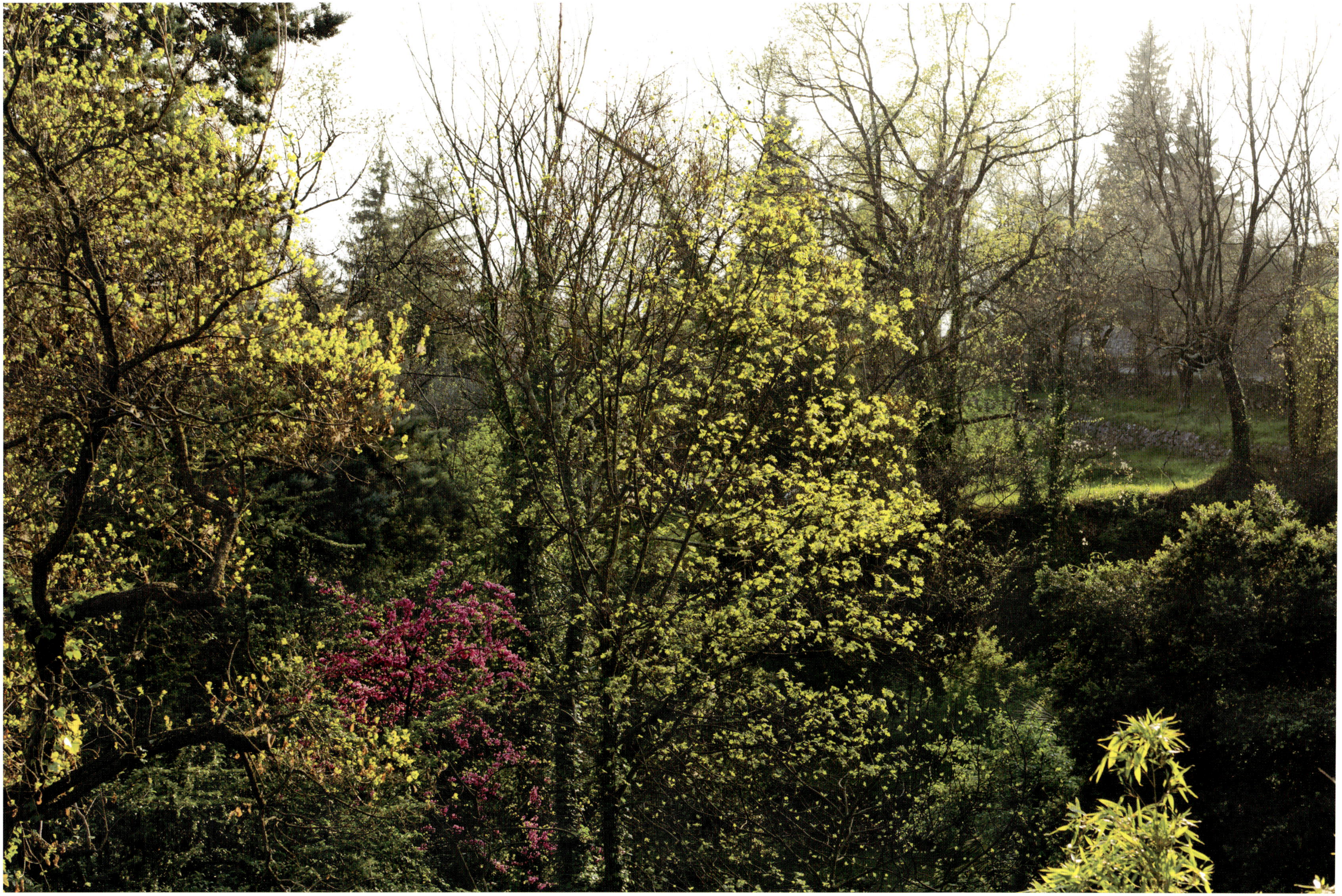

PLATE 18

WE ARE LOOKING, LOOKING. WE CAME HERE TO LOSE OURSELVES AND YET WE FIND, OF COURSE, THAT that is impossible. Every blade of grass, every river, every moon is part of who we are. We pass a field of uprooted trees and they feel like our tribe. Who, what, yanked them from the soil and lay them down to die? And is that what frightens us about having uprooted ourselves—that we, too, will lay down and die?

In the morning we climb the stone steps to the top of Bonnieux, where a twelfth-century church stands rooted to its spot. From its tower, four bells slowly toll, not in any recognizable rhythm—and yet the meaning of the rhythm is all about recognition, because the bells are tolling for a local man whose funeral we look down to in the valley. We see the mourners gathering. The door of the hearse is open, and even from this distance one can see the coffin. The bells, each solitary tone, gasp and gasp again, as if the bell ringer is listening for eternal vibration. The last note sounds and we enter the church. I try, in my lacking language, to tell the bell-ringer how moved I was by the sounds he made. He tells us they were the sounds of the last breaths leaving the body.

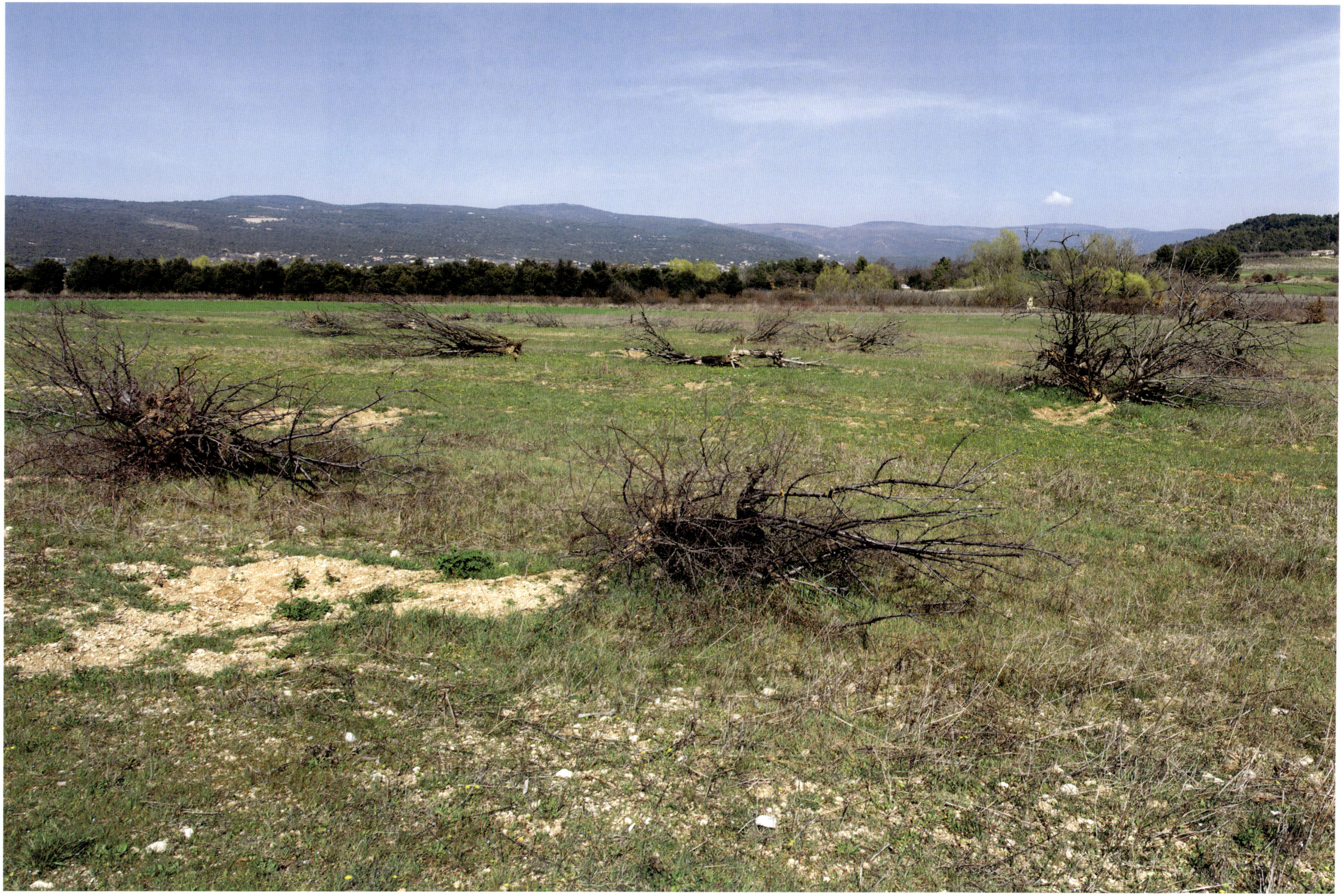

PLATE 19

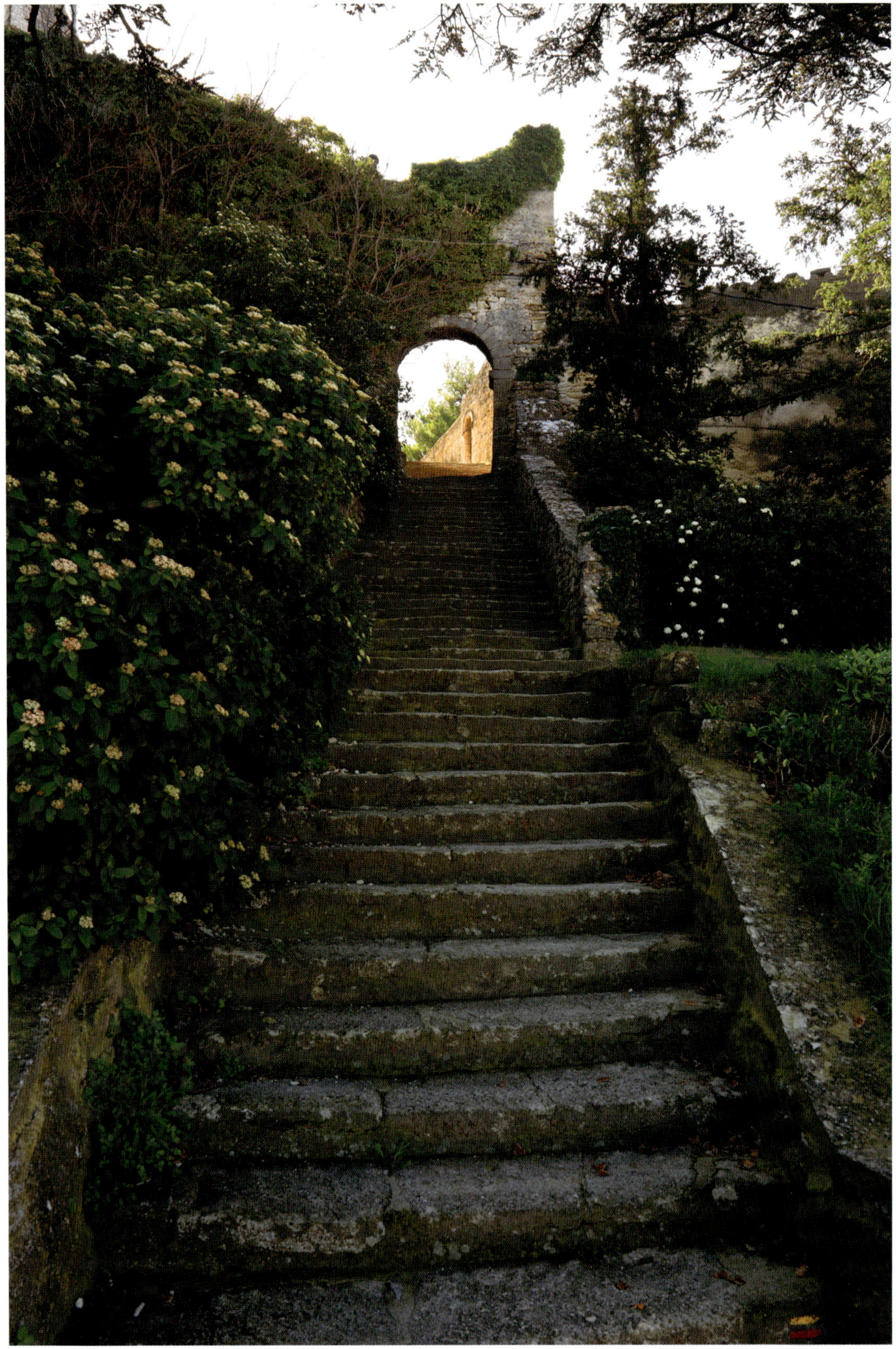

PLATE 20

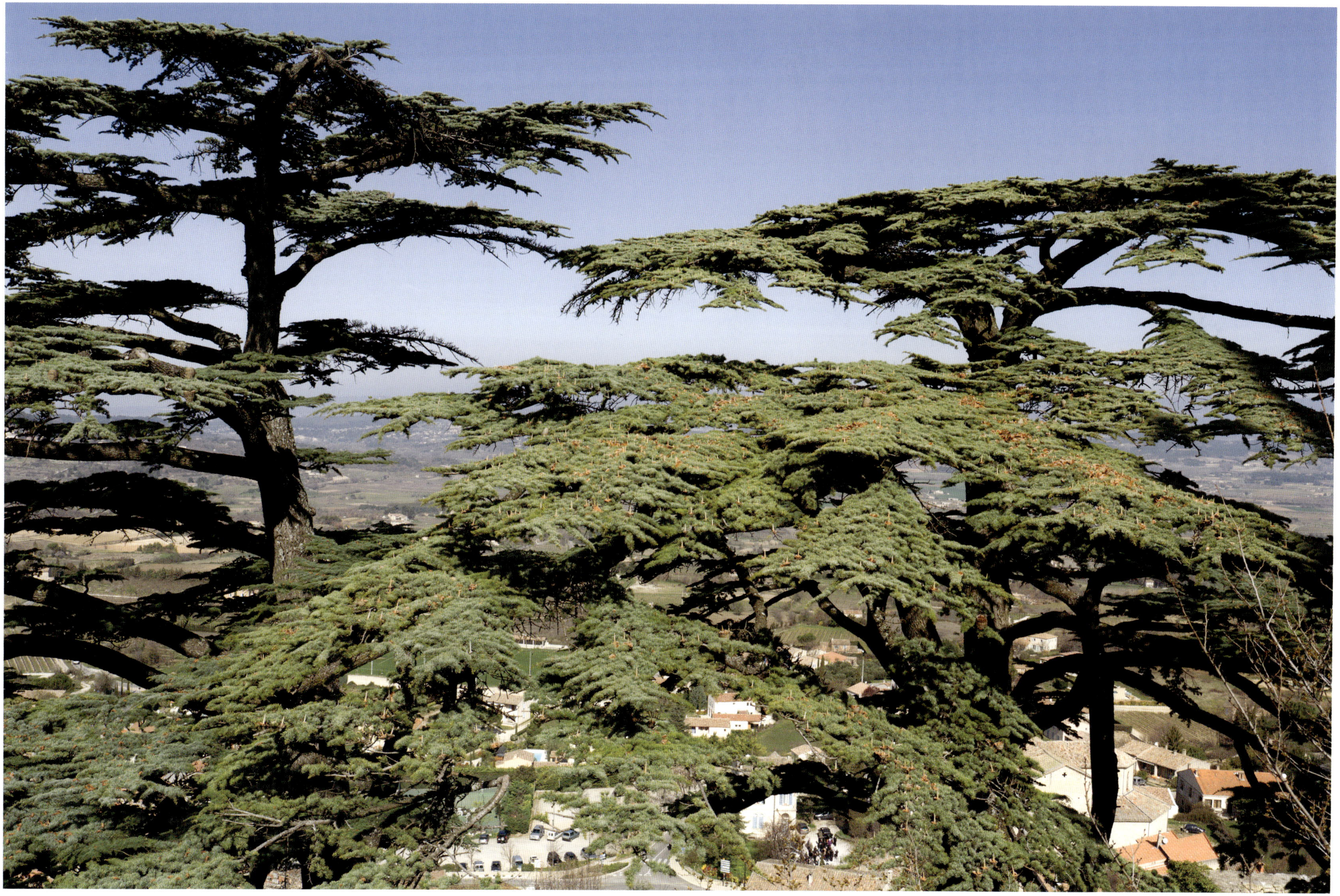

PLATE 21

PLATE 22

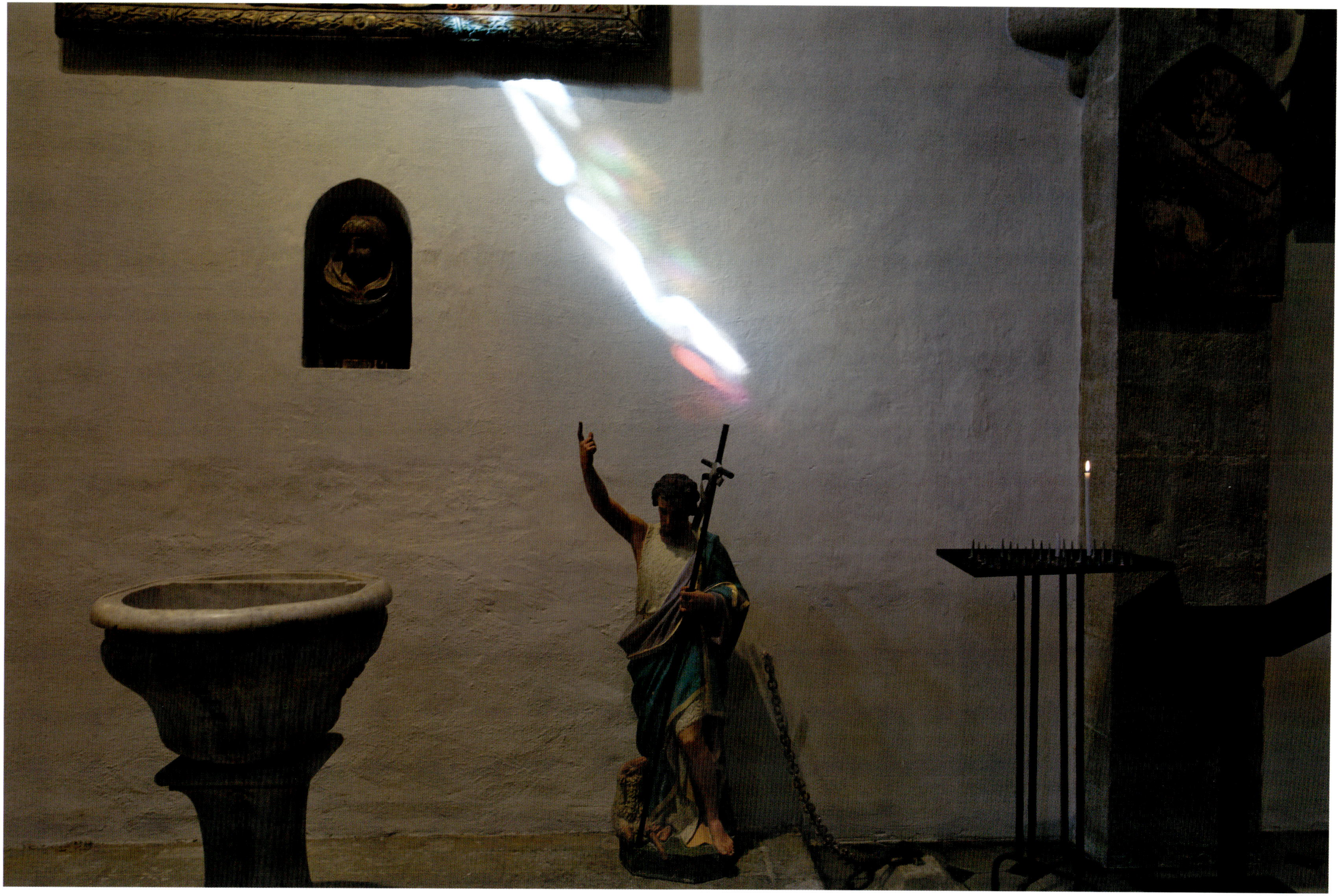

WE JOURNEY ON TO AIX-EN-PROVENCE. IN THE CENTER OF TOWN WE STOP AT A CAROUSEL, ENTRANCED. What is it about a carousel that is so captivating? Maybe what touches us most is that there is still a need for such a simple experience. Maybe it's comforting in this age of video games and nonstop digital addiction to find that something as whimsical and old-fashioned as this is still sought after. I look at the various modes of transport going round and round—horses, carriages, trains, cars, motorcycles, planes—and the toddlers and young children riding them, their parents waving goodbye to them each time they circle around as though sending them out into the world over and over again. Don't we all need to be transported? To be taken onward into our dreams of adventure?

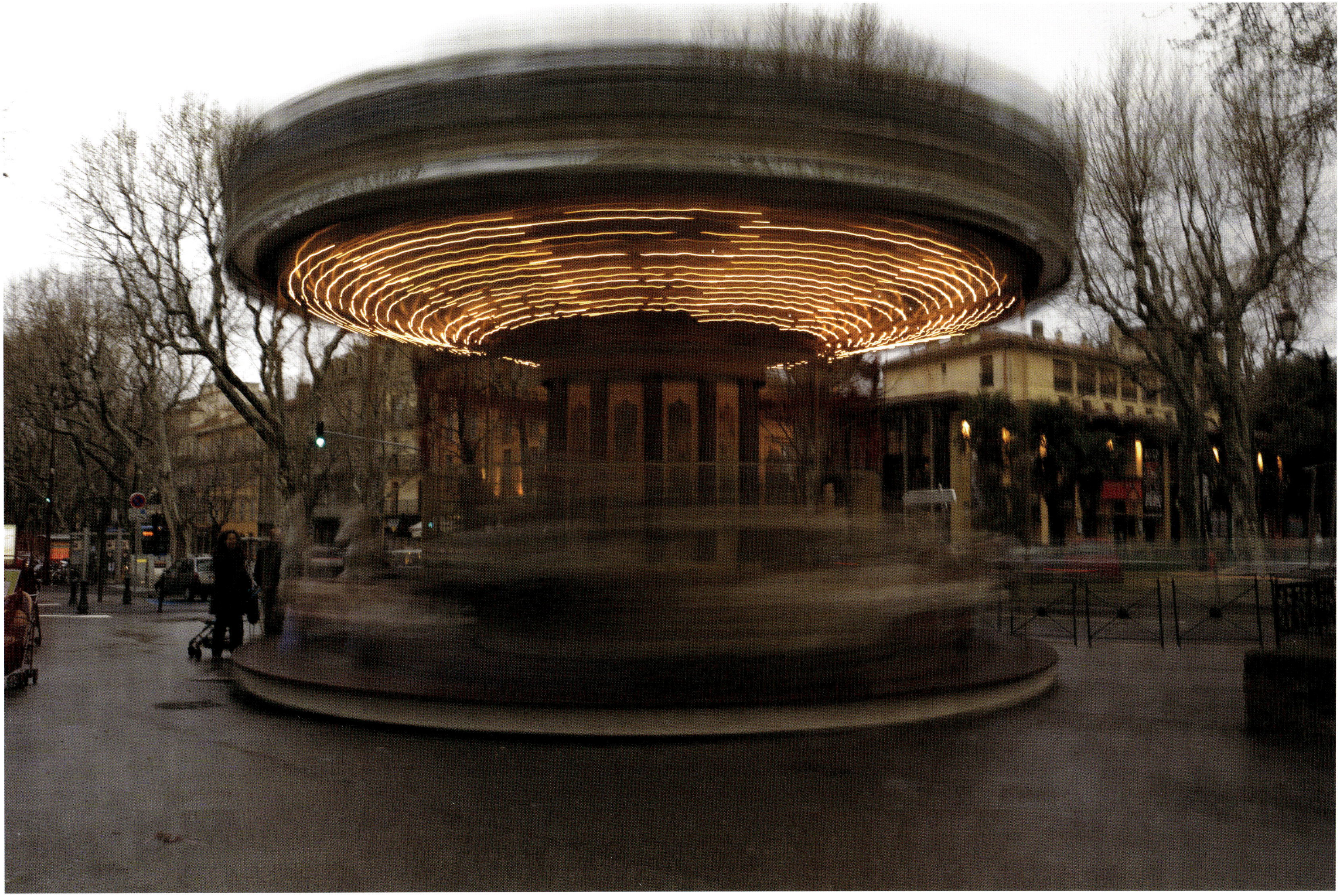

PLATE 23

THIS MORNING WE ARE TRANSPORTED YET AGAIN—THIS TIME, IN CEZANNE'S STUDIO. IT'S HOLY IN HERE, and one longs to surrender to the light and vision and ritual, the never-ending search to articulate the inexplicable. It's a gray day, as gray as the walls, which gives the whole experience a dreamlike, floating reality.

In Cezanne's garden I pick a single flower of myrtle and walk the paths he trod, and then we leave him there and take the back road to Vauvenargues. The day is mixed: broody, fast-moving skies; a weak sun trying to break through. It, like us, is looking for an opening. We look and look and remark to each other on the difficulty we're having in seeing something that takes our breath away. We stop here and there, searching. We become aware of our "need" and have to keep letting go. We have to trust that what we're looking for will appear when we least expect it.

We continue to climb up into the mountains, and as we round a sharp bend, a rocky ledge calls to me. I have no idea what it is that beckons me, yet am impelled to follow this instinct. I climb over a railing and find "my" rock. I sit and look out to the mountains and valleys, still wondering what is it about this place that makes me feel at home on the planet? I look around and see I am surrounded by wild thyme! The gift is right there at my feet in the form of a metaphor. And indeed, sitting in the vast landscape, one understands the larger sense of being surrounded by time. How many centuries ago was this area underwater? How long did it take for these rocks to forge themselves? How many tectonic upheavals took place? I pick huge bunches of thyme and heartened, we travel on.

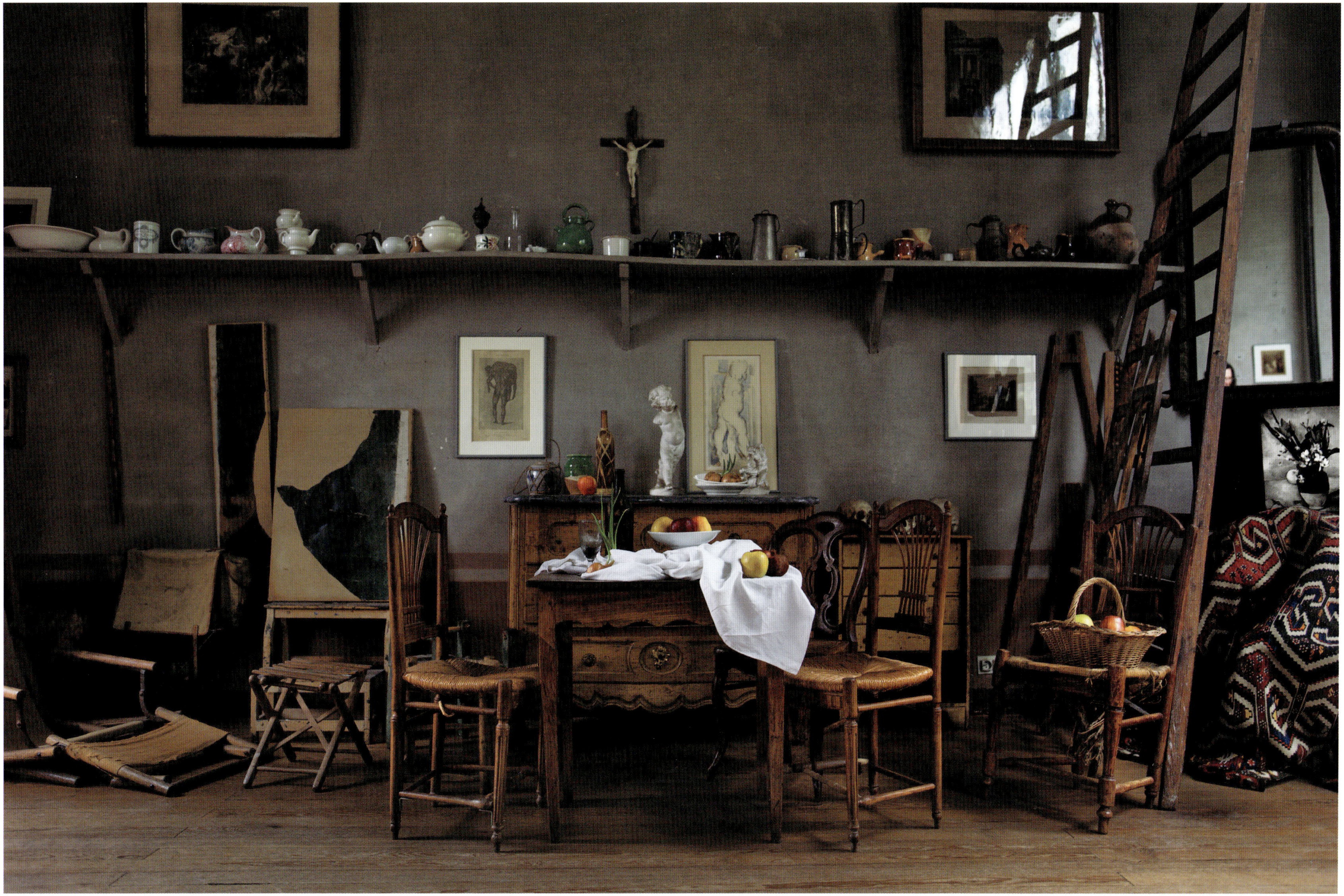

PLATE 24

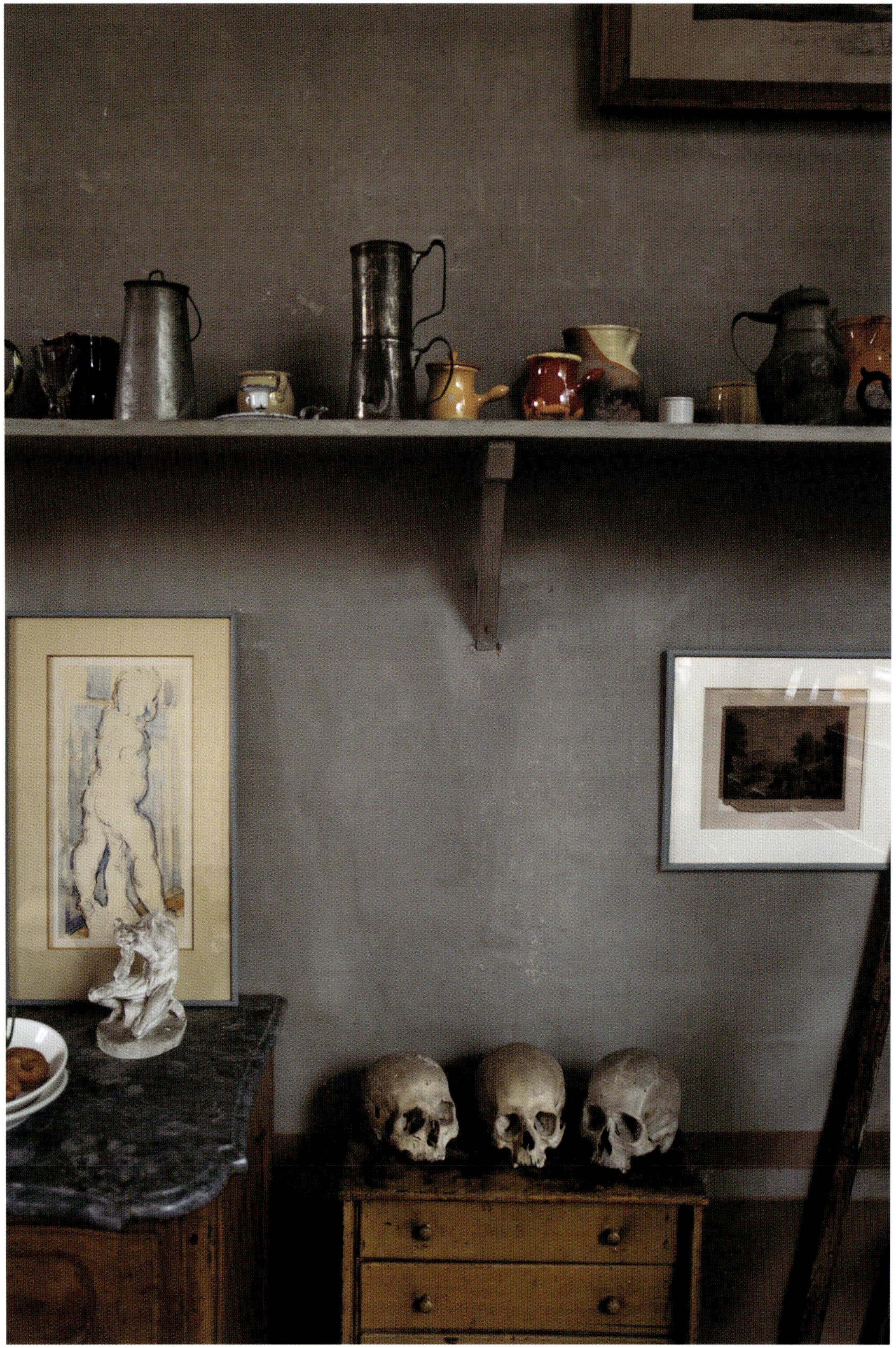

PLATE 25

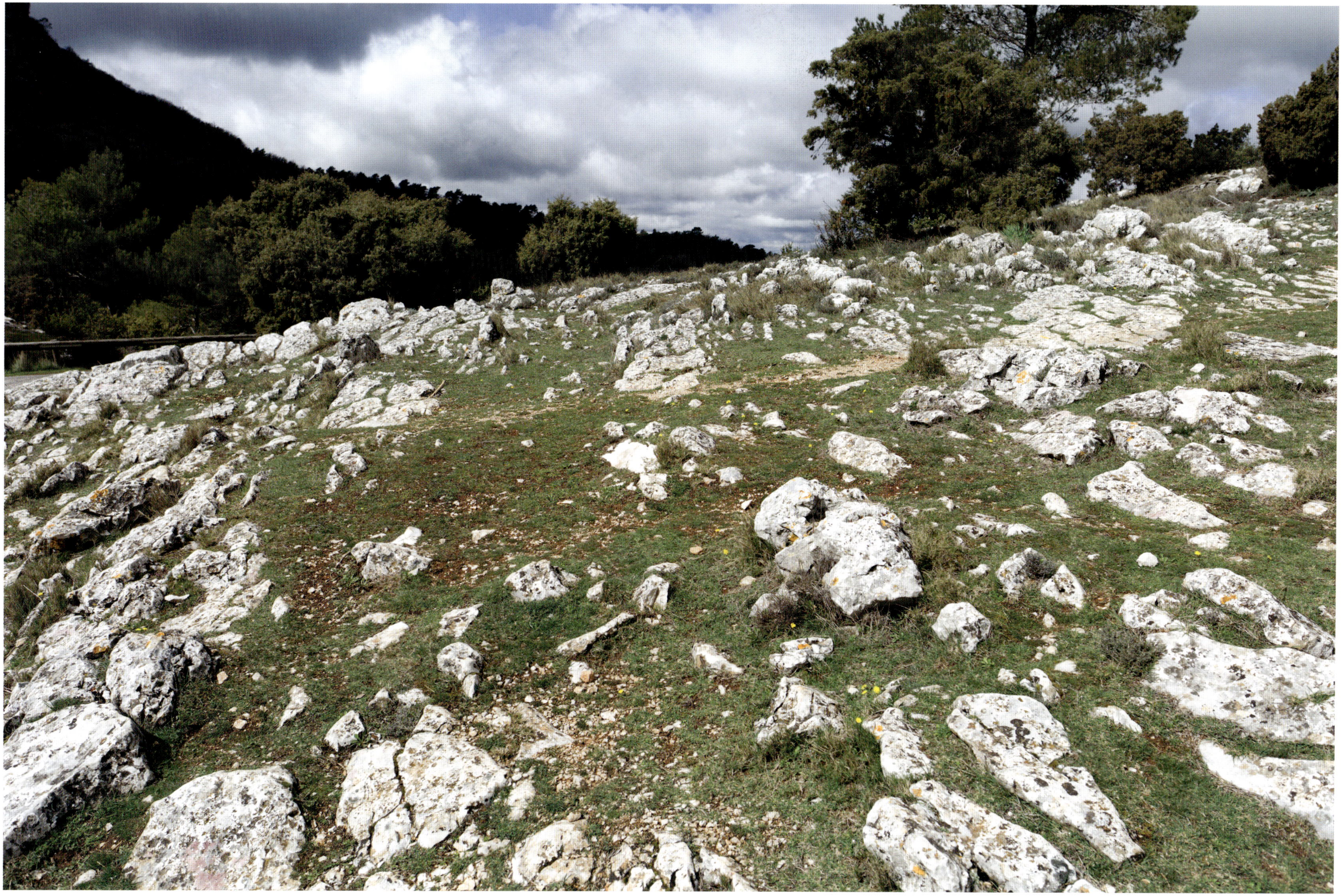

PLATE 26

PLATE 27

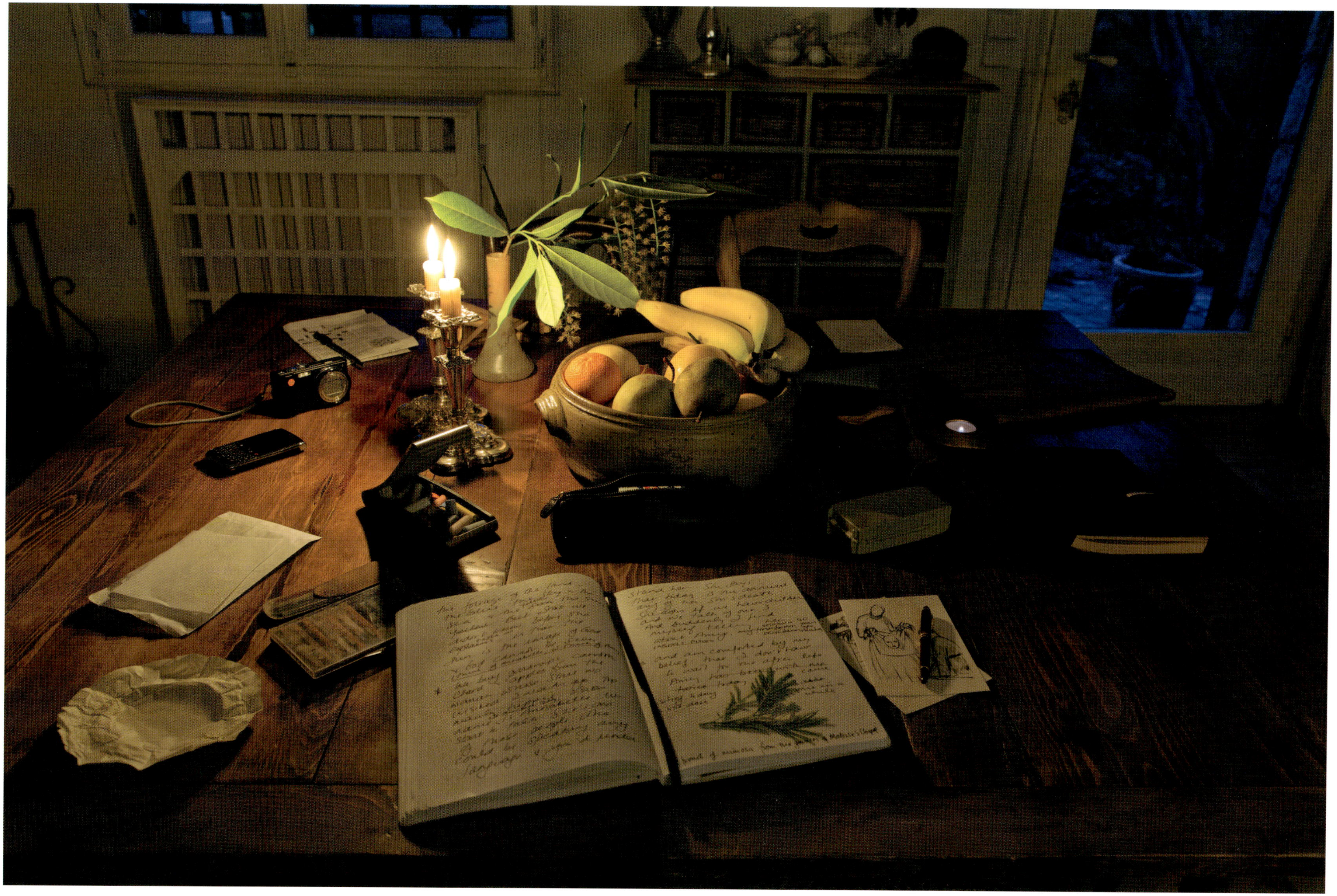

AFTER AN EARLY BREAKFAST, WE TAKE OFF FOR NICE. SATURDAY IS TRIPLE-MARKET DAY: BOOKS, FLOWERS, FOOD.

It's a happy city today, full of that Saturday feeling that some cities do so well—Nice, in particular. There are still only a few tourists as the season hasn't started yet, but the natives are as carefree as any vacationer. We amble through bookstalls, browsing here and there: old books on Provence, portraits of those who worked the land. At another stall Tintin rules, while at another an antique book is held open to a page of watercolored figures naked from the waist down.

The French are already at the bistros with their coffee, croissants, and cigarettes. I think of the first time I came to France, back in the sixties when I was eighteen. I hitched around Europe for three months with a friend, the two of us smoking Gauloises and ordering café au lait in grammar-school French. Yes, it's all changed a lot since then, like everywhere, and yet here, today, in the old town of Nice, much remains. The French are so beautifully French.

We wander on to the flower stalls; sunlight streams through the canvas awnings onto bunches of peonies—some in a coral shade new to me—roses, tulips, lilies, irises, and many other blossoms whose names I do not know. Oh, and the food stalls! Glistening olives, plump sausages, melting cheeses, fruits, vegetables, nuts, pastries, and breads.

We return to the square of booksellers and lunch outside at a brasserie. We feel suspended as only travelers can: no plan; no needs; no language; hardly a thought—just the being, right here, right now, in Provence.

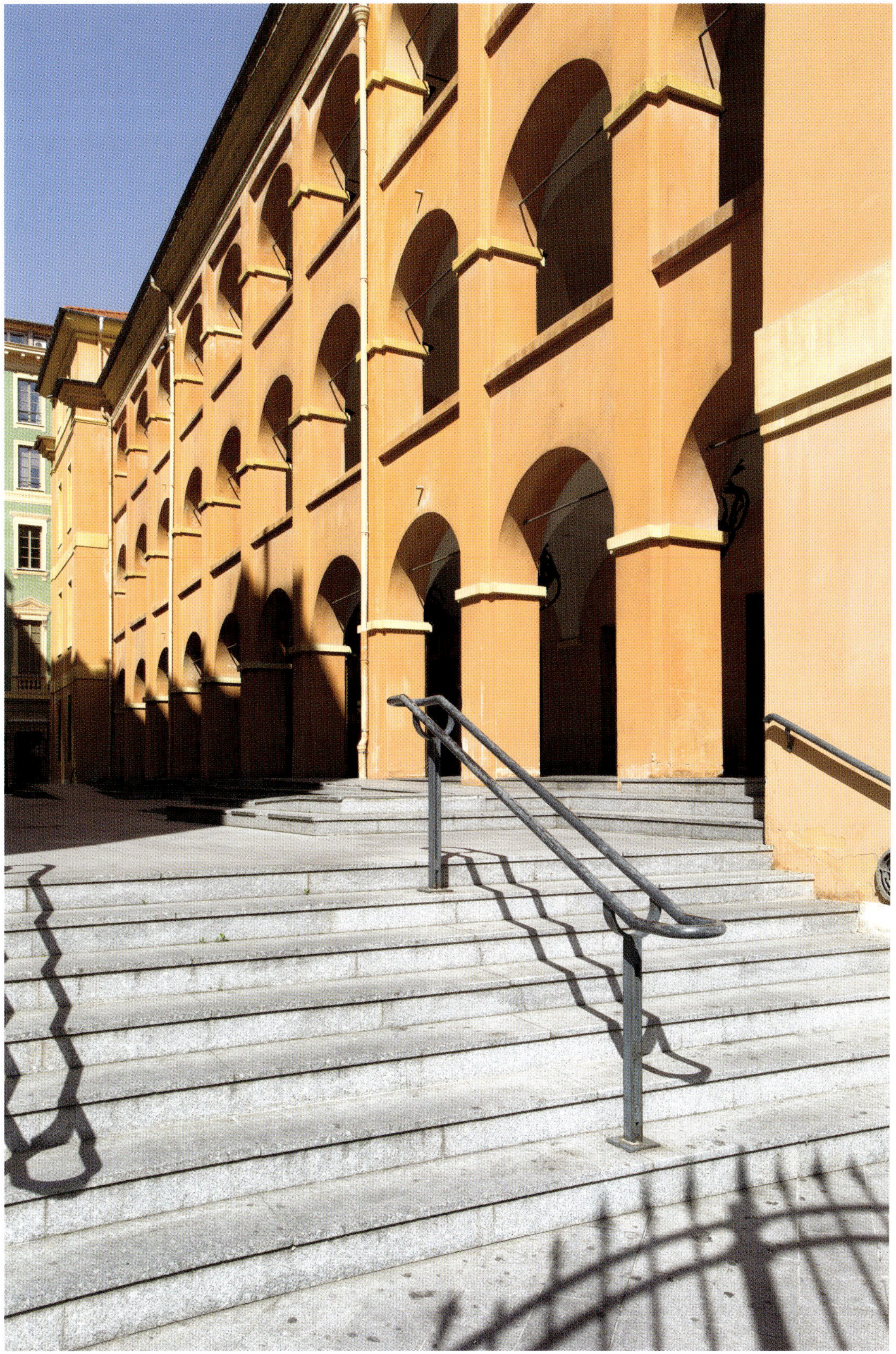

PLATE 28

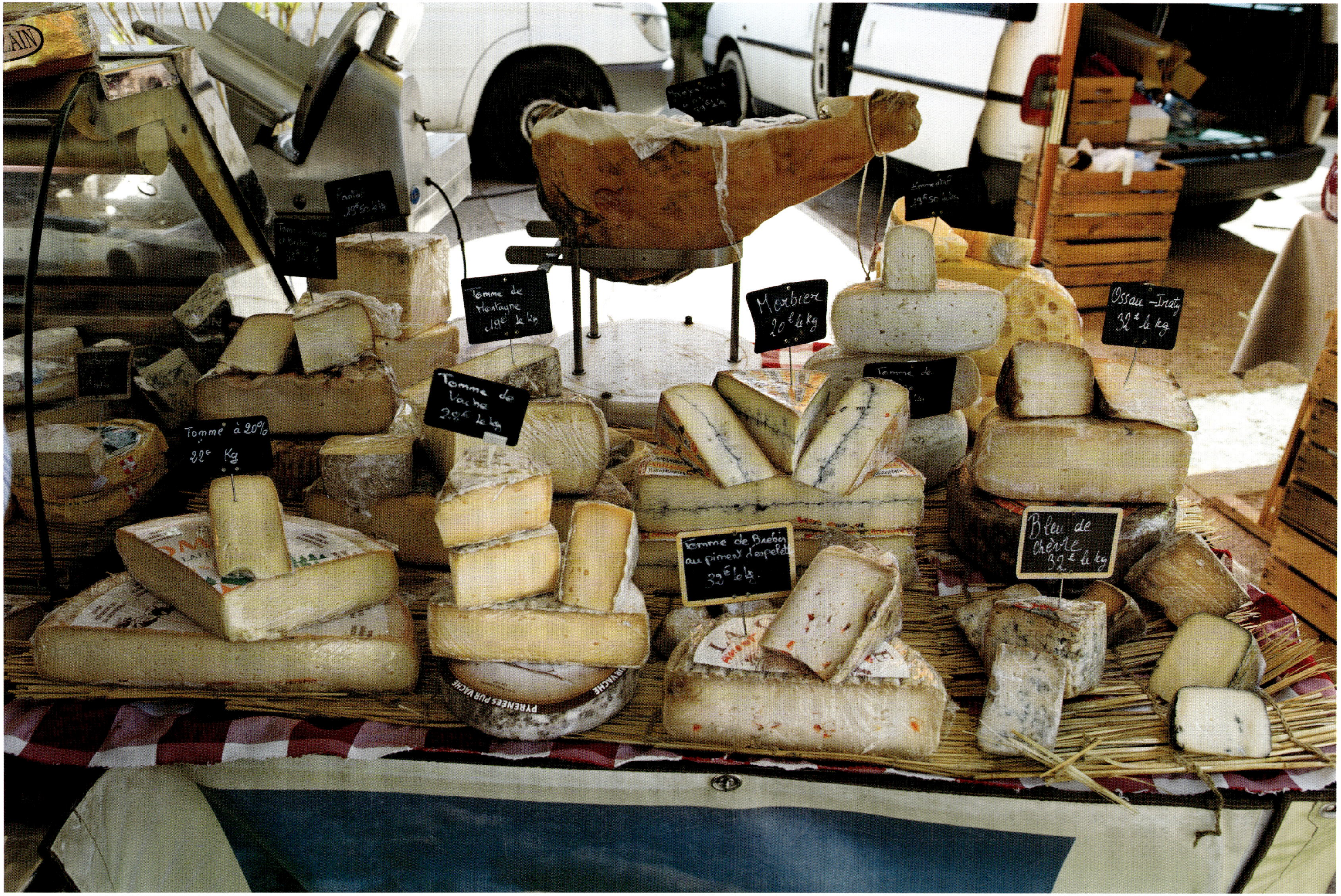
Tomme de Montagne 19€ le kg
Tomme à 20%
22€ Kg
Tomme de Vache 22€ le kg
Morbier 20€ le kg
Ossau-Iraty 32€ le kg
Tomme de Brebis au piment d'espelette 32€ le kg
Bleu de chèvre 32€ le kg
PYRENEES PUR VACHE

PLATE 29

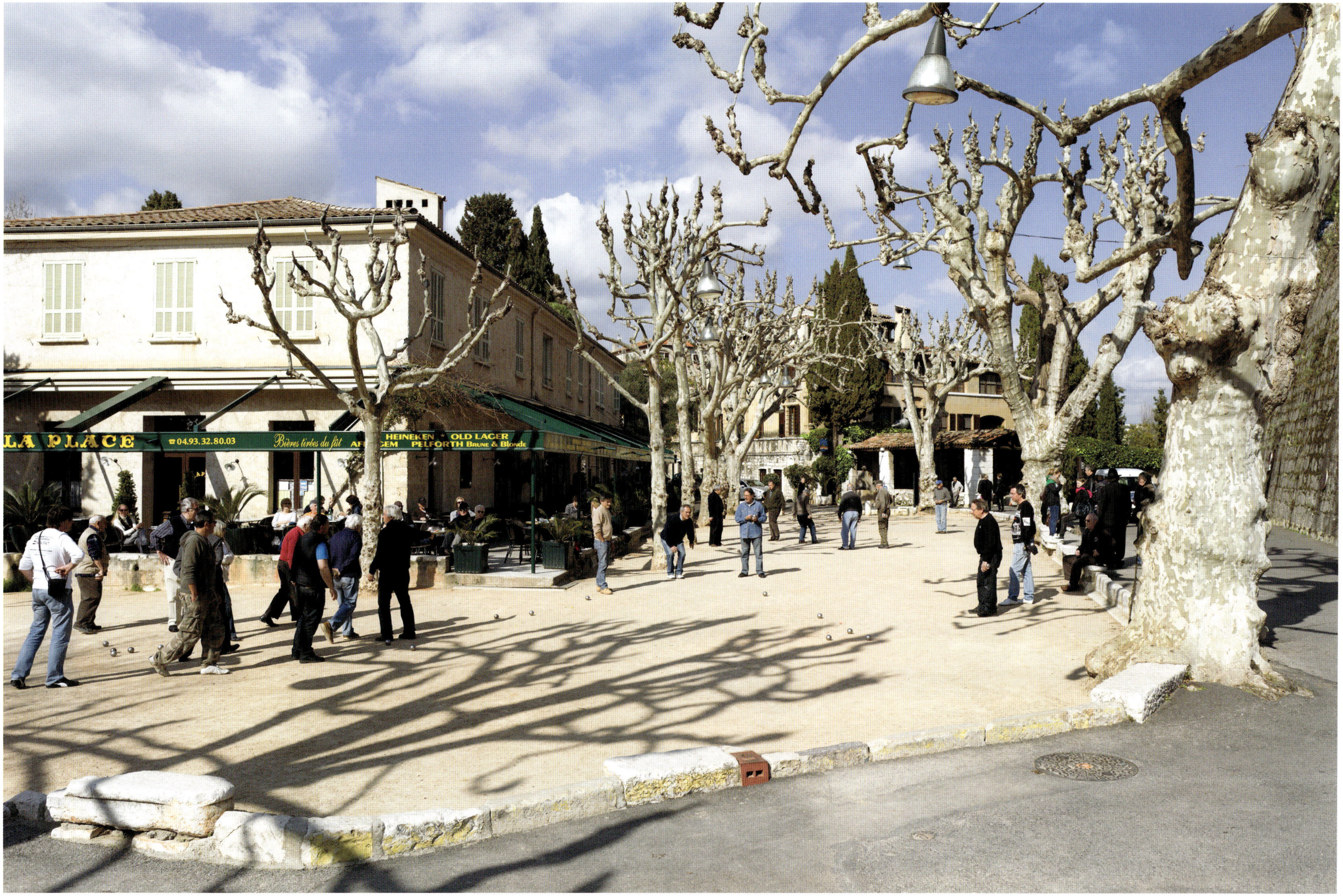
LA PLACE
04.93.32.80.03
Bières tirées du fût
HEINEKEN * OLD LAGER
PELFORTH Brune & Blonde

PLATE 30

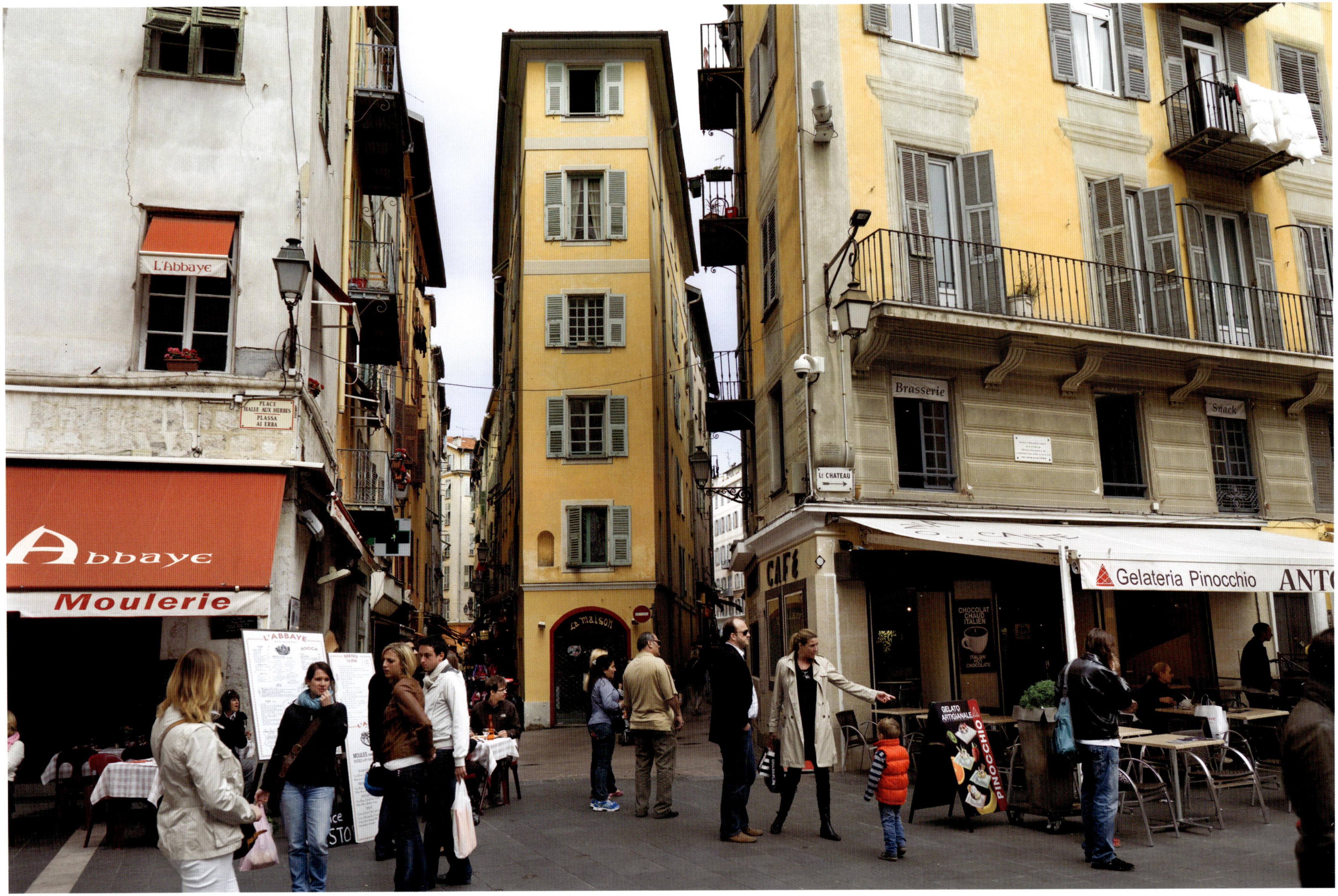
L'Abbaye
PLACE
HALLE AUX HERBES
PLASSA
AI ERBA
Abbaye
Moulerie
L'ABBAYE
SOCCA
La Maison
Brasserie
Snack
Le CHATEAU
CAFÉ
Gelateria Pinocchio
ANTO
CHOCOLAT
CHAUD
ITALIEN
ITALIAN
HOT
CHOCOLATE
GELATO
ARTIGIANALE
PINOCCHIO

PLATE 31

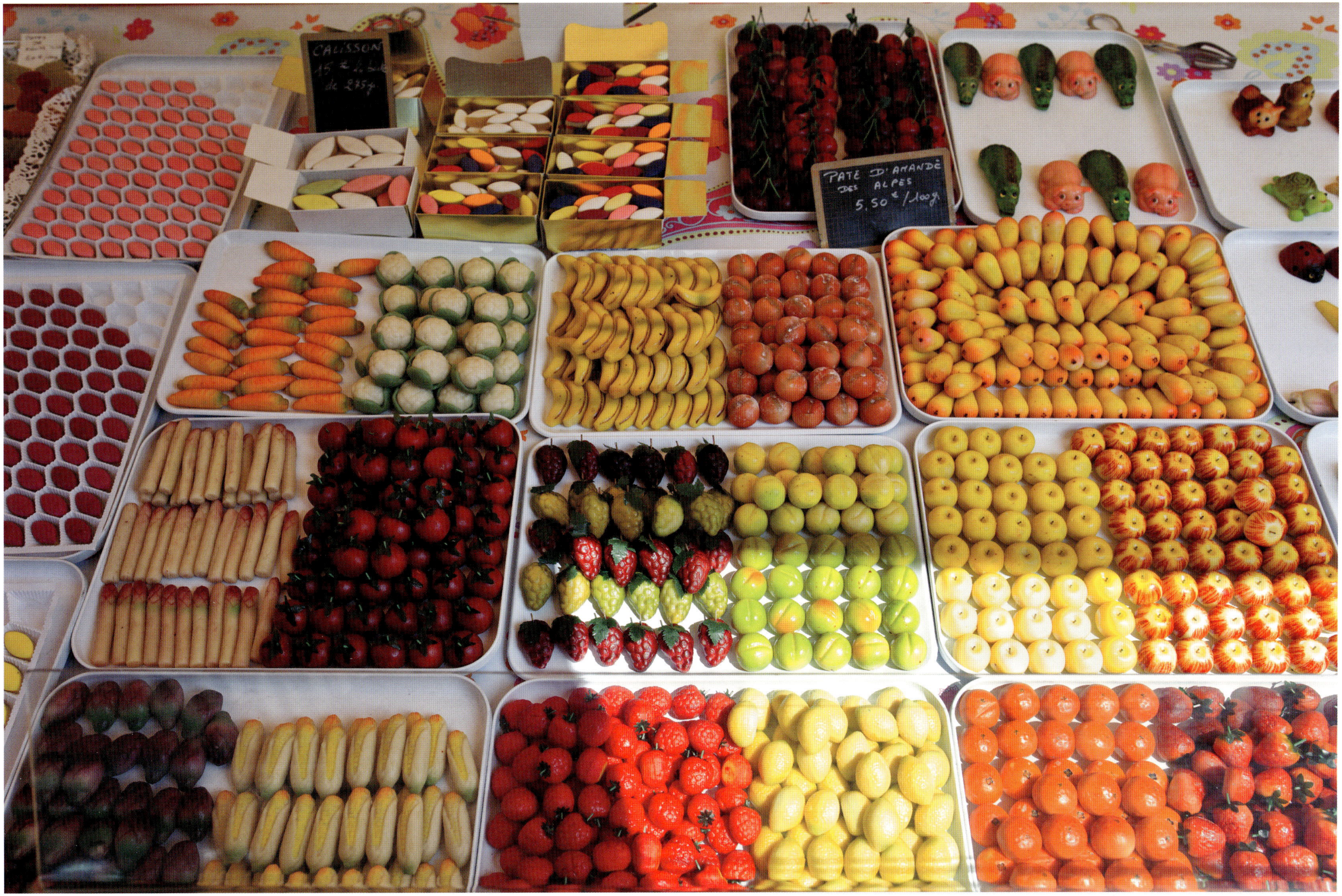

PLATE 32

April

WE'RE BACK IN BONNIEUX AND DECIDE TO TAKE AN AIMLESS RIDE IN THE SURROUNDING COUNTRYSIDE. The morning is as gloomy as our mood: the sky glowering, the mistral still at its malignant play; the air cold down to the bone. Yet in spite of all this it is a day alive with color. The wisteria, lilac, and iris are dressed in shades of mauve and purple—shades that are often associated with death, but which Mother Nature flaunts in the season of birth.

Two fields of newly tilled earth lay side-by-side, one the color of sand, the other closer to rust. A backdrop of ocher hillsides sets off a meadow of rape, its yellow buzz almost vicious in intensity, while next to it, a crop of robust young wheat is so green it vibrates. At the far edge of one field a line of bottle-green pines stand in dark solemnity, while over there rows of shiny new grape leaves are all atwitter on their old stumps of vine. And then we round a corner in an old hill town and are hit with a shock of magenta from a flowering Judas tree. These living colors create their own light, a light which is all the brighter beneath the gray tarpaulin sky.

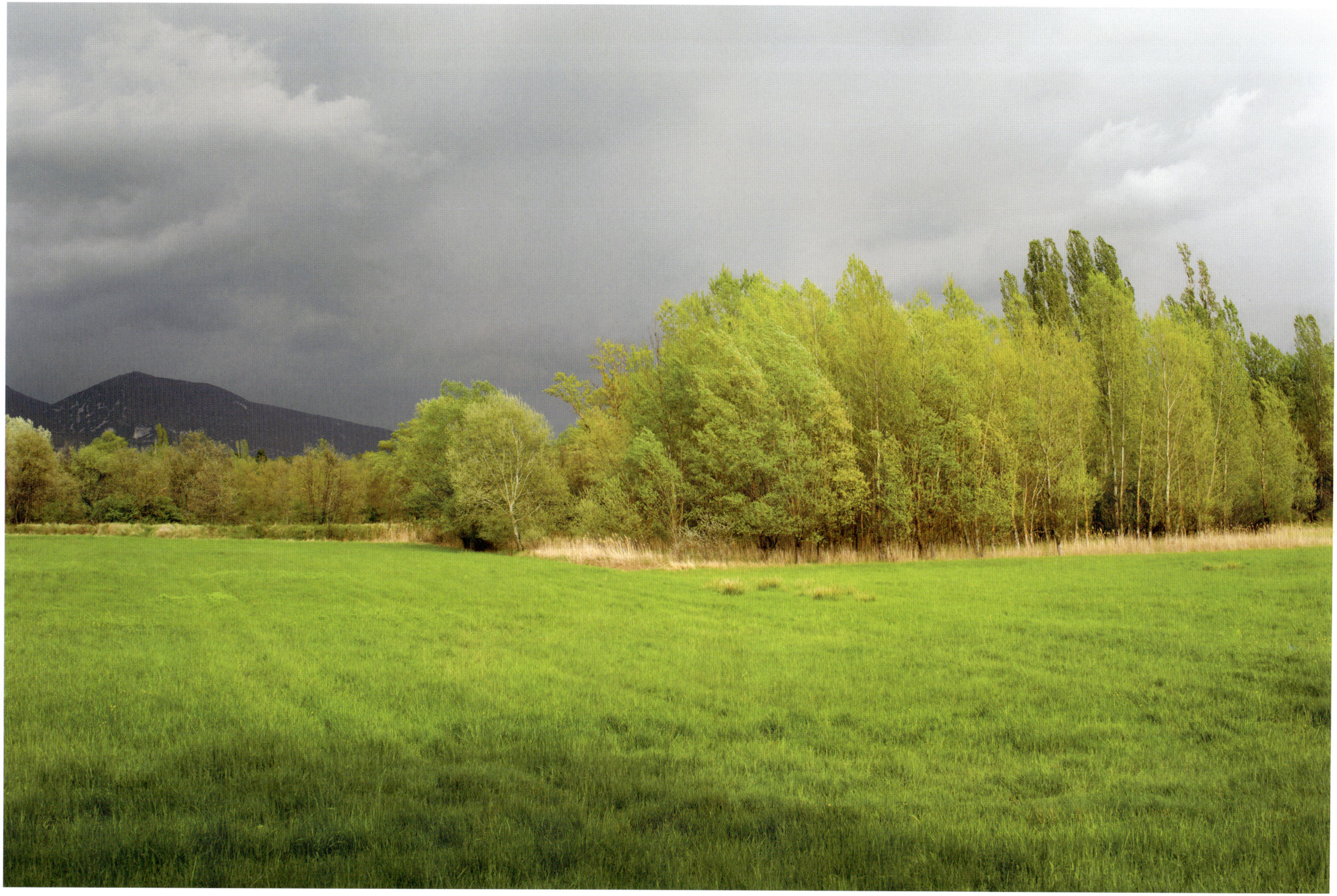

PLATE 33

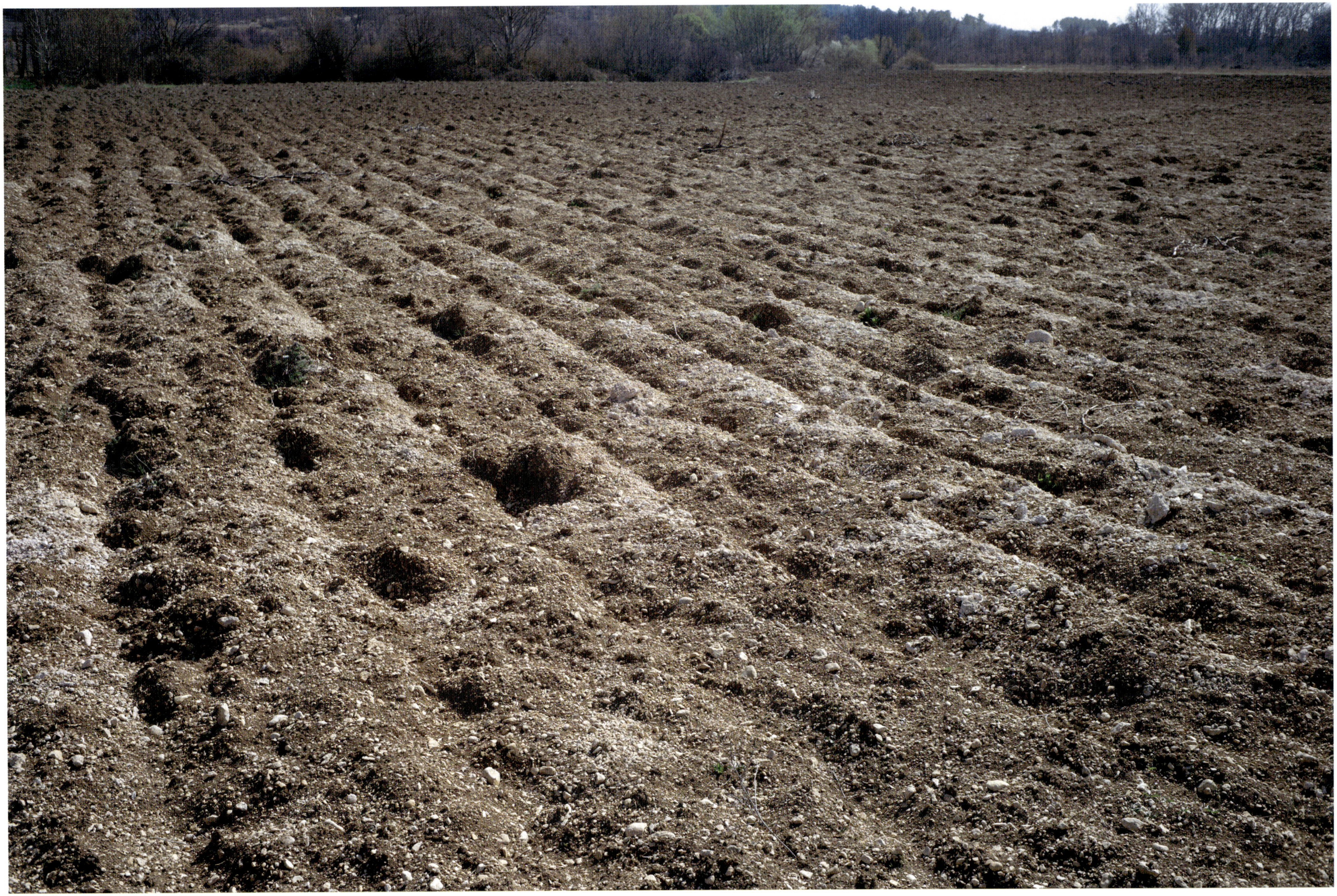

PLATE 34

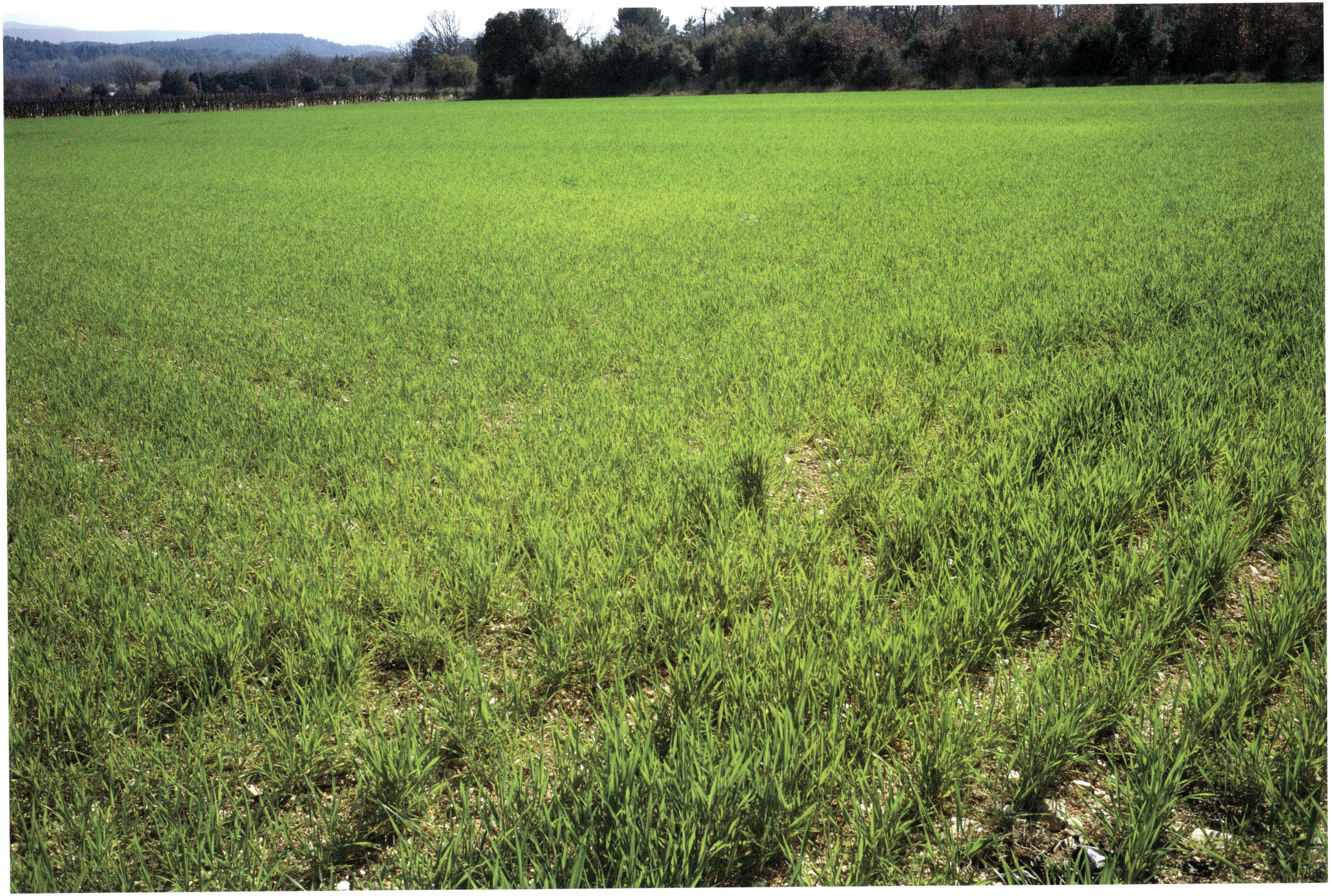

PLATE 35

PLATE 36 (OVERLEAF)

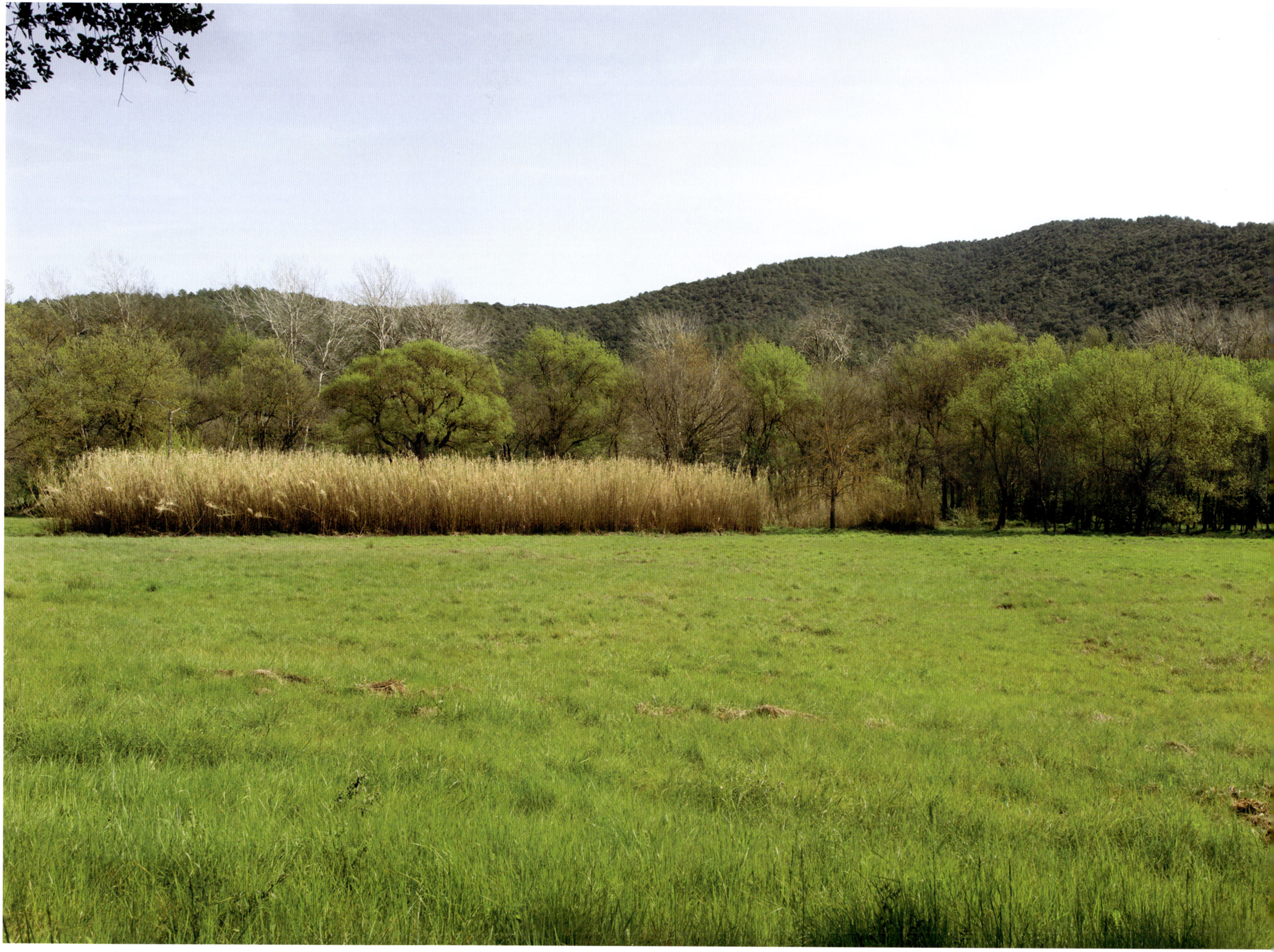

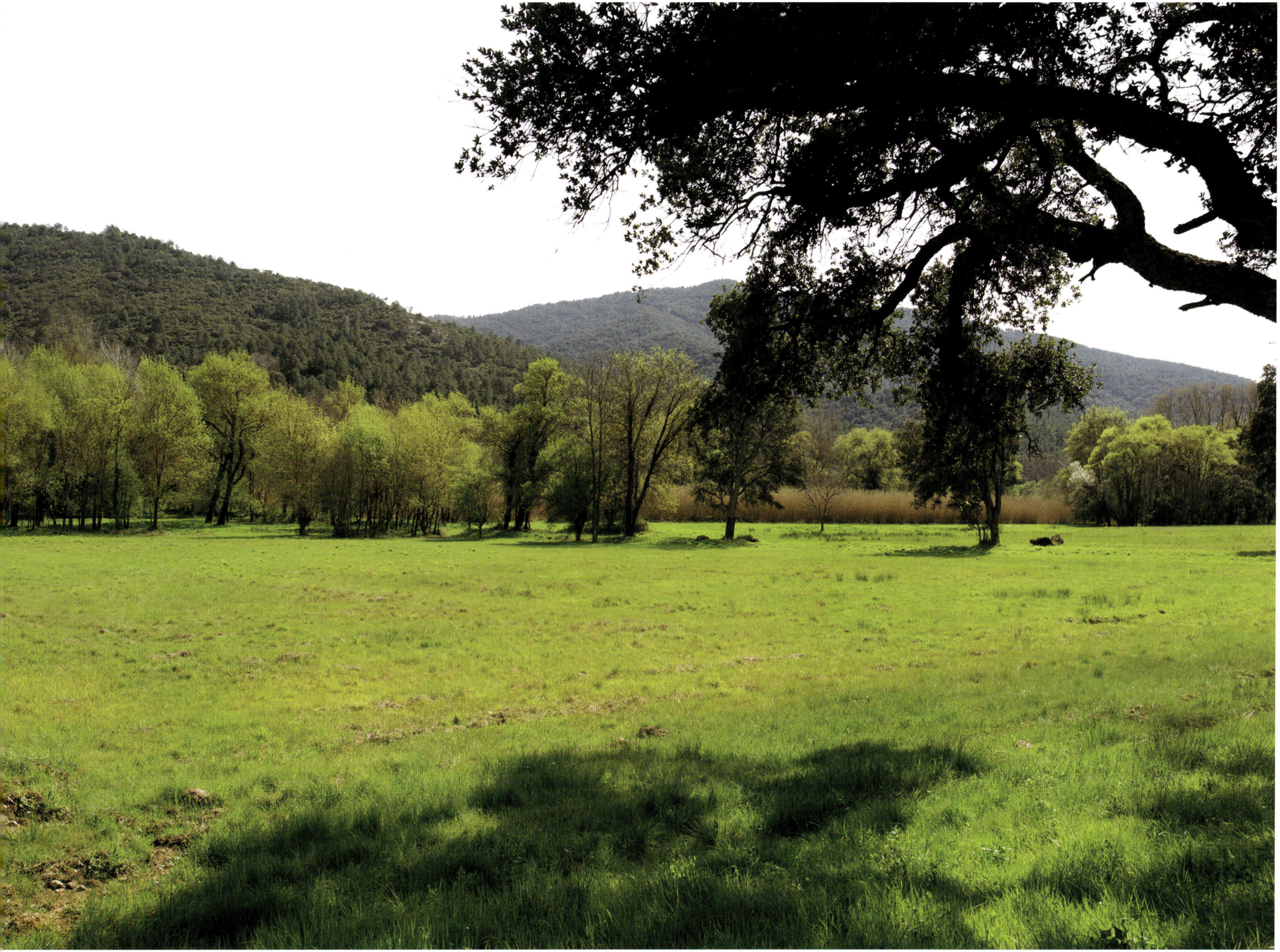

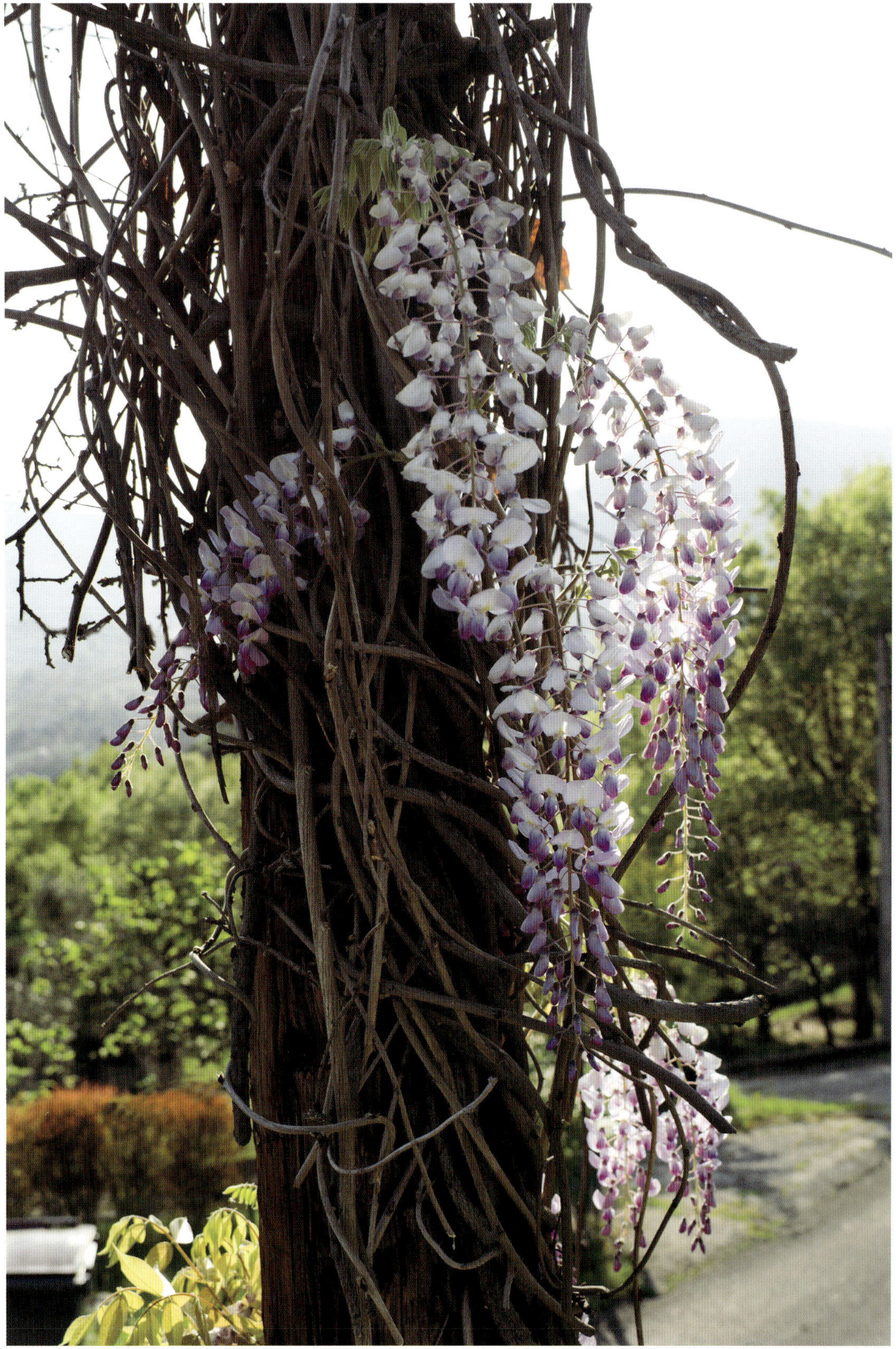

PLATE 37

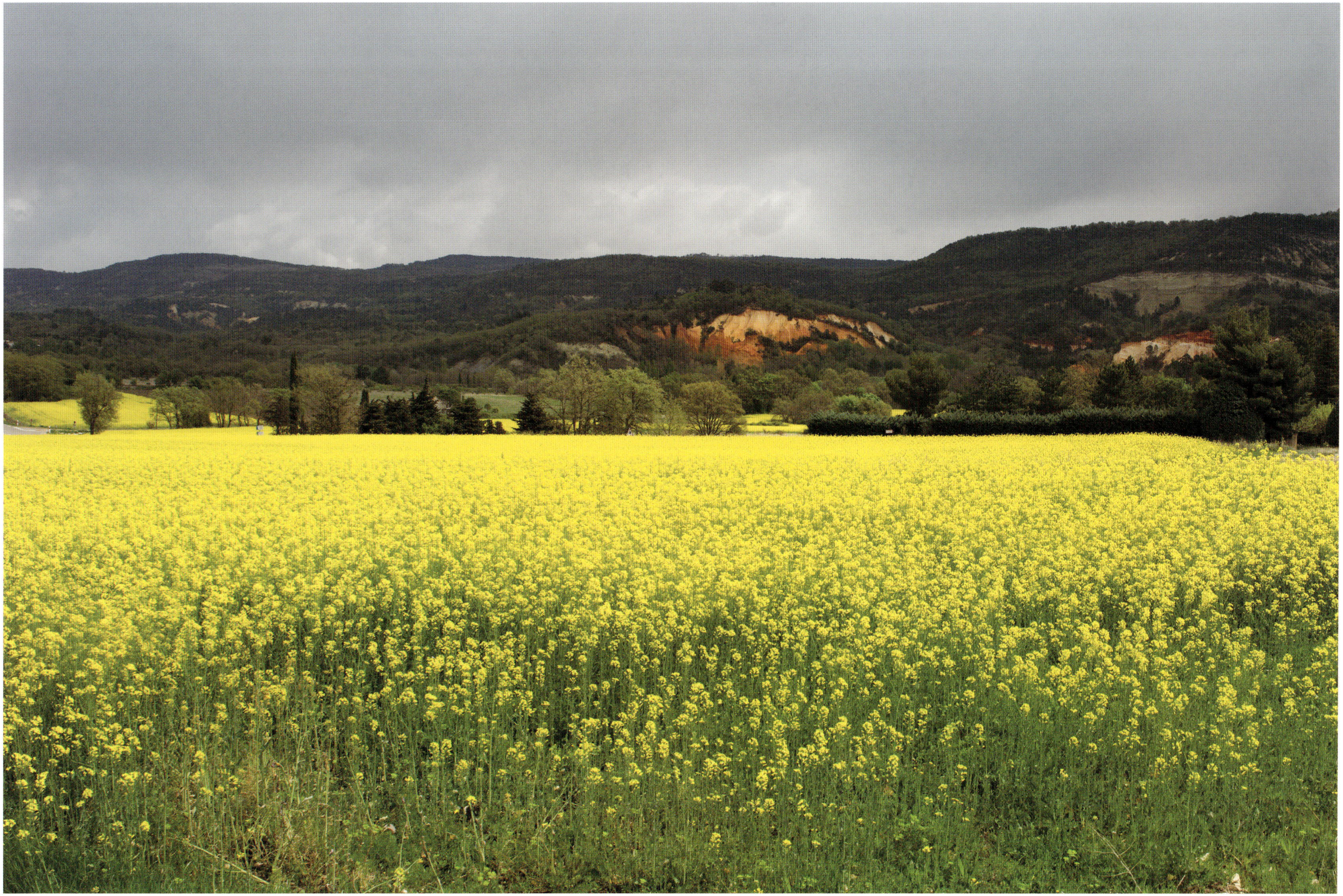

PLATE 38

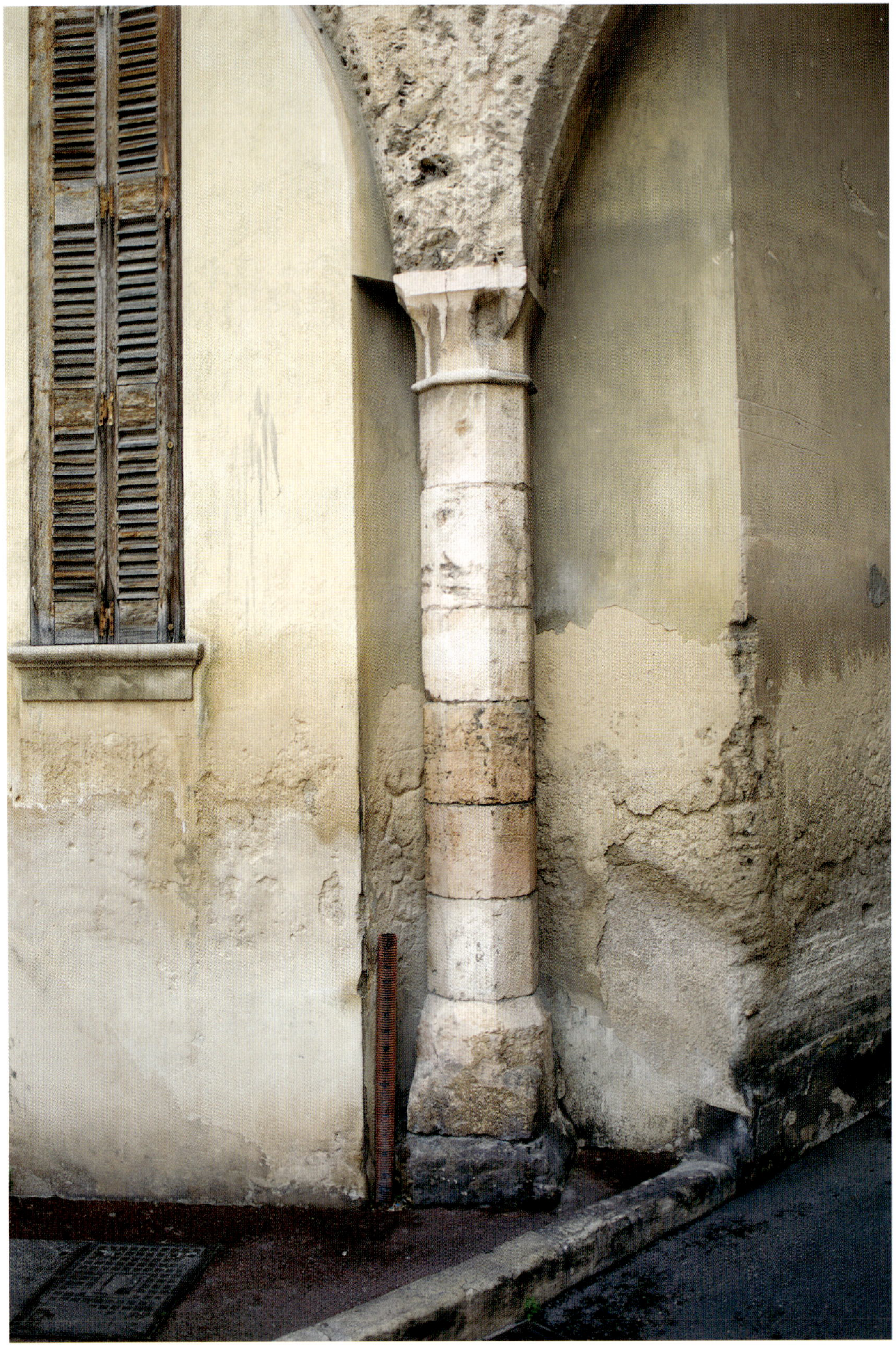

PLATE 39

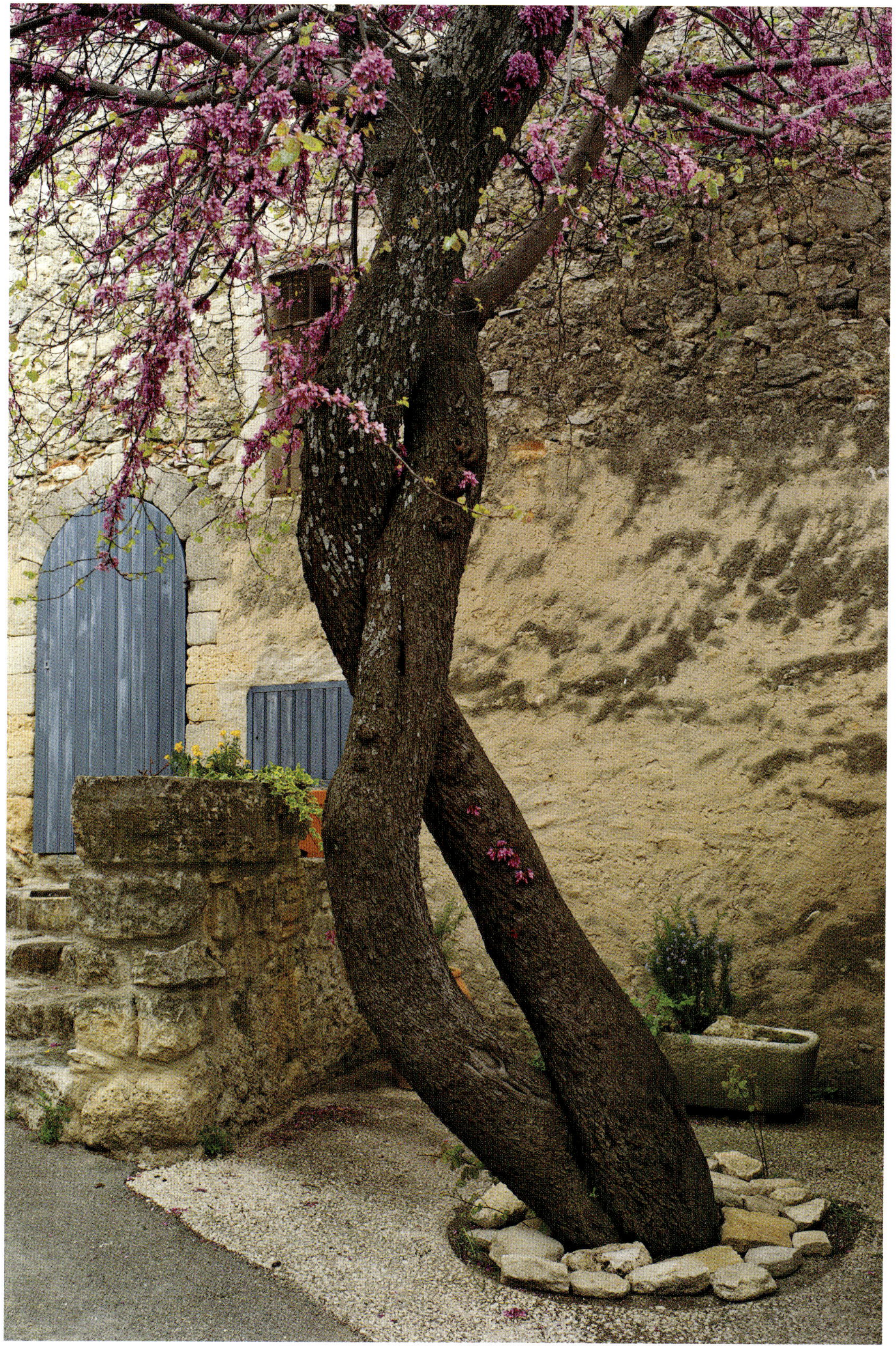

PLATE 40

WE SAIL ON THROUGH THE COUNTRYSIDE THROUGHOUT THE LATE AFTERNOON, THROUGH RAIN CLOUDS and sunshine, through fields and villages, and then, just outside the town of Apt we see a tree that takes our breath away: an enormous tamarisk, decked out in her spring crinoline, a tattered chiffon of the palest pink, slightly gray with age. She shivers and shimmies in the breeze in full glory, against a sky now turned to gunmetal.

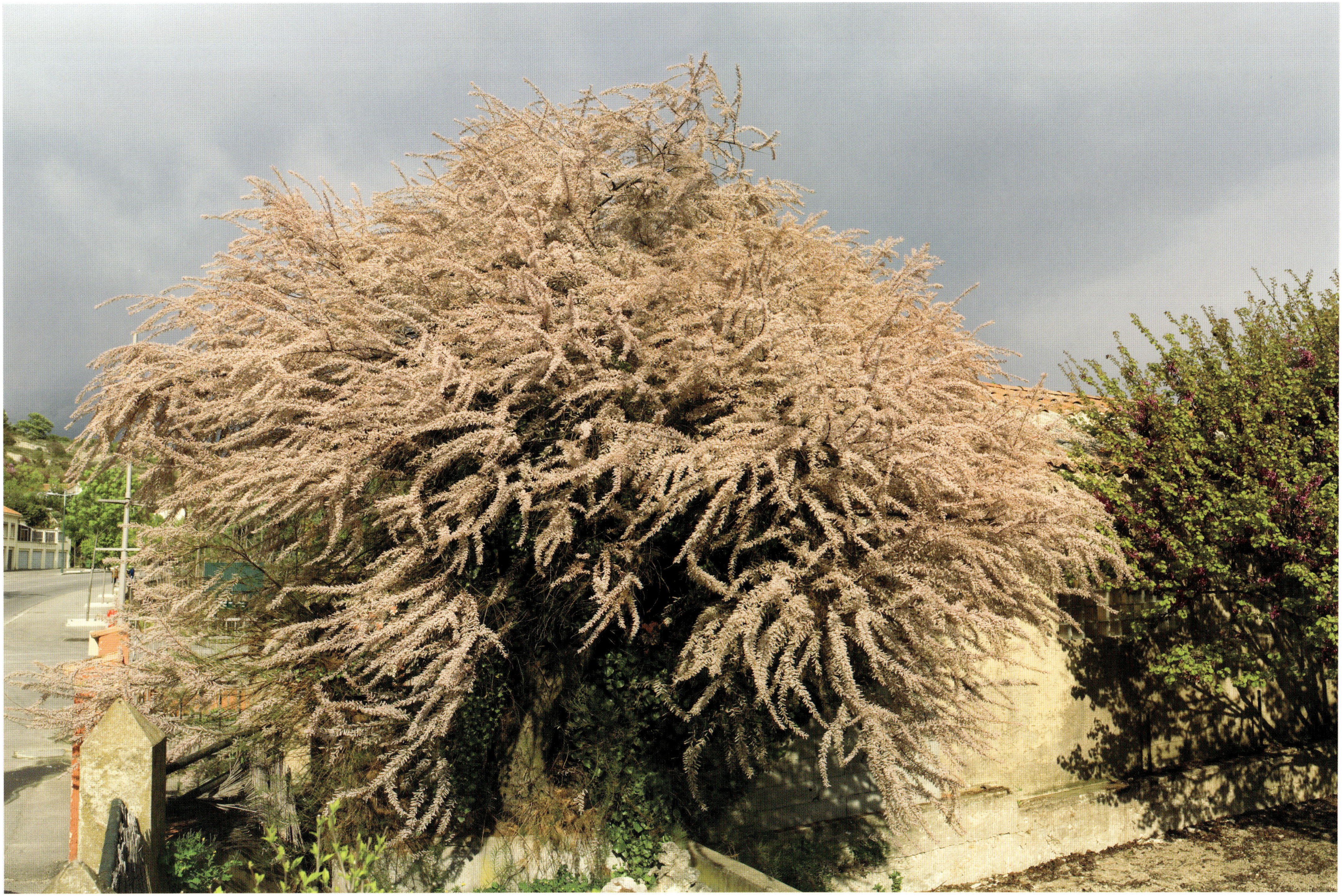

PLATE 41

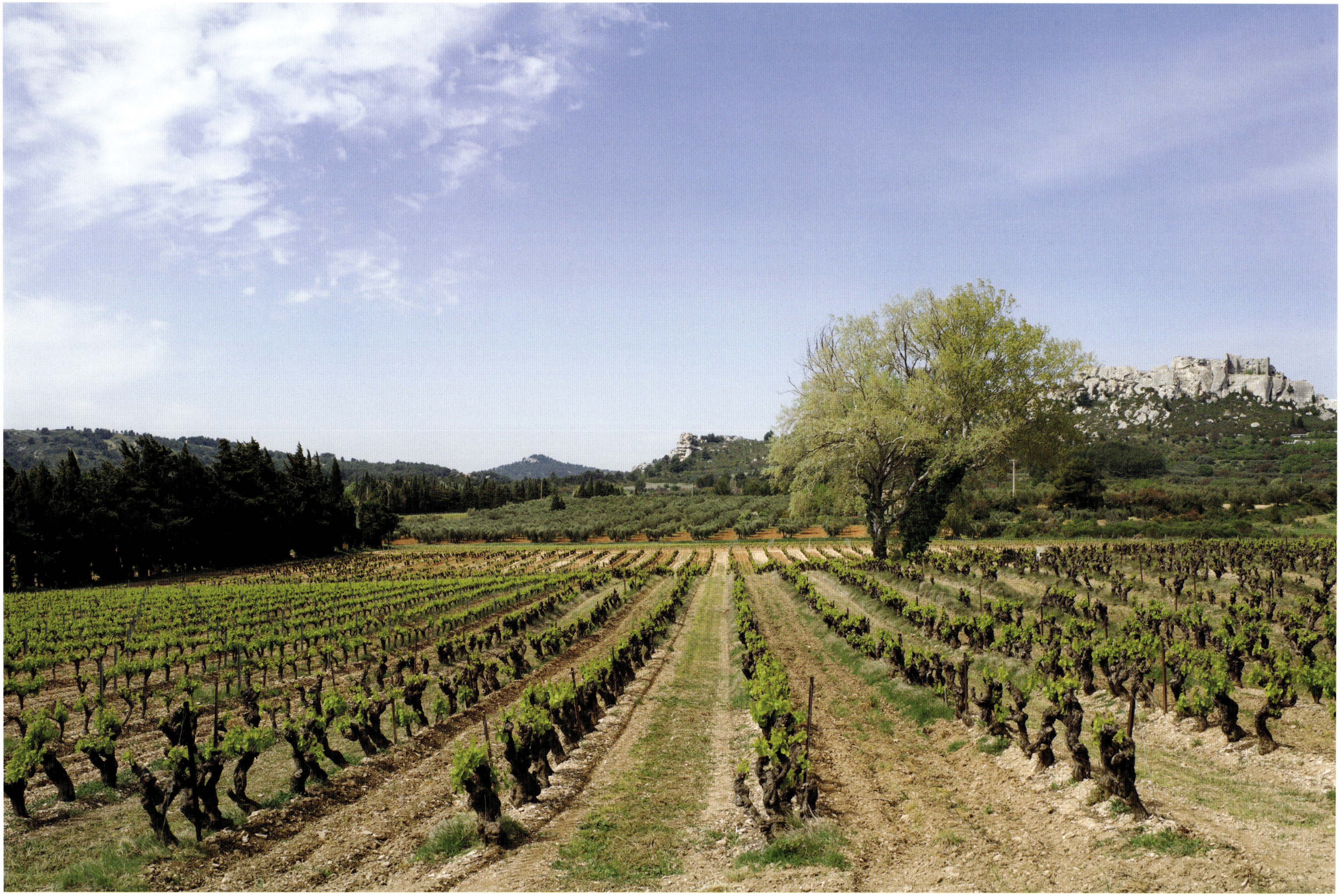

PLATE 42

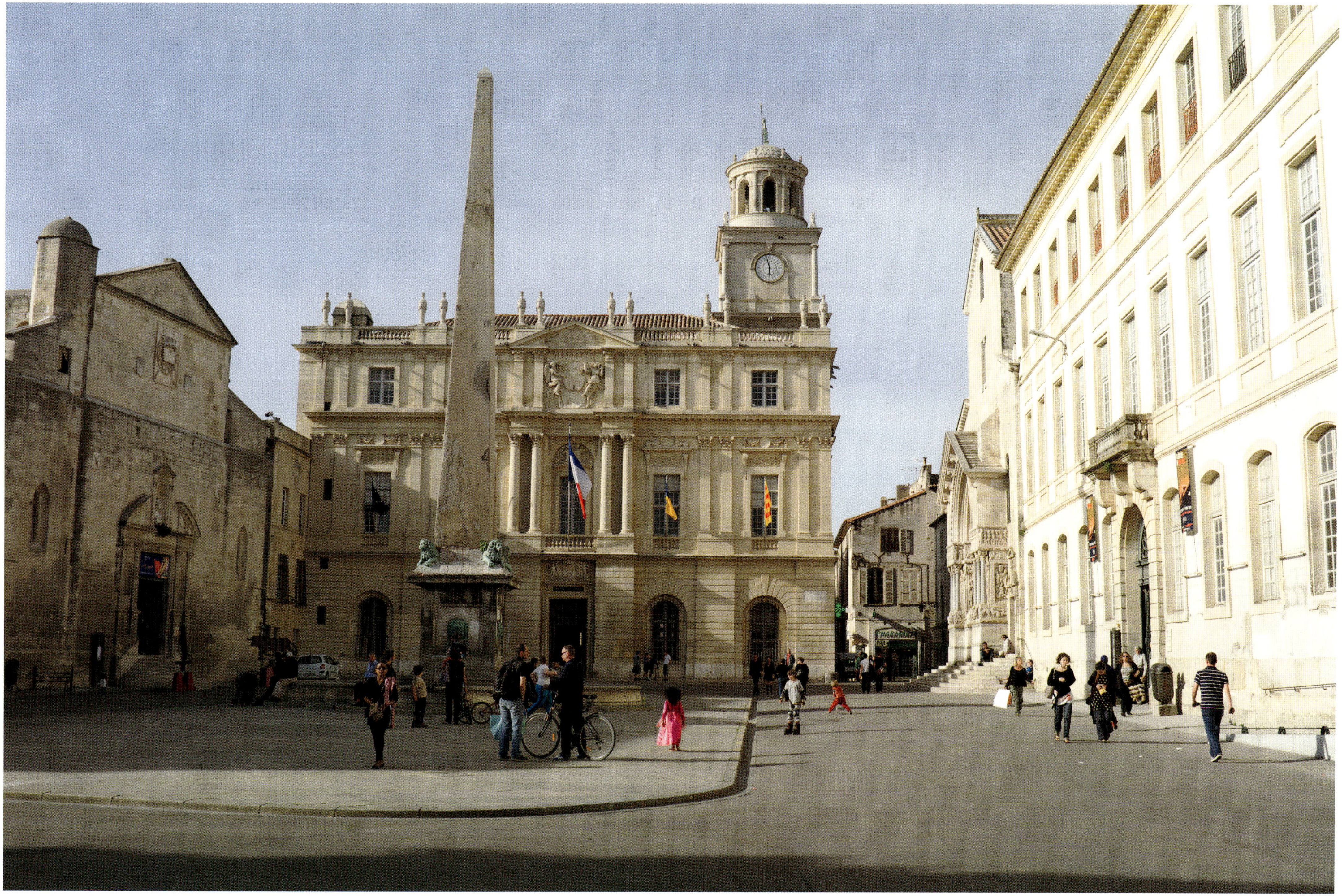

PLATE 43

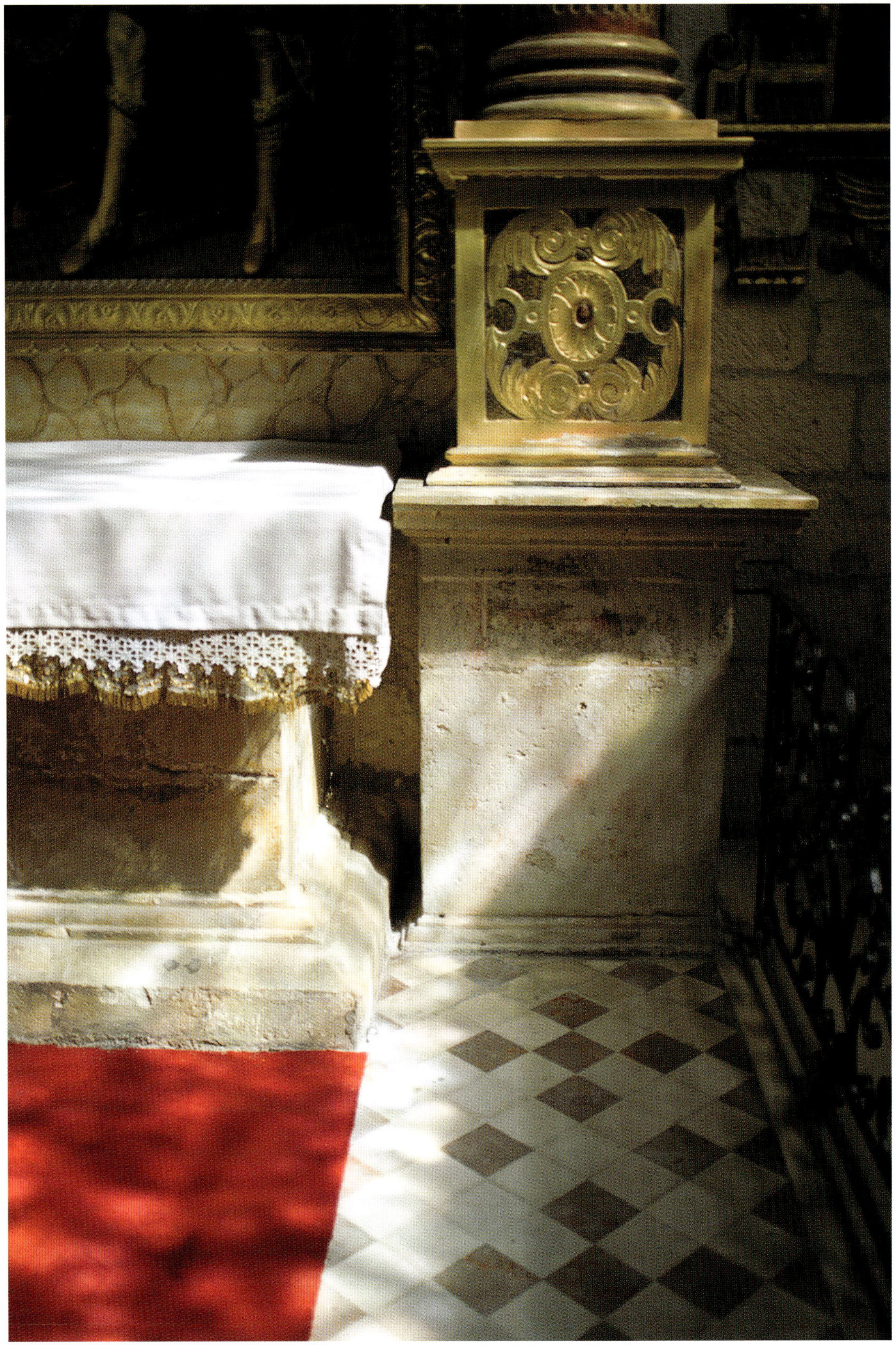

PLATE 44

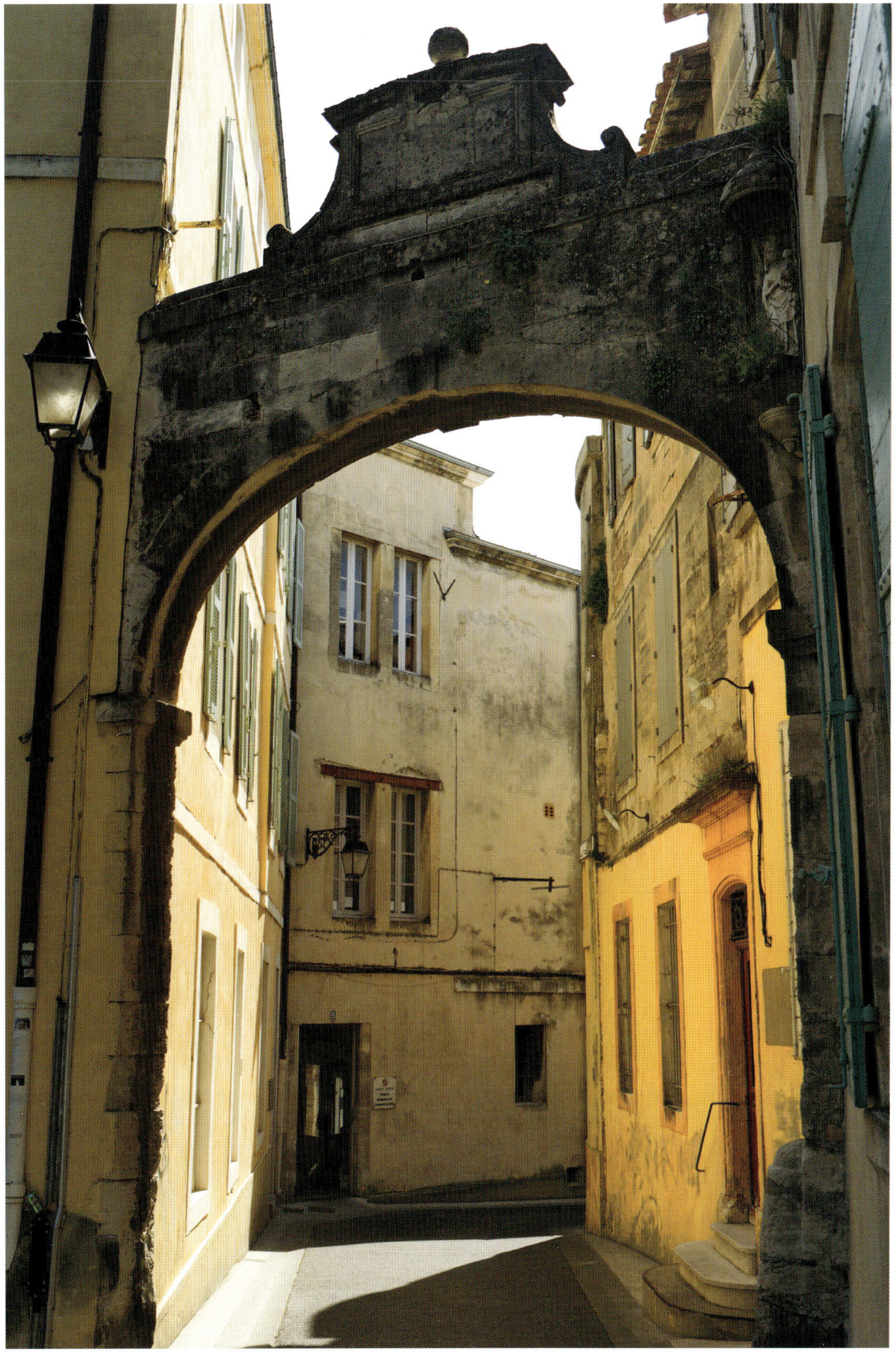

PLATE 45

I WON'T GO INTO HISTORY AS IT'S NOT WHAT I DO, AND IT'S READILY AVAILABLE ON THE INTERNET, BUT history abounds here in Arles—from the Roman amphitheater built during the first century CE to the haunts of Vincent van Gogh. And it is the physical remains of all this history that is so comforting. This morning I come out of a cathedral, sit on the sunny steps looking across the square to more ancient buildings and think, well, if all this has survived for so long, through centuries of tribulations and pestilence, maybe this poor old world can survive a little longer.

A class of adolescent school kids stands dazedly where centuries before Roman solders had marched. We aimlessly wander the labyrinthine streets, knowing we can't get lost, which allows for timeless exploration—destination unknown. We buy an old piece of handspun cloth. We watch the locals, carrying briefcases or shopping baskets—and, of course, baguettes—and realize what it is we've come to love about all these old towns: the French love them. More than that, they treasure and respect their history. It is natural for them to live modern life among the ruins and ancient dwellings. Every corner you turn you get another glimpse of breathtaking houses, raddled stone, crumbling pillars, faded shutters, plants growing out of every crevice, laundry hanging from a window. There is no conformity, no straight lines or grids, no street wider than a wagon, only centuries of tradition.

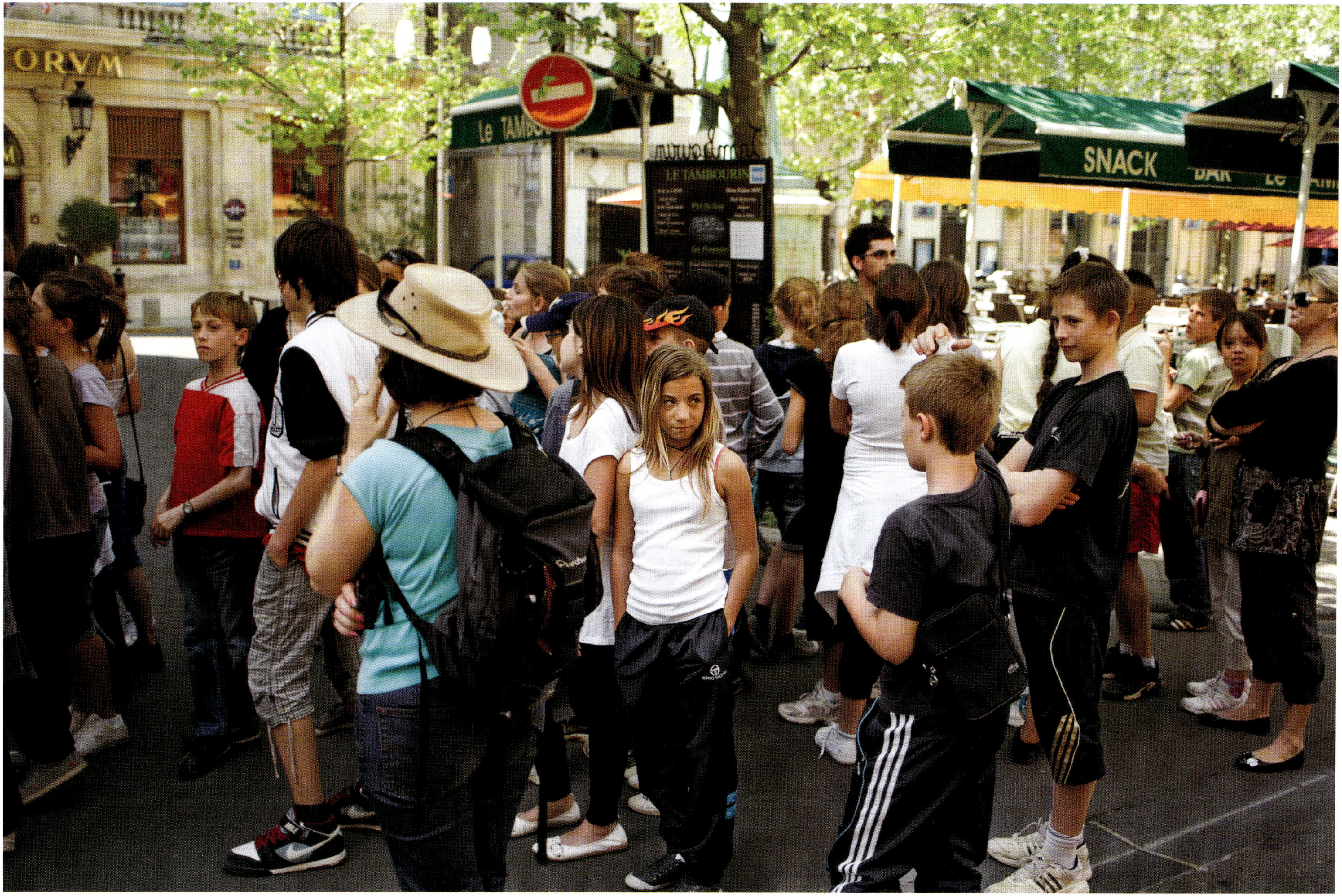

PLATE 46

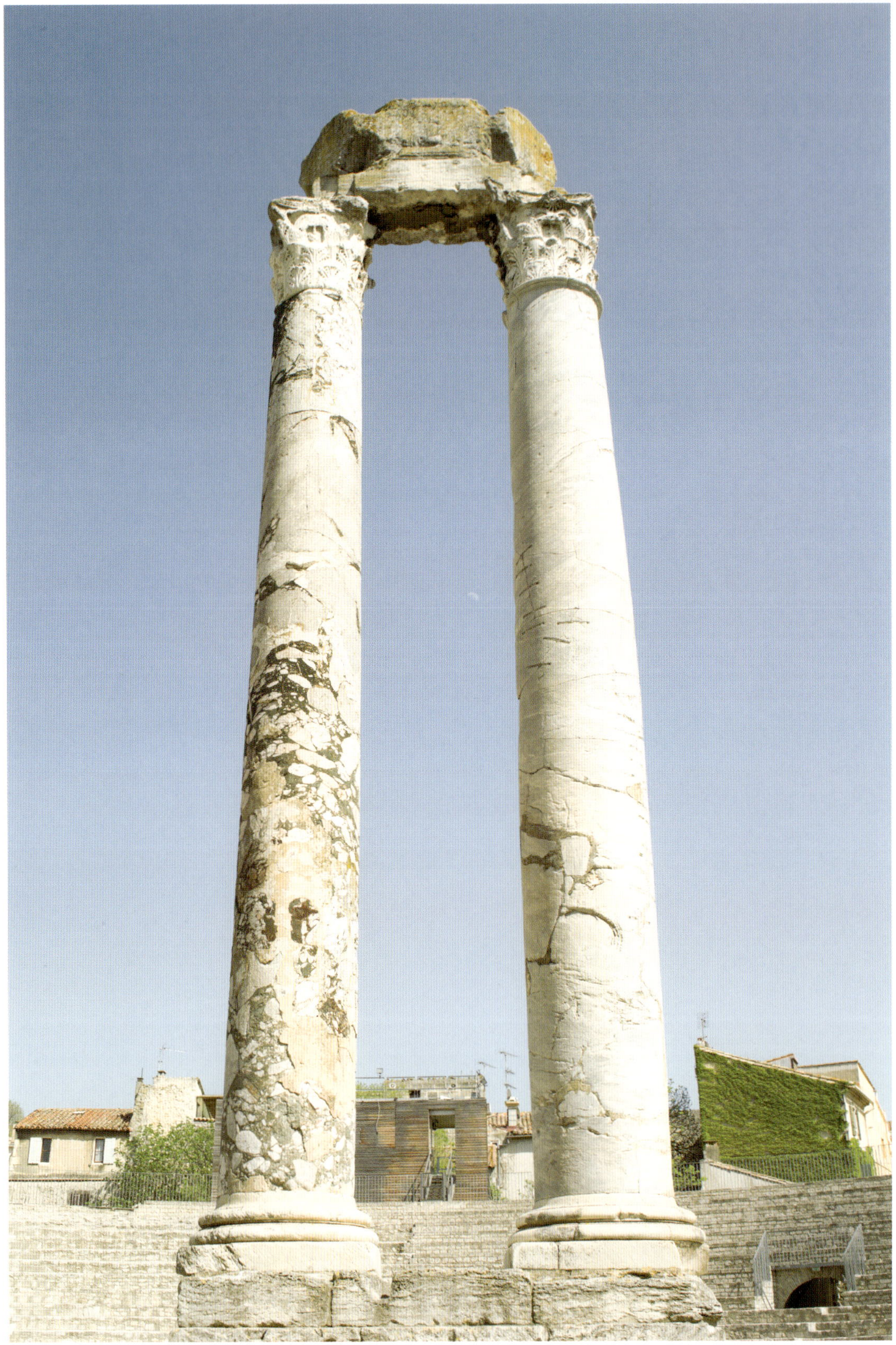

PLATE 47

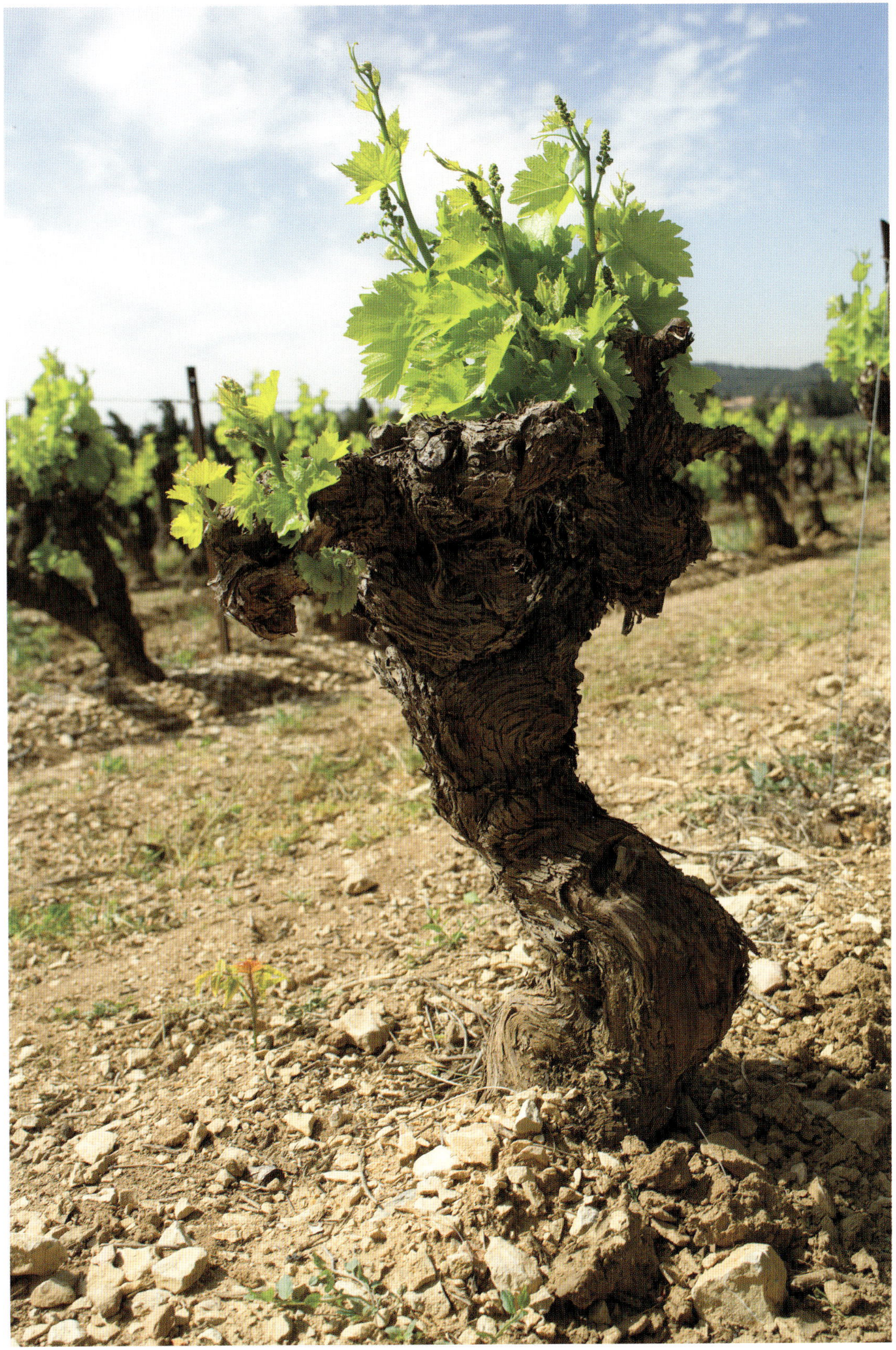

PLATE 48

VAN GOGH'S SPIRIT IS PALPABLE IN THE ROOM; A RESTLESS ENERGY THAT HAS ONE PACING TO AND FROM THE window and the door and back to the window to gaze out at the peace of the garden, which one wants to believe may have been of solace to the artist. And yet it is the chair that breaks one's heart, quietly sitting there, as though waiting for the man who stood in the world and gave it back to us in all its mad beauty.

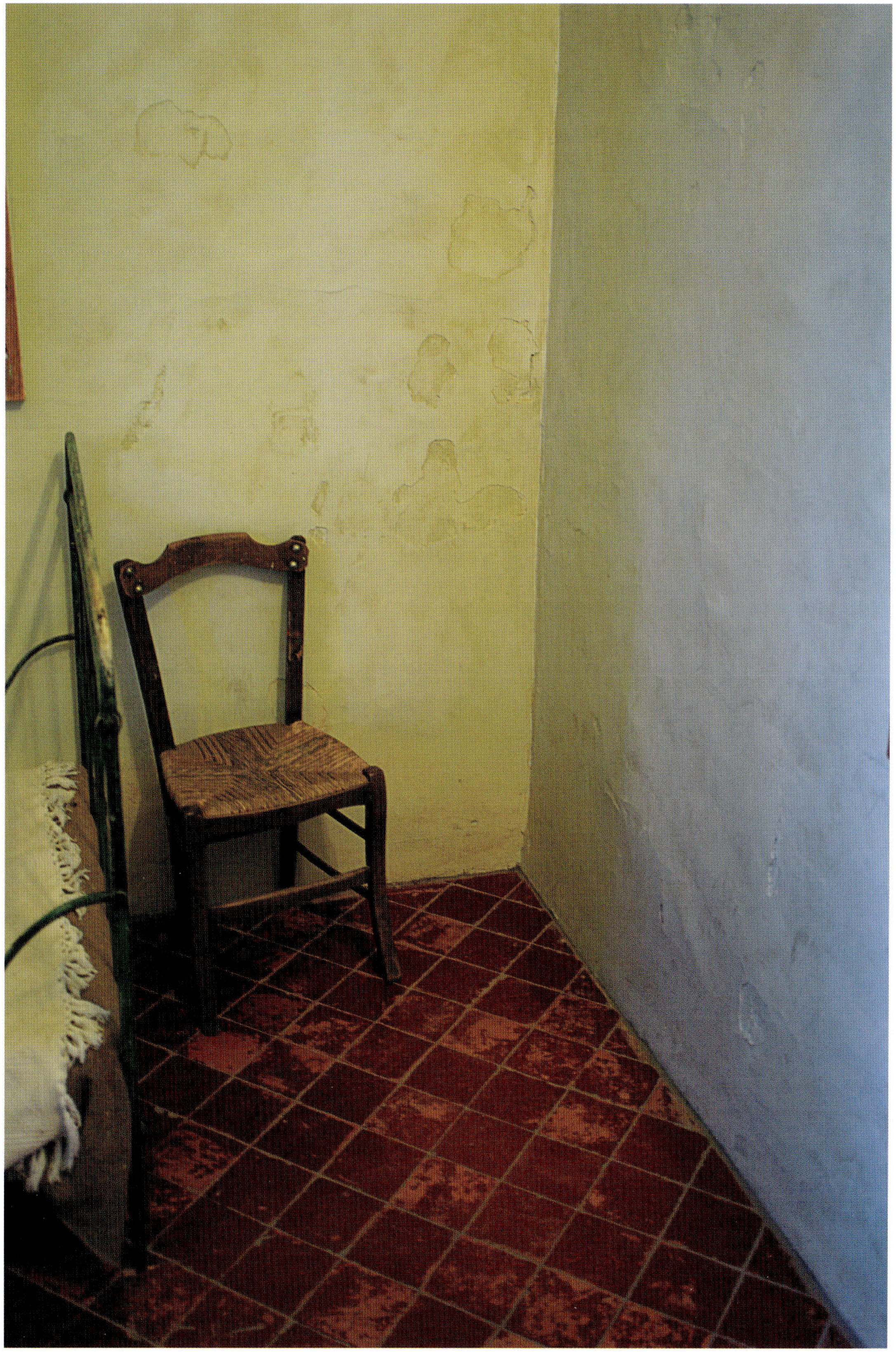

PLATE 49

PLATE 50

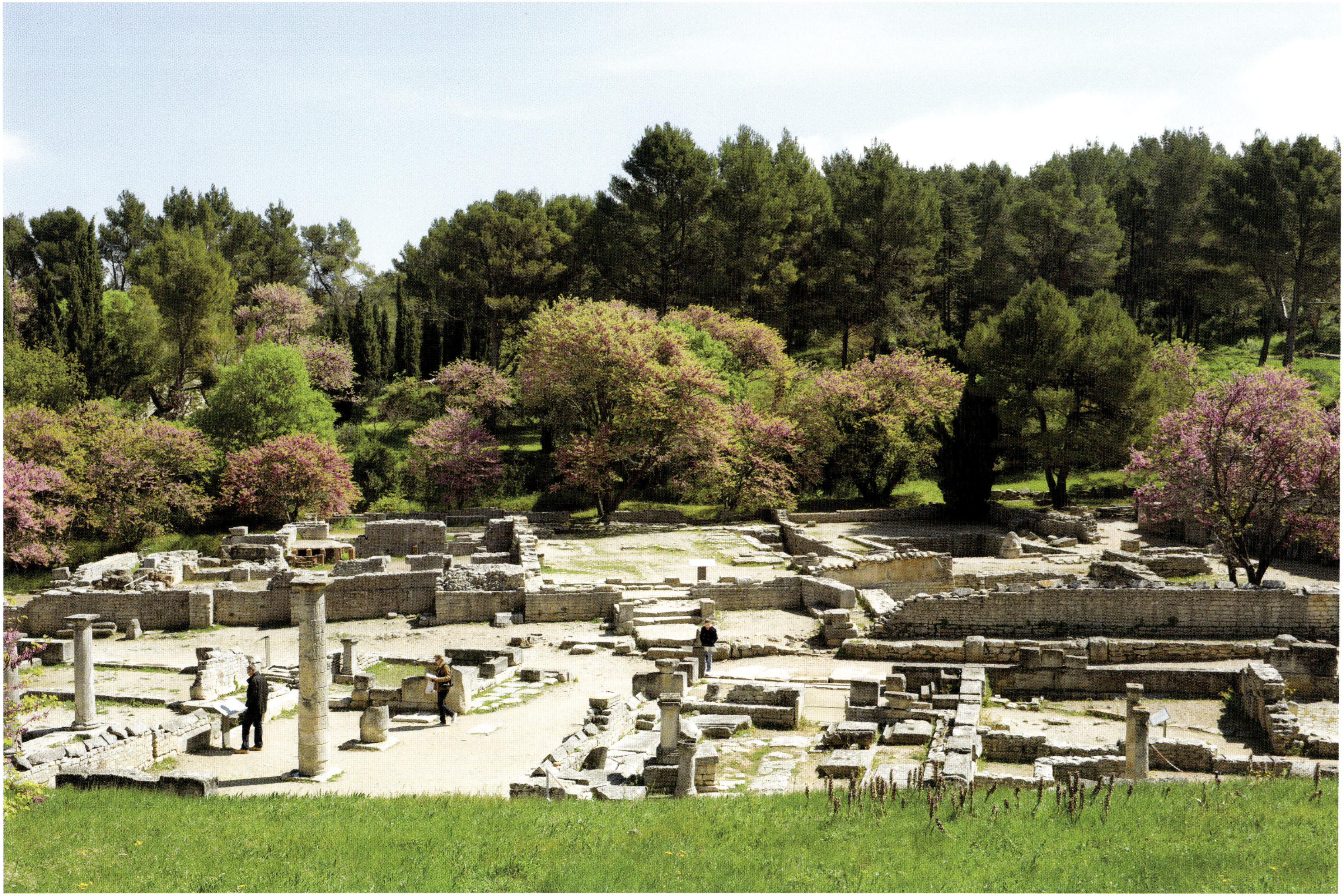

WE ARE SITTING ON OUR TERRACE AT LES TROIS SOURCE, A THIRTEENTH-CENTURY BED-AND-BREAKFAST AT the foot of Bonnieux. The mistral has departed, the hour serene and sunny. We watch the last of the day's light interact with all that comes within its realm, and the nature of this light strikes me with all the clarity of a sudden epiphany. As we've said before, on this Provençal adventure we have had to let go of our images of Tuscany, where the quality of light was an integral part of our experience. As we described in our Tuscany book, there the light had a warmth to it that held you and the landscape in its embrace. We had been missing that quality here.

The sun is low in the sky, but not yet disappeared below the hills. And so it is that the treetops, just about level with our second-floor terrace, are illuminated. Suddenly trees that had seemed fairly nondescript are scintillatingly revealed: the myriad clusters of spring catkins resemble a sea of starfish outlined in fairy lights. It is breathtaking, and the two of us sit as if in a spell, watching as every few seconds the slightest breeze loosens grains of pollen, sending off little backlit puffs of mossy green smoke.

What I come to understand about Provençal light is that it is piercing. It goes straight to the heart of everything and illuminates its essential nature. It pierced my heart in such a way as to make me want to stay forever.

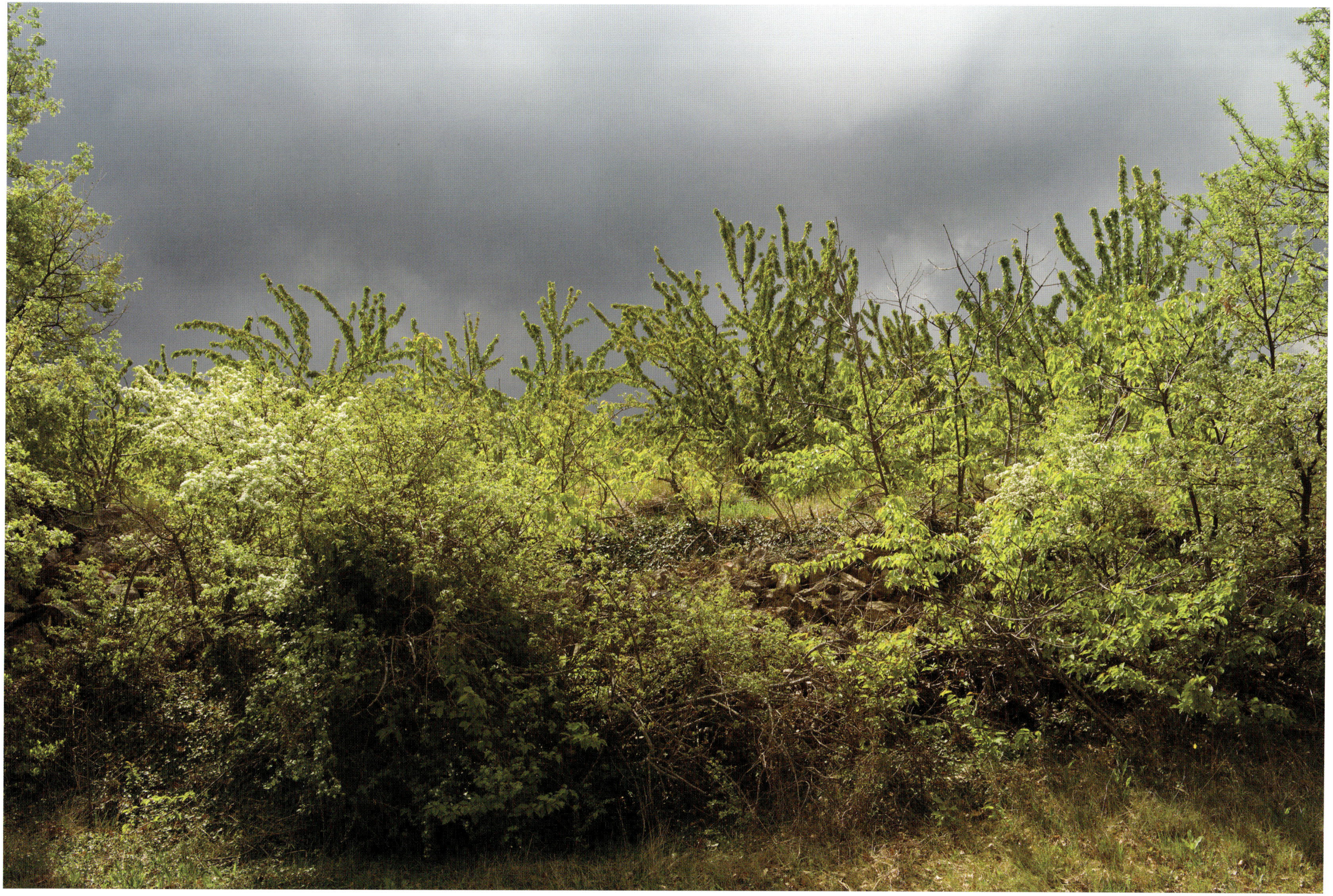

PLATE 51

PLATE 52

PLATE 53 (OVERLEAF)

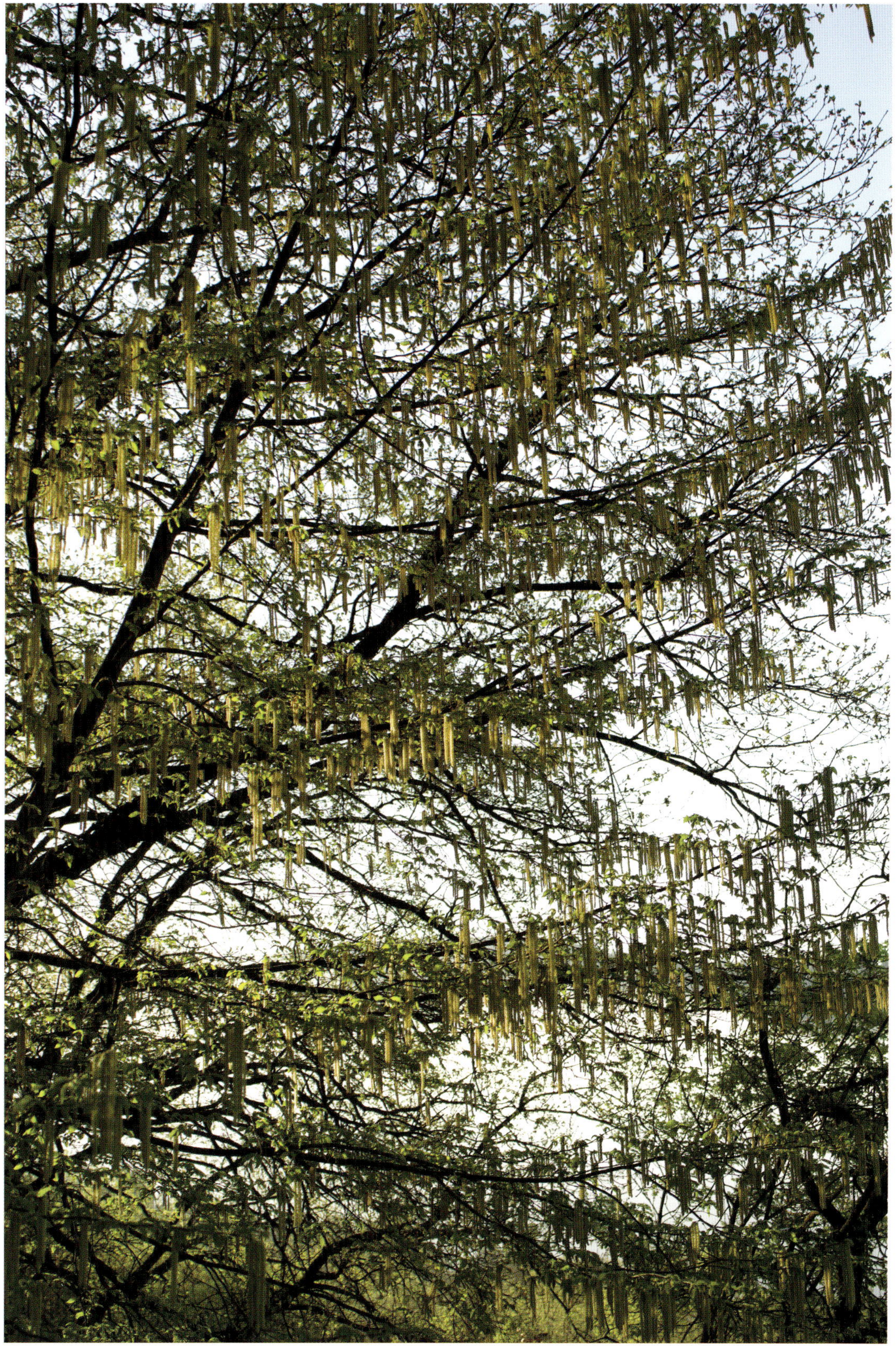

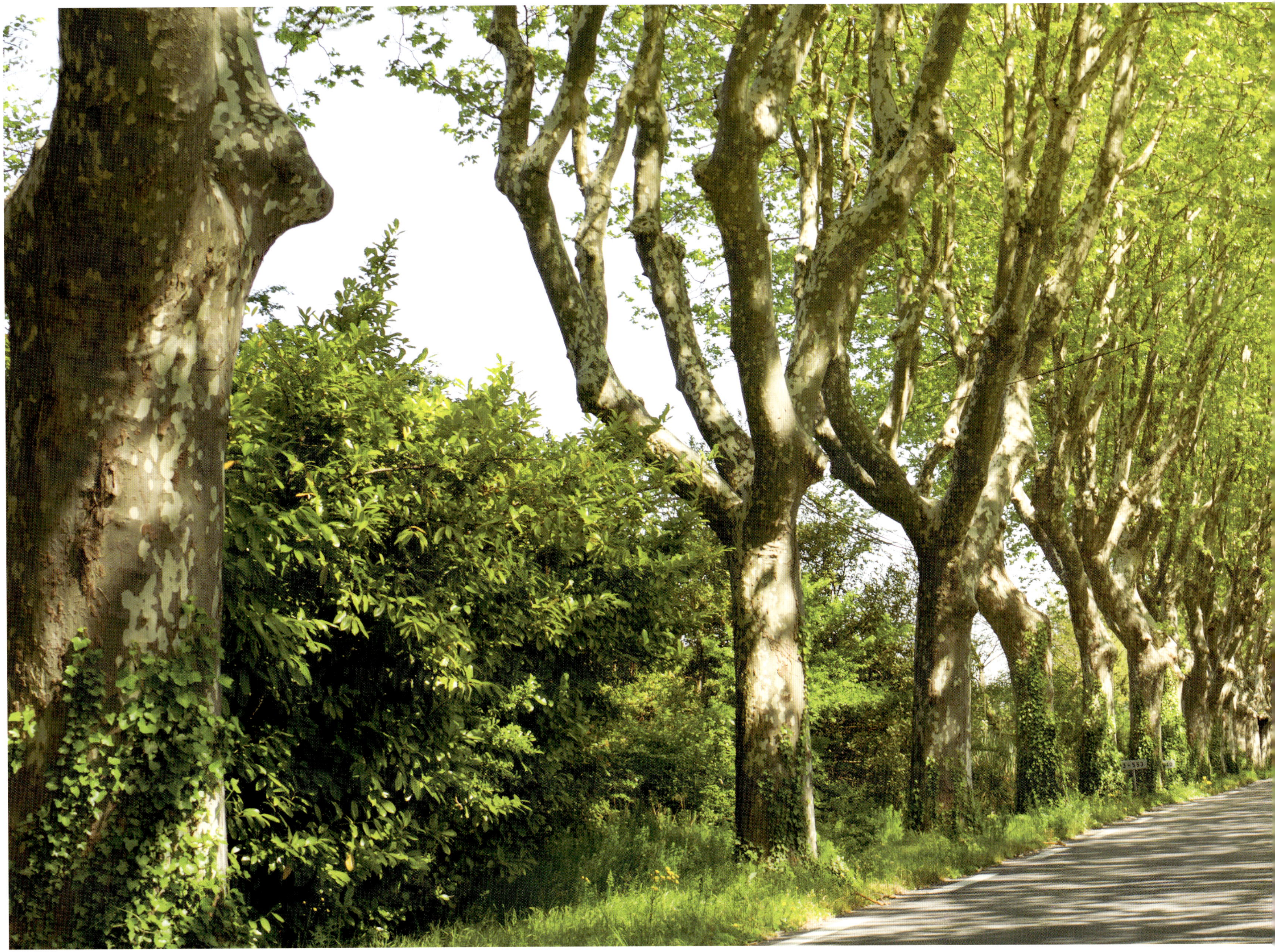

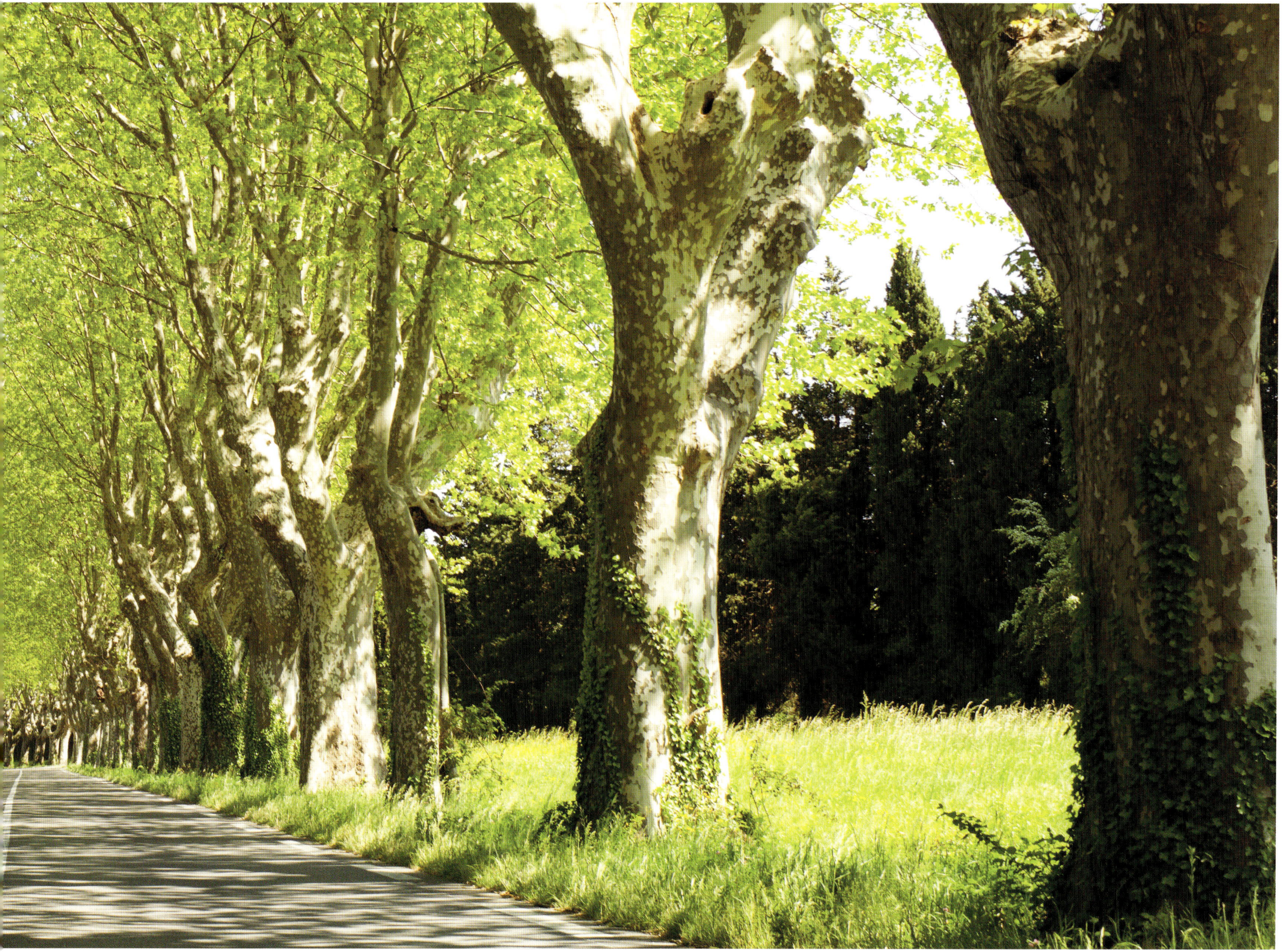

TODAY WE VISIT THE SMALL VILLAGE OF SAINT-JEANNET, HIGH UP IN THE MOUNTAINS ABOVE NICE. The mistral is on the move again, its cool wind separating itself from the warmth of the day.

We choose a street to explore and find ourselves in a small square, which is flanked on its long side by the impressive stone wall of the town's church. In front of us, a fountain spouts its music. All else is quiet.

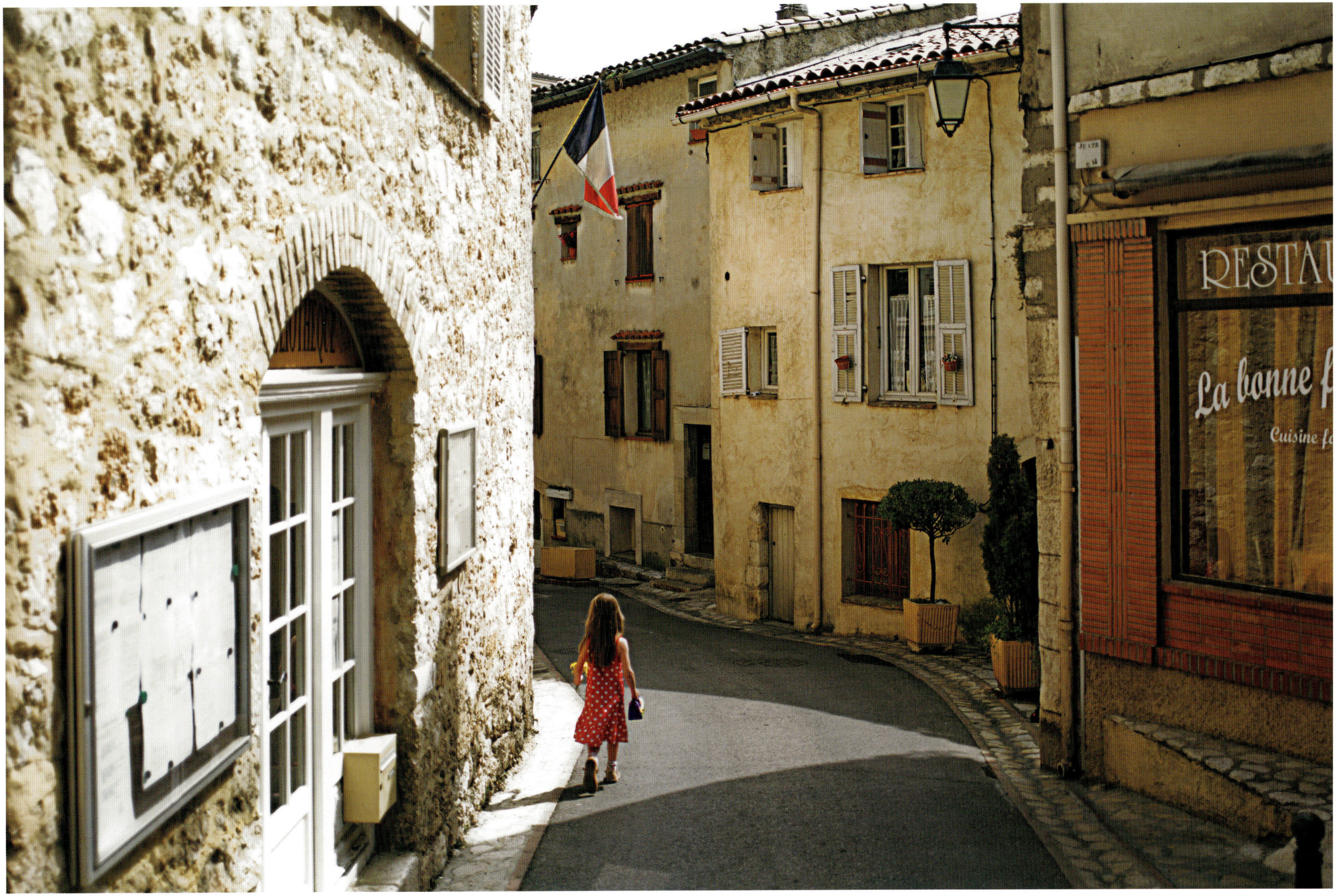

PLATE 54

WE ENTER THE CHURCH AND ALMOST SWOON FROM THE INCENSE STILL BURNING FRESH. WHO WAS HERE? Where did they go?

And there is the crucifix, just there to the right, in front of the altar.

It doesn't matter what you believe in, or how many Christs hanging from the cross one has seen in a paltry lifetime, there is still something totally mesmerizing about this figure nailed to the fear and doubt of others. And today, on this Good Friday, 1,978 years after the event, one is both horrified at what man continues to do to man and amazed at the pain each of us is able to bear.

We wander down a few more streets until the houses peter out and we reach the far side of the village. We are about to turn around, but something impels us to follow a path, which probably eventually leads up into the wilderness of the mountain. The air is perfumed, and there, right in front of us, stands a tiny stone chapel, its door open.

I don't know if I will ever be able to articulate the experience of being inside that space. I want to say it was the holiest of places, having not to do with religion, but sanctuary.

I sit on one of the humble chairs. I read a prayer and am touched that it is addressed not to God, but to a Universal Mother.

Joel has stepped outside, and when I turn to follow him I see a rope draped over the open door. Of course I pull it! And at the end of the pull comes the gentlest of bells, its sweet, small note already carried up the mountain to the heavens.

We stand in silence listening to the wind, which, though roaring down from the mountain, leaves us unscathed, the linden trees sheltering us beneath their shivering leaves.

Time dissolves. Thoughts disappear. There is only being.

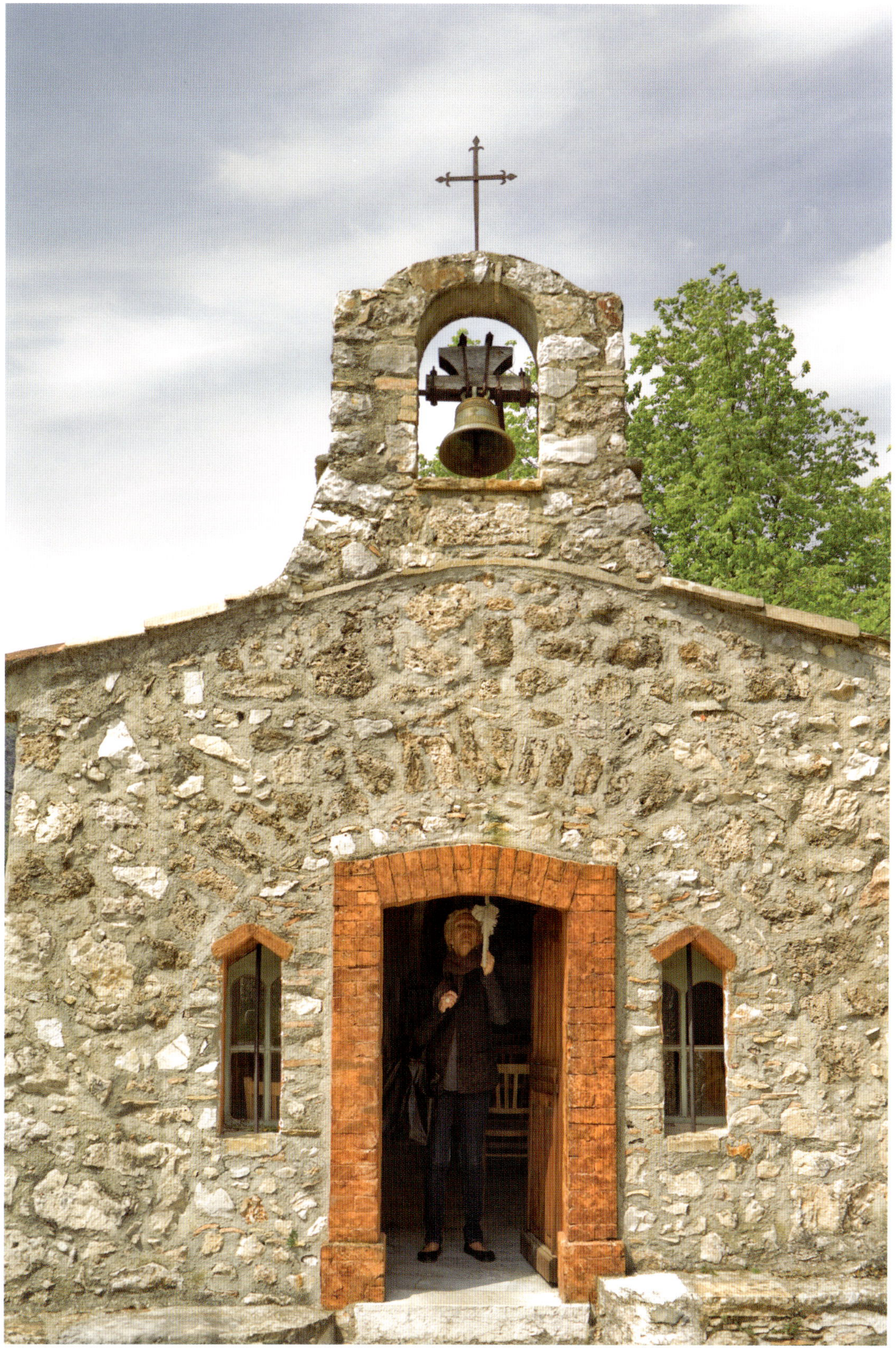

PLATE 55

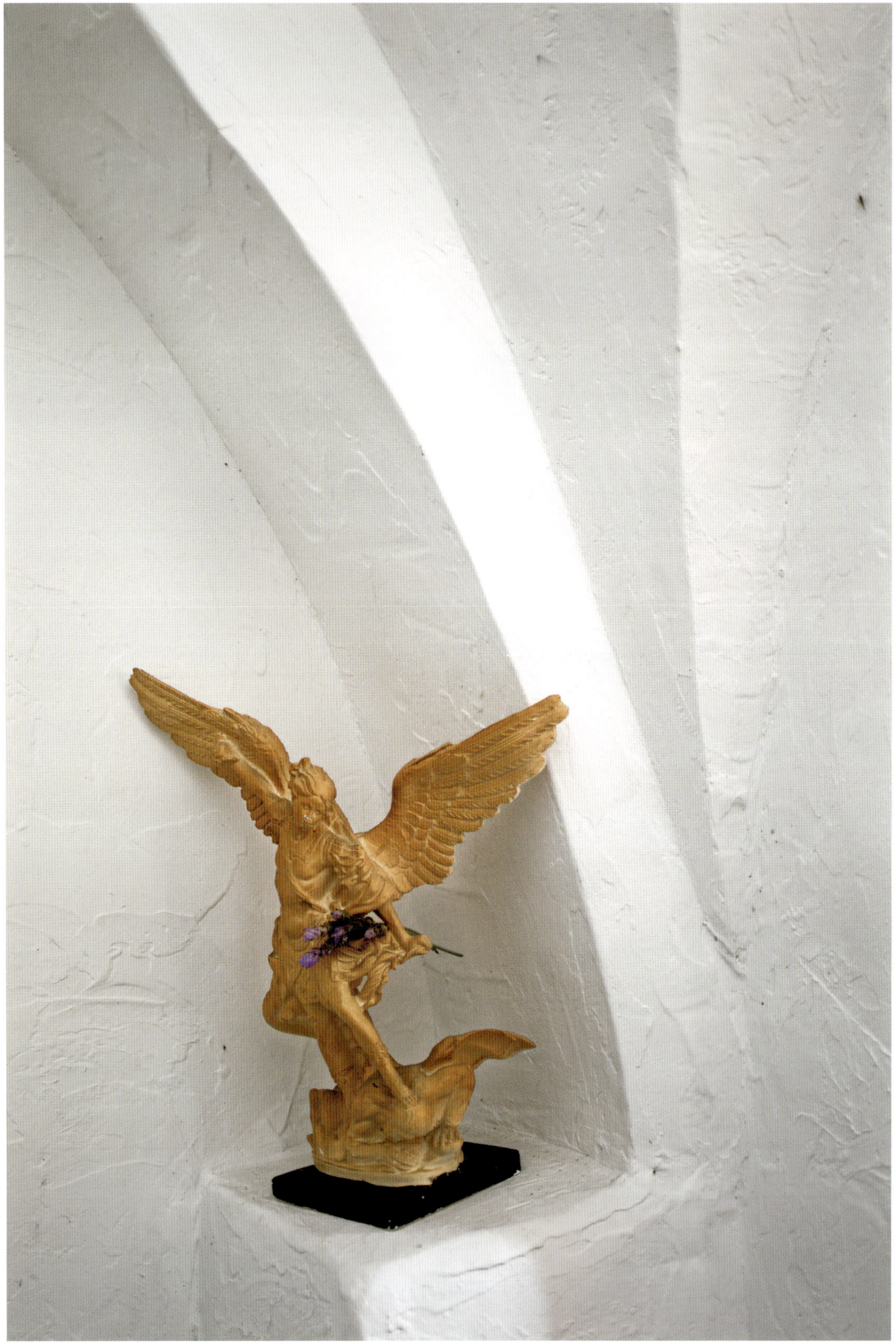

PLATE 56

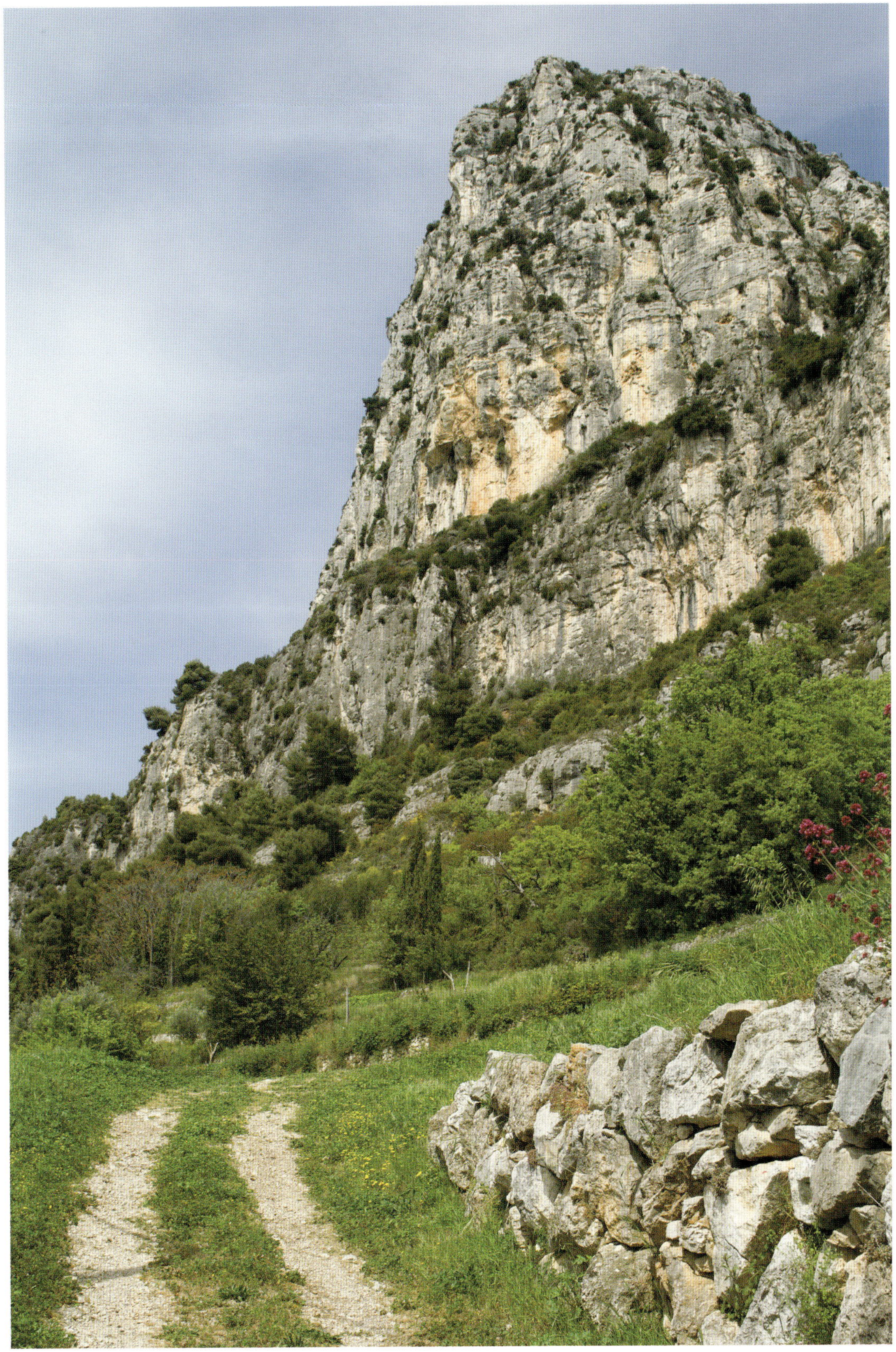

PLATE 57

SUMMER

June

WE HAVE RETURNED TO LES TROIS SOURCES, FRESH—OR RATHER NOT SO FRESH—OFF THE PLANE. AS WE WAIT for our room to be prepared, we picnic under the mulberry tree in the courtyard, a lunch of baguette, Brebis and Banon cheeses, apples, and best of all, cherries from the orchard. Sated and unpacked, we set the alarm for a two-hour nap and disappear into the depths of exhaustion. When we awake, the best we can do is stumble to the pool, stopping under several cherry trees along the way for juice-laden fortification.

Oh, these cherries: black ones whose skins are as soft as their flesh; orange ones that pop in the mouth with a tang; crimson ones that taste like long-ago childhood. The place is literally dripping with cherries and we are convinced this is the fruit that got Adam and Eve into trouble. Surely it wasn't a Granny Smith.

We manage two laps apiece without drowning and maybe ten minutes in the sun before realizing we are too fragile for the heat of the day. So we drive into the village for dinner supplies and sit out on the terrace with our feast, gratefully free of menus, waiters, music, and chatter.

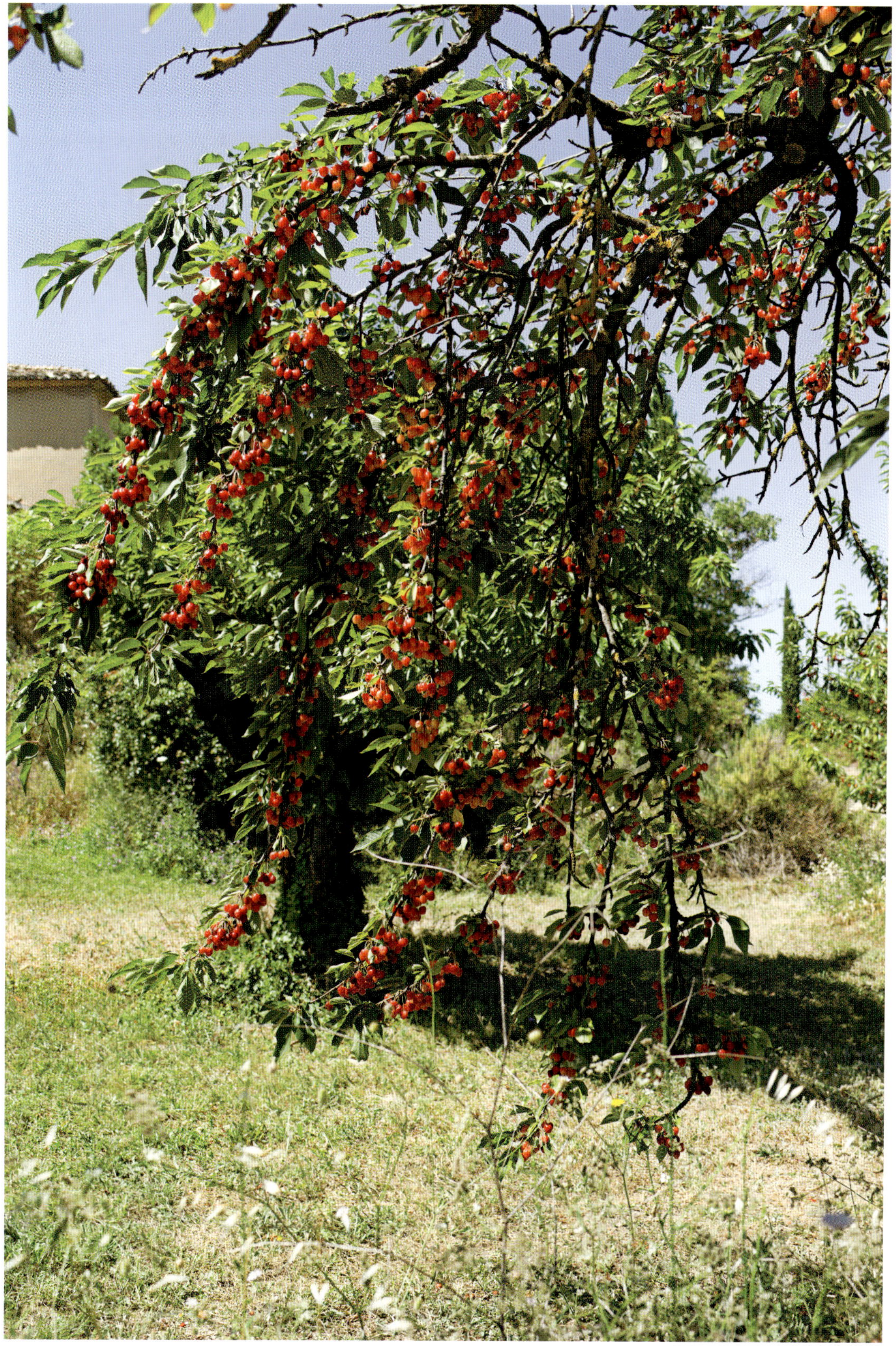

THESE SIMPLE MOMENTS IN LIFE, WHEN YOU REALLY PAY ATTENTION TO YOUR NEEDS AND REALIZE HOW little you need to feel complete are, for us, moments of utter joy and gratitude. To sit on this terrace again with an evening breeze at play and look out over the wild landscape of Provence is almost too much to take in. The sun begins its lazy descent and we decide to take an evening walk on the property. And so it is that we round a corner of the building and come upon our first lavender field.

The lavender: it almost brings us to our knees. That gasp of perfume-laden blue lit by the low sun. What seems like a million stems are frenzied by the wind, yet their flowers still offer soothing calm—unlike we mortals who, whipped into our own frenzies, so easily forget our own essence. Not so the lavender. No mistral can rob it of its essence. We walk into the middle of it, bend low to inhale it, and pick enough to season our bath, press to our temples, and place under our pillows, letting its gentle spirit waft through our dreams.

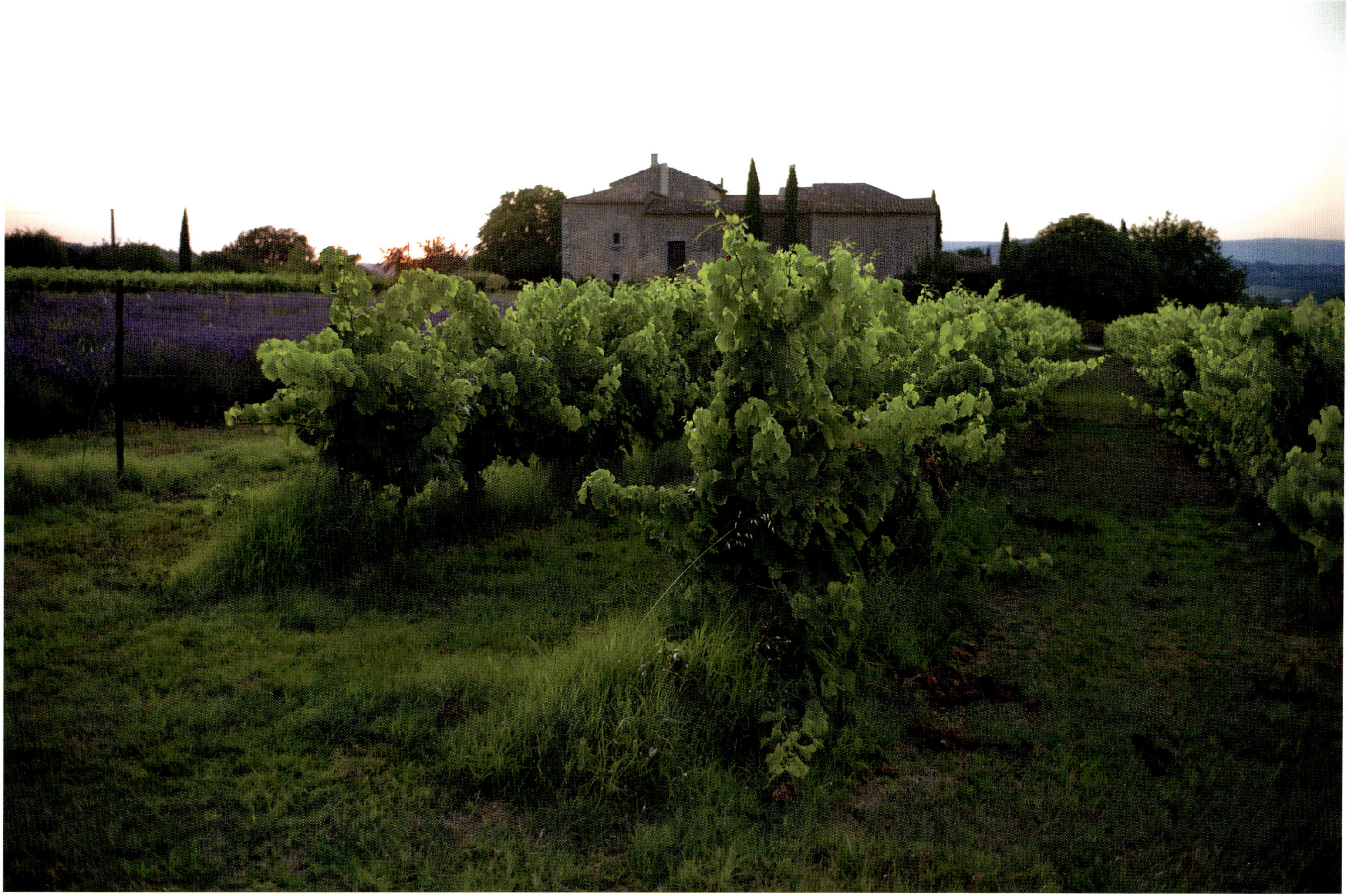

PLATE 59

PLATE 60 (OVERLEAF)

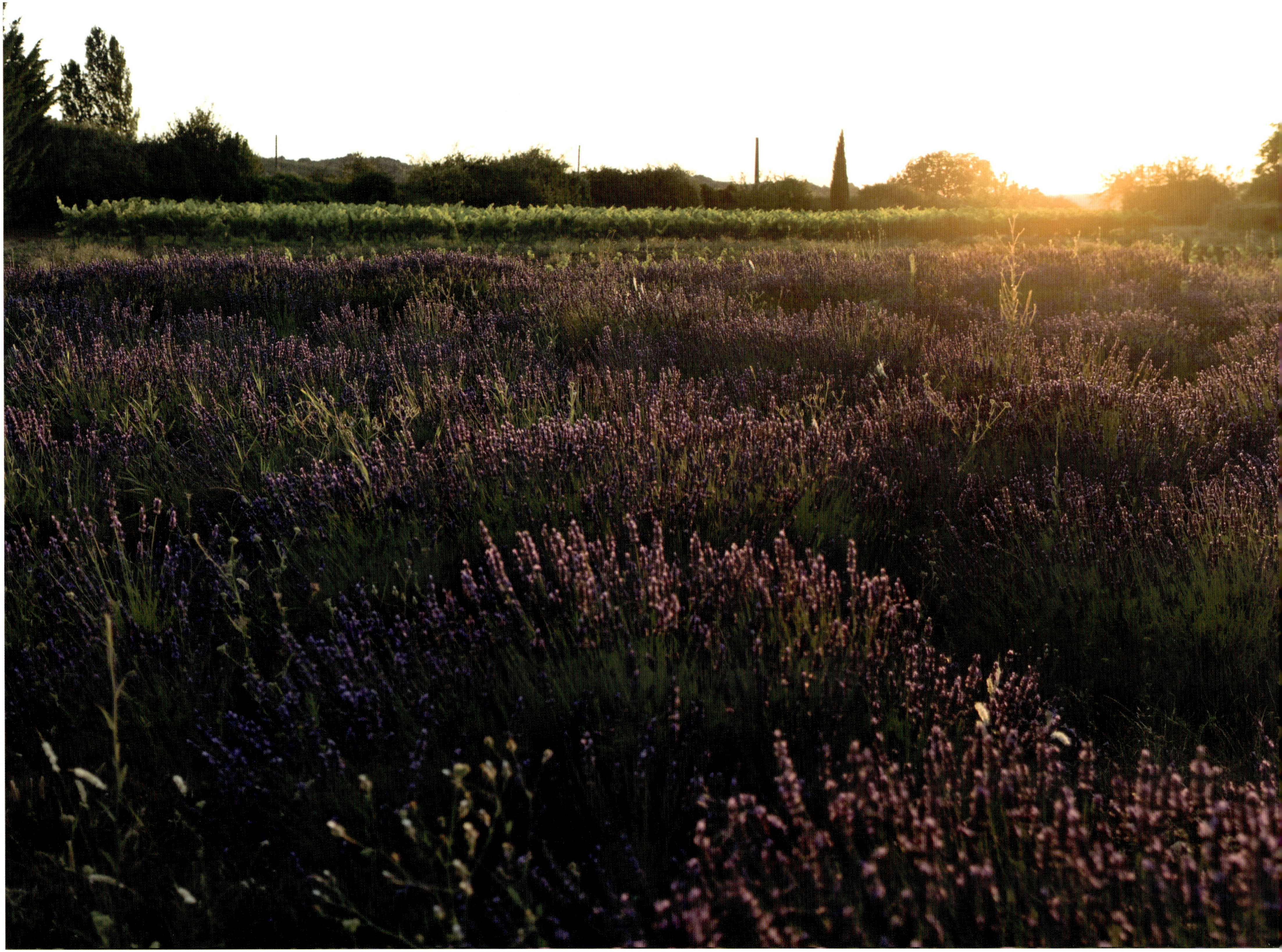

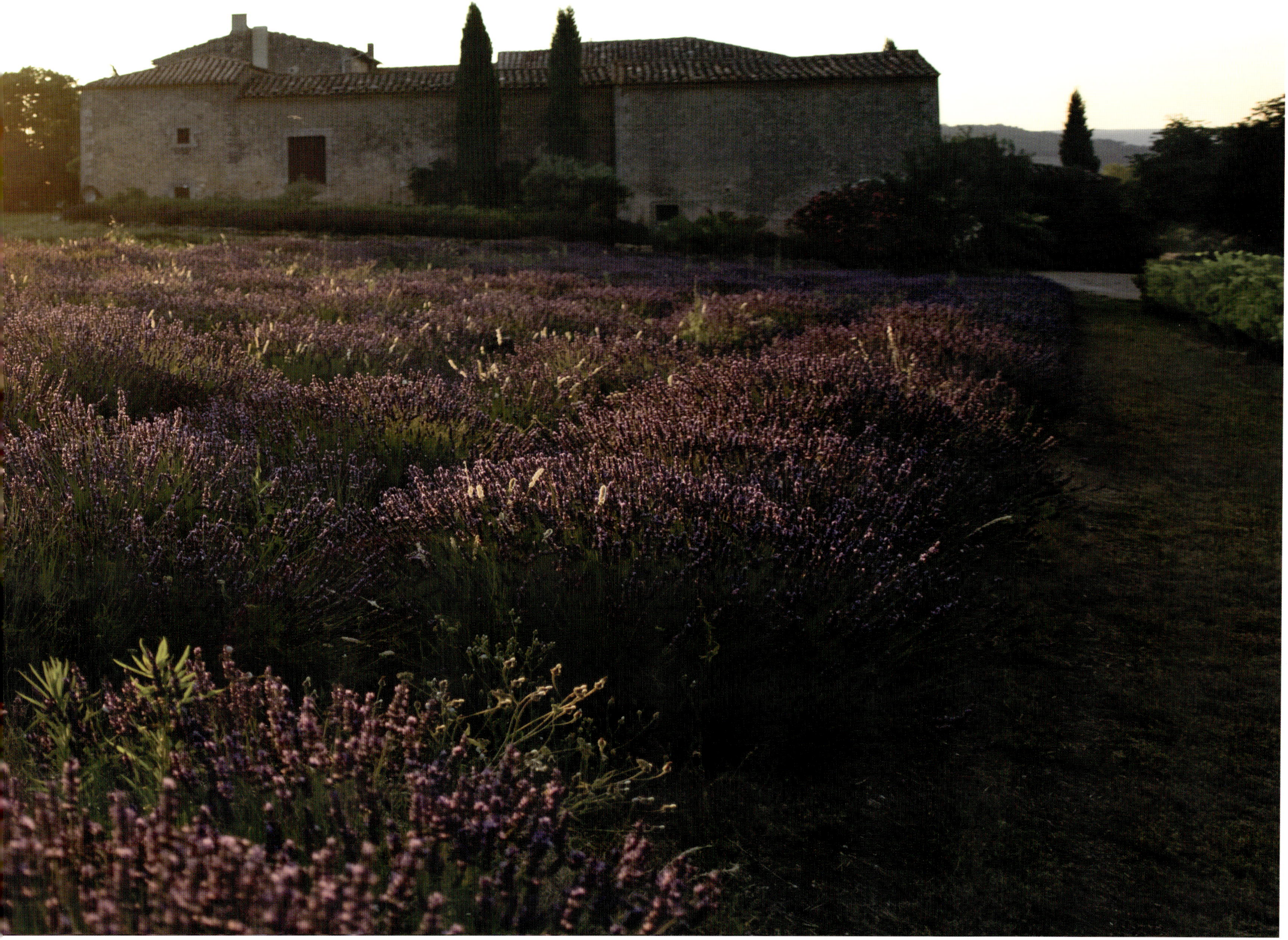

PLATE 61

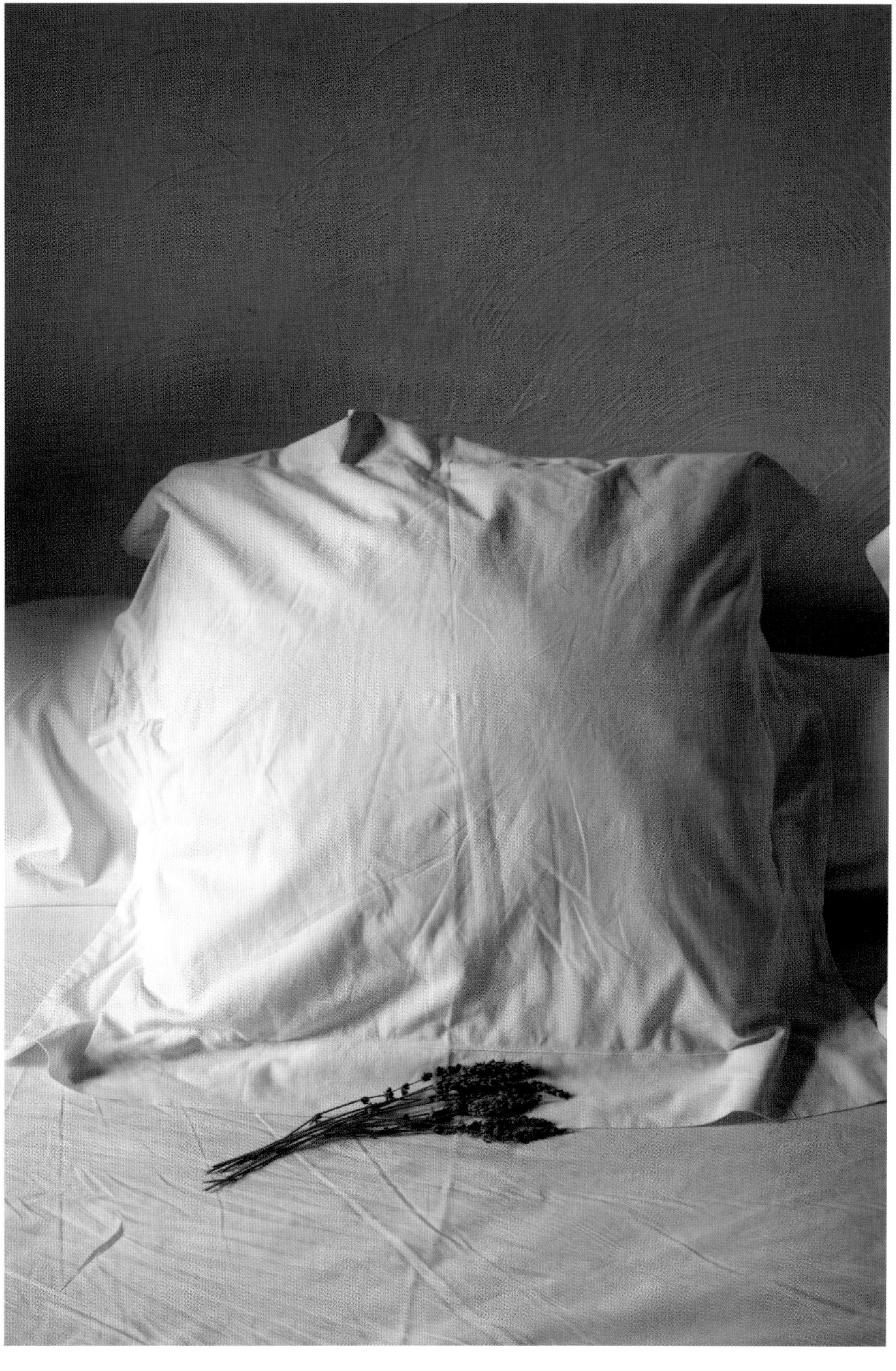

July

WE SET OFF FOR SAULT IN THE LATE MORNING, DRIVING ALONG BACK ROADS LUSH NOW WITH SUMMER, passing field after field of lavender, the clichéd image of Provence that we had decided against including in the book when we first began this journey. We had made a similar pact when embarking on our *Tuscany: Inside The Light* book—no sunflowers! And in fact that book has only one photograph of them: a field in late autumn whose sole survivors are dried on the stalk, heads bowed like defeated soldiers.

It's always a problem for artists, be they photographers, painters, or writers—how to avoid the cliché. It's an interesting word, from the French *clicher*, meaning "to stereotype." We have all seen countless photos of lavender fields. Unfortunately, the majority of those photos are not imitative of the original, but overexaggerated versions of the real thing. Those saturated blue skies over almost violent purple fields may take some folks' breath away, but to actually be here and "see" them is a whole different reality—they are far more subtle and complex.

It occurs to us that for some people, real lavender fields might be a disappointment if they're expecting them to look like those photos. Thanks to digital manipulation, we have come to think of overhyped reality as actual reality. But there are some things, many things, in this world, that have to be seen in person to be experienced. And to really "see" is to be willing to stand and breathe it in, to let the surface image deepen by taking the time necessary for the eyes to see beyond the first hit.

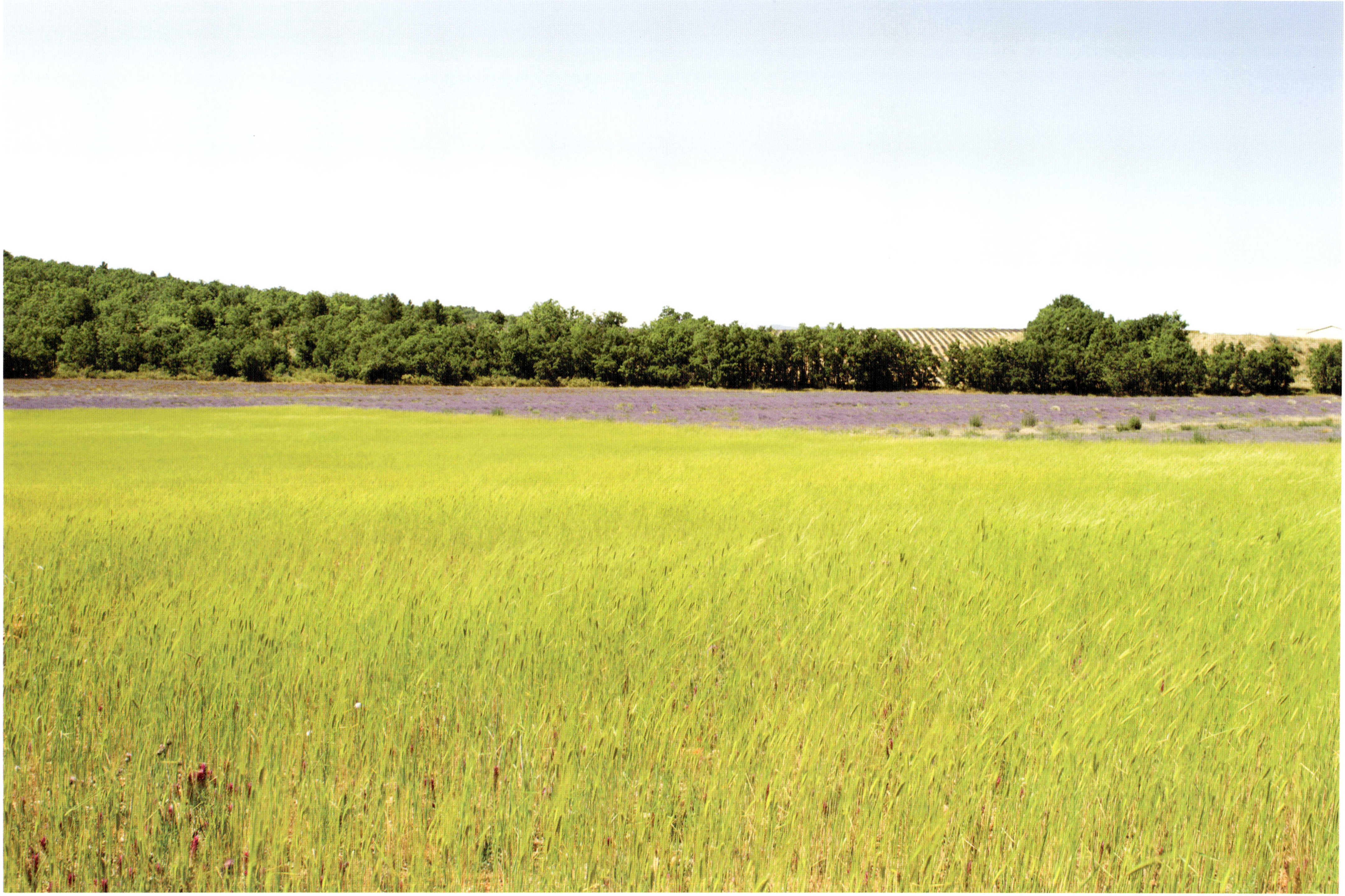

PLATE 62

THE FIELDS WE SEE TODAY TAKE OUR BREATH AWAY NOT JUST BECAUSE OF THE COLOR, BUT ALSO BECAUSE of the variety, abundance, and simplicity of the rows. The colors range from blush, to, well, lavender, to indigo, to purple, to almost charcoal. There is not only variety of color but also formation—some stems dense with close-knit spears of flowers while other stems carry their flowers loosely in random clusters. And the scents, carried in the oils of the petals, are as varied as the flowers themselves. Some give off a faint scent reminiscent of grandma's hanky, while the most pungent fill your lungs with the power of camphor.

Most of us are aware that lavender is known for its calming, healing properties. Most of us have smelled dried lavender, in an eye pillow perhaps, or a sachet for the drawer. Some of us have drizzled drops of lavender oil into a bath or used it on the temples to massage away a headache. Imagine being surrounded by it a million-, trillion-fold. Imagine breathing this fragrant air during the weeks of lavender bloom. It is impossible not to pick and press and inhale all day because it is everywhere. Not just in the fields cultivated for production, but in every garden—private or public—and in traffic circles, planters, parking lots, and best of all, wild. One could say that lavender is the essence of Provence, and it is hard for us to believe that we nearly robbed ourselves of this experience because of our "artistic" snobbery.

By the time we arrive in Sault, we have stopped countless times to pick and squeeze and sniff, filling the dashboard with flower-laden stems that we squeeze some more as we drive, holding our fingertips to our nostrils for yet another inhalation. Perhaps this is why in Provence, everyone, everywhere, seems so relaxed and happy . . . they are all drunk on lavender! One does not really mind if lunch takes a long time to arrive to the table and the bill takes even longer. Just sit and relax and smile and eventually one's needs are met.

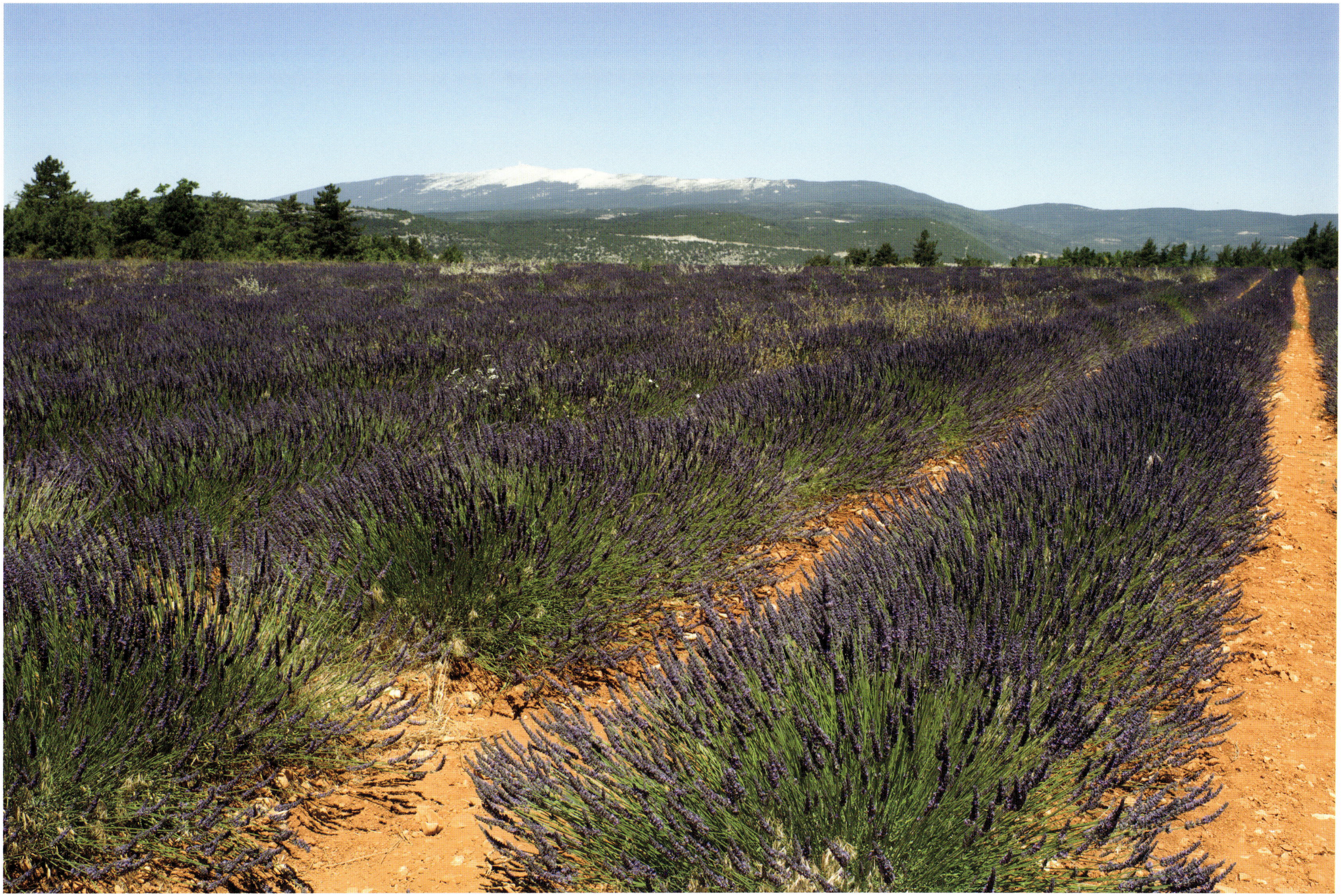

PLATE 63

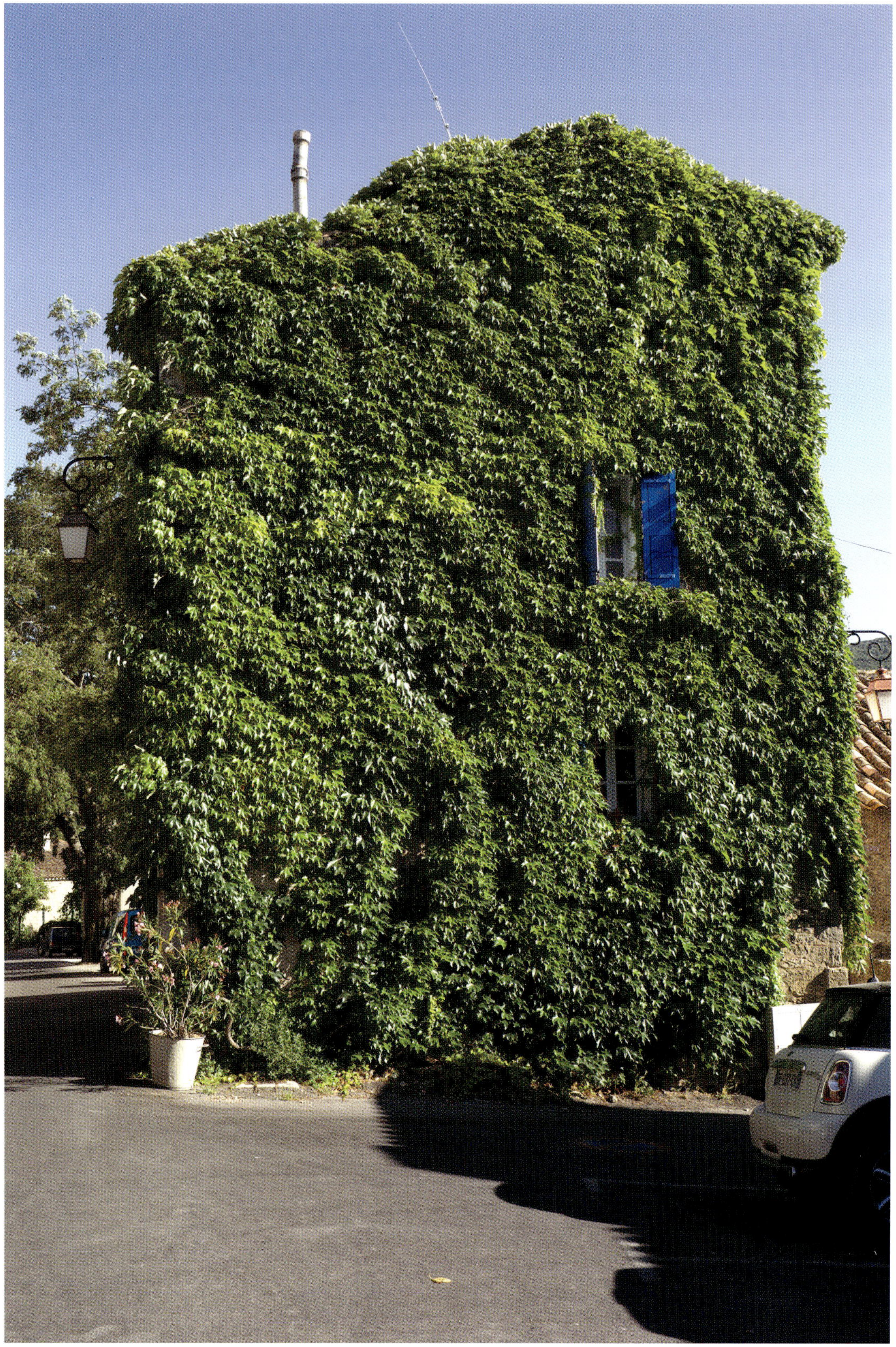

PLATE 64

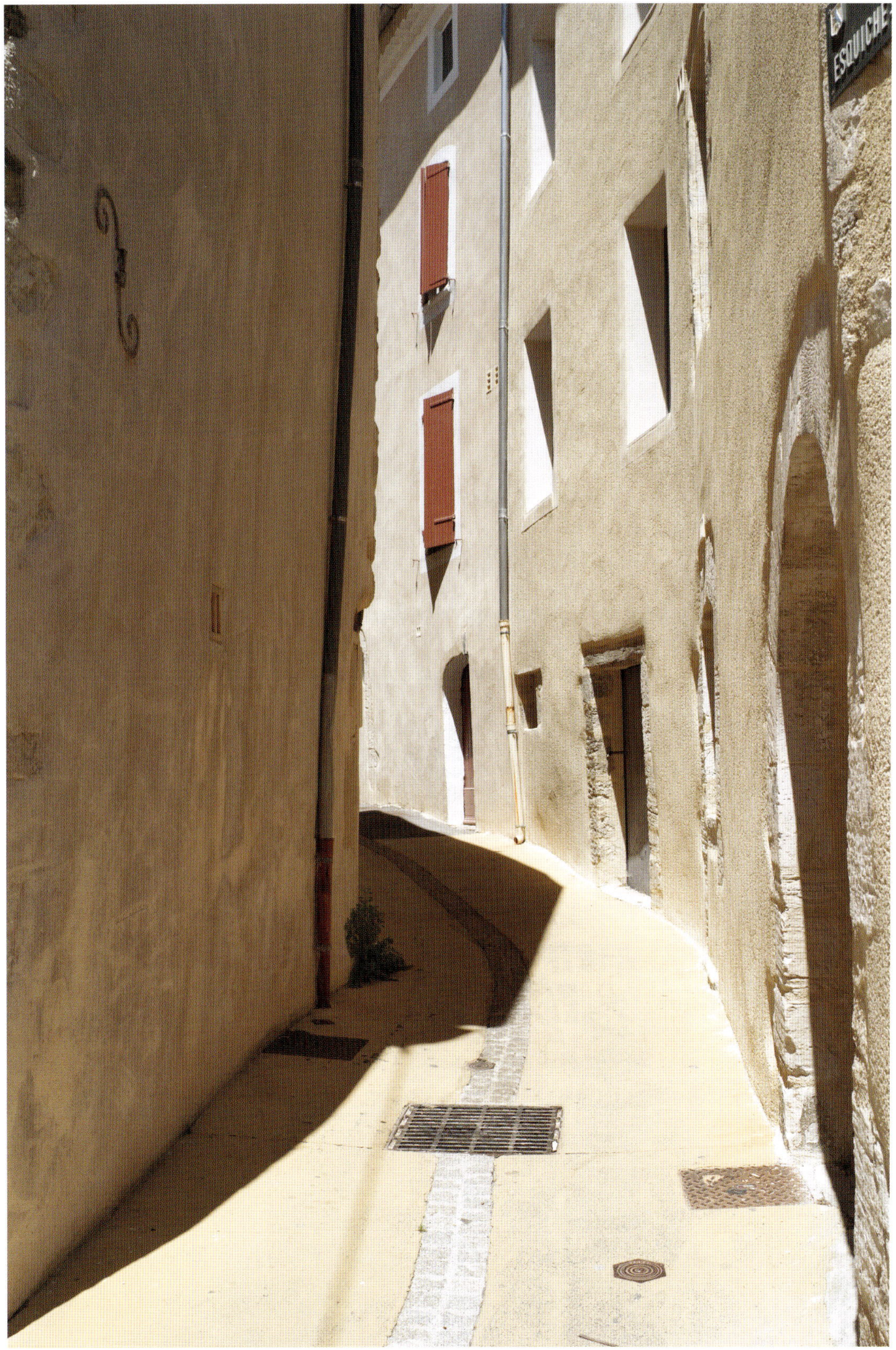

PLATE 65

SAINT-TROPEZ IS EVERYTHING YOU EVER IMAGINED . . . AND LESS . . . AND MORE. WE WERE HERE IN THE spring when it was still a sleepy town inhabited mostly by the natives. The architecture and scenery are stunning, but now it's tourist season and like every beautiful spot in the world during tourist season it's hard to actually see the place during the day and night. But the early mornings are ours! The streets running with water sluicing the night away. The shuttered peace. Streets deserted, except for locals shopping for produce (by eleven there will be a different kind of shopping going on, for high fashion and jewelry and some atrocious art).

A short walk through soft light takes us to La Tartine Tropezienne for the best omelets, pain au chocolat, and café au lait. Then a stroll back to La Ponche, our hotel. Situated in the old part of town away from the harbor, we have the Brigitte Bardot room, which we chose solely for its terrace. I guess we have a thing for terraces and this one is, for us, the quintessential, timeless, Saint-Tropez experience.

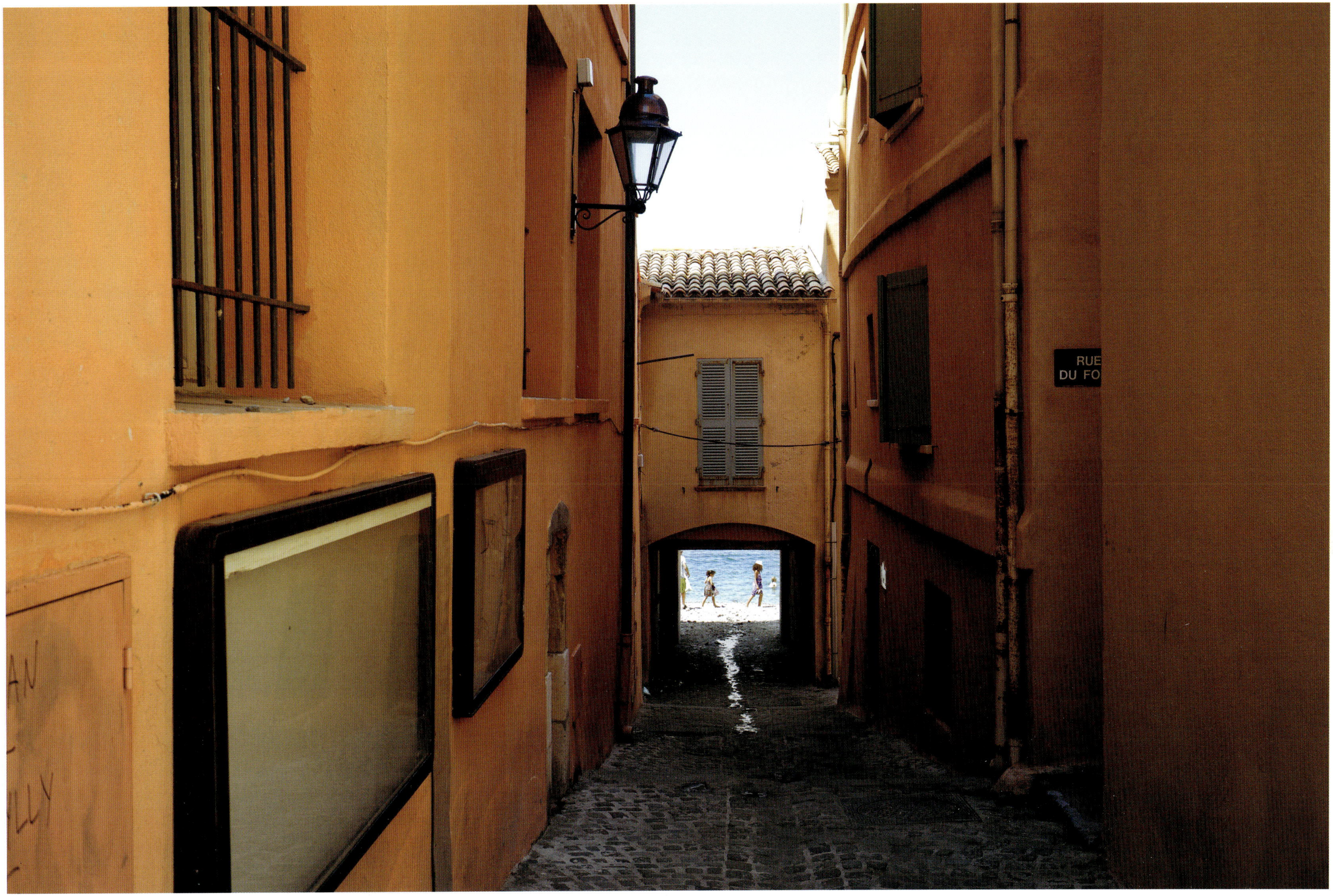

PLATE 66

PLATE 67 (OVERLEAF)

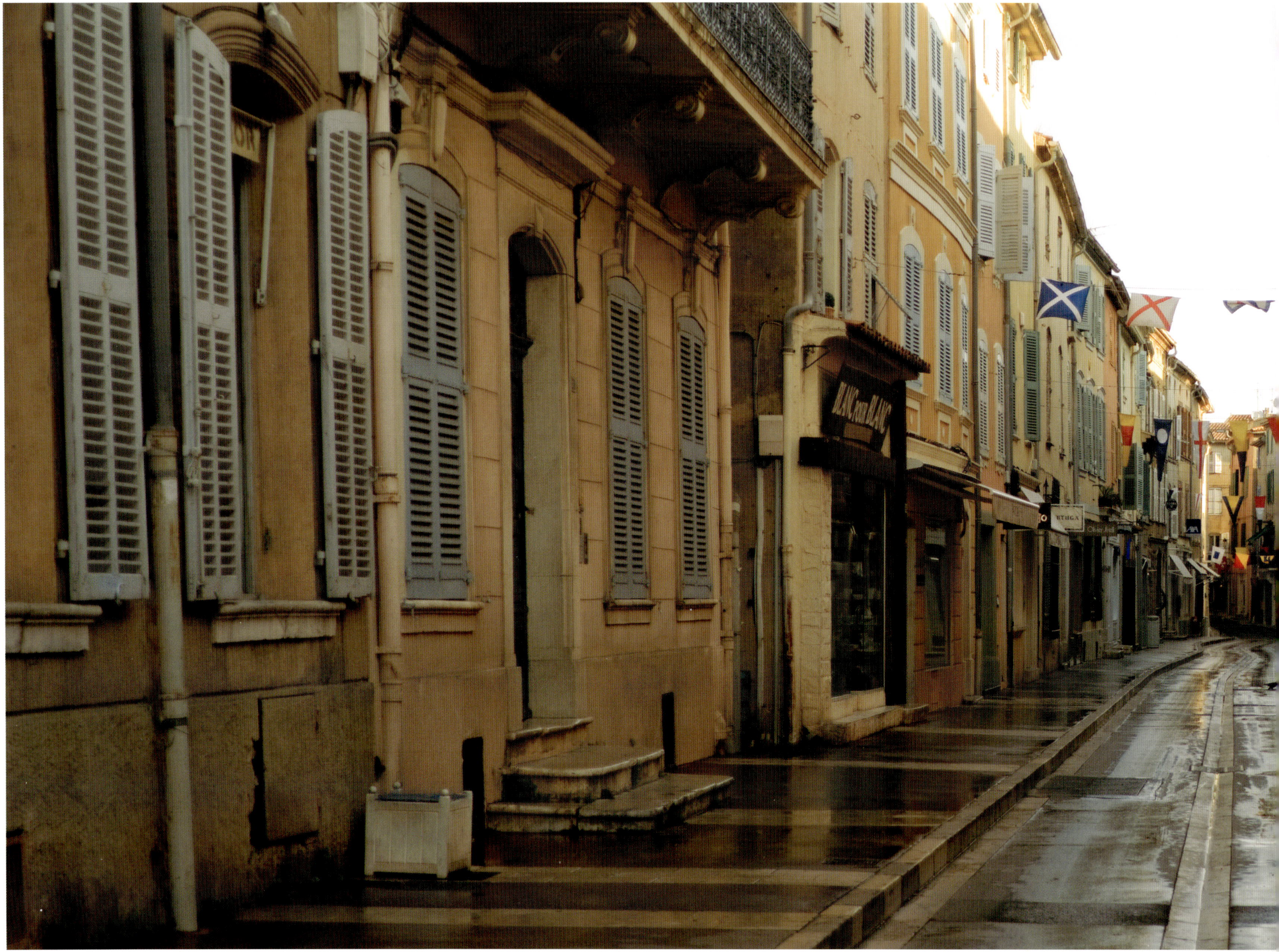

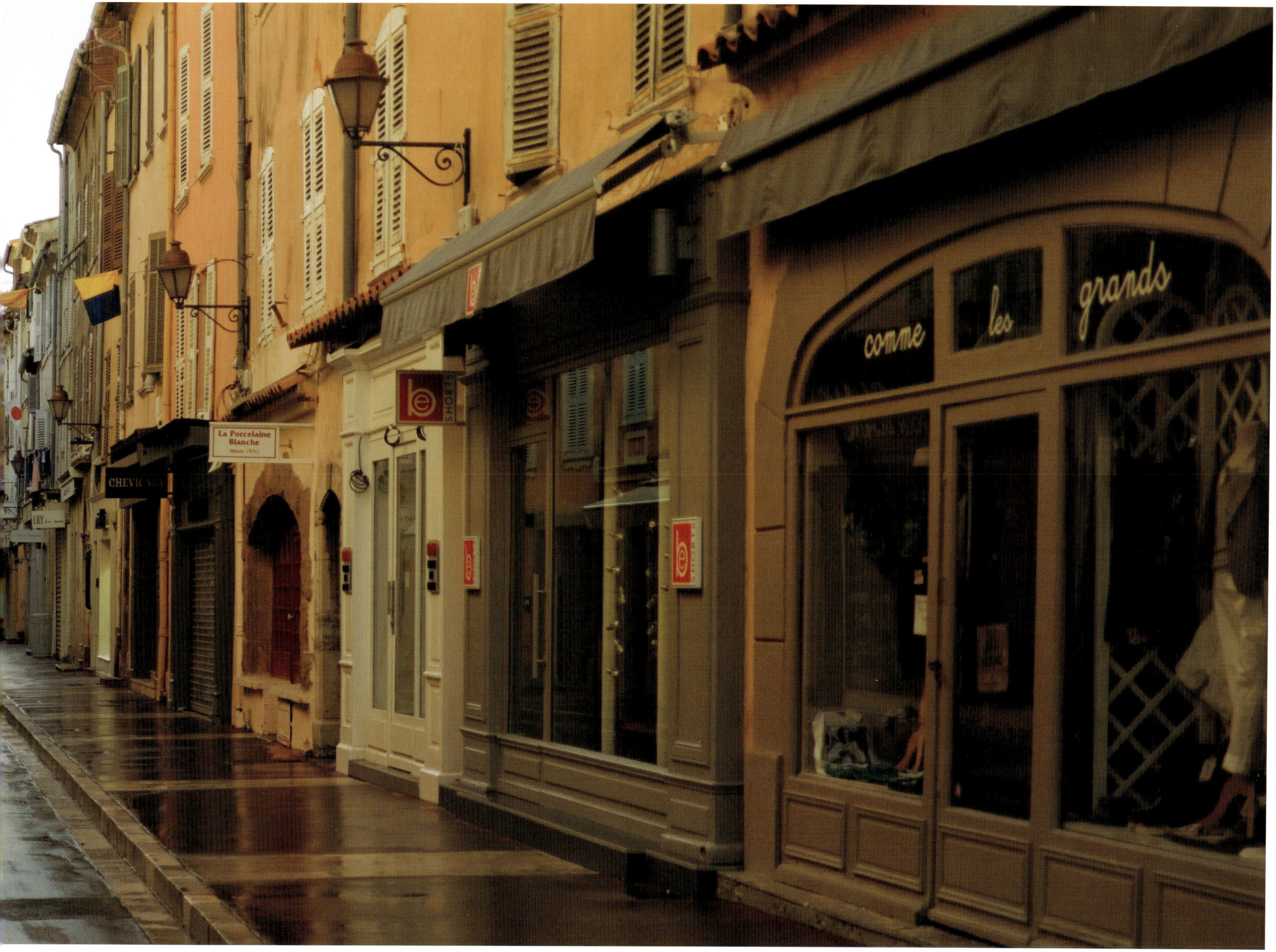
La Porcelaine
Blanche
SHORTS
comme les grands

SURROUNDED BY A MAD CHORUS OF TILED ROOFTOPS AND CHIMNEYS AND OVERLOOKING THE SEA, we spend a fair amount of our three-day visit on the terrace. We sit out on it every night, often serenaded by an accordion player strolling the square below, from where the happy chatter of diners at several outdoor restaurants plays like easy-listening. We dine above it all by candlelight, watching the long evening play across the sky. For dessert, vanilla ice cream, which we devour while gazing out to sea, gasping in delight as an old-fashioned vessel sails into view to the chime of bells from the nearby tower, until finally, sated by all that is good in life, we reluctantly leave the terrace and gratefully sink into bed, our eye pillows redolent with perfume from the lavender we picked just days ago.

When you first approach the outskirts of Saint-Tropez, it's quite vulgar—the highway is lined with big-box stores, car and boat dealerships, and plastic outdoor furniture. Driving past all this, the spirit sinks. Then you enter the town proper, and see throngs of tourists looking for something else to buy and your heart sinks some more. But you push on and come to the square, where in the spring the pollarded trees looked like powerful fists but now, leafed out in their summer finery, they dapple the light and spare you from the sun, so that you can quite easily sit on a bench for half an hour and watch the same men playing boules whom you watched in April. And there, across the square—squeezed in between Fendi and Armani—is the tiniest of shops, where we will buy our salad ingredients and fruit. The woman who owns (or rents) the shop is perhaps in her mid-seventies and proud of her produce, as well she should be, as she brings it fresh from her garden every morning. These little vignettes, or *aperçus*, as I like to call them, lift the spirit every time. It's what we love about the French, this willingness to work hard to continue a way of life that is fast disappearing everywhere. And yet they aren't romantic or sentimental—far from it. I would say this is a country of pragmatists: they know you can't stop "progress" but they also know you don't have to, in the name of progress, get rid of that which has tradition and value.

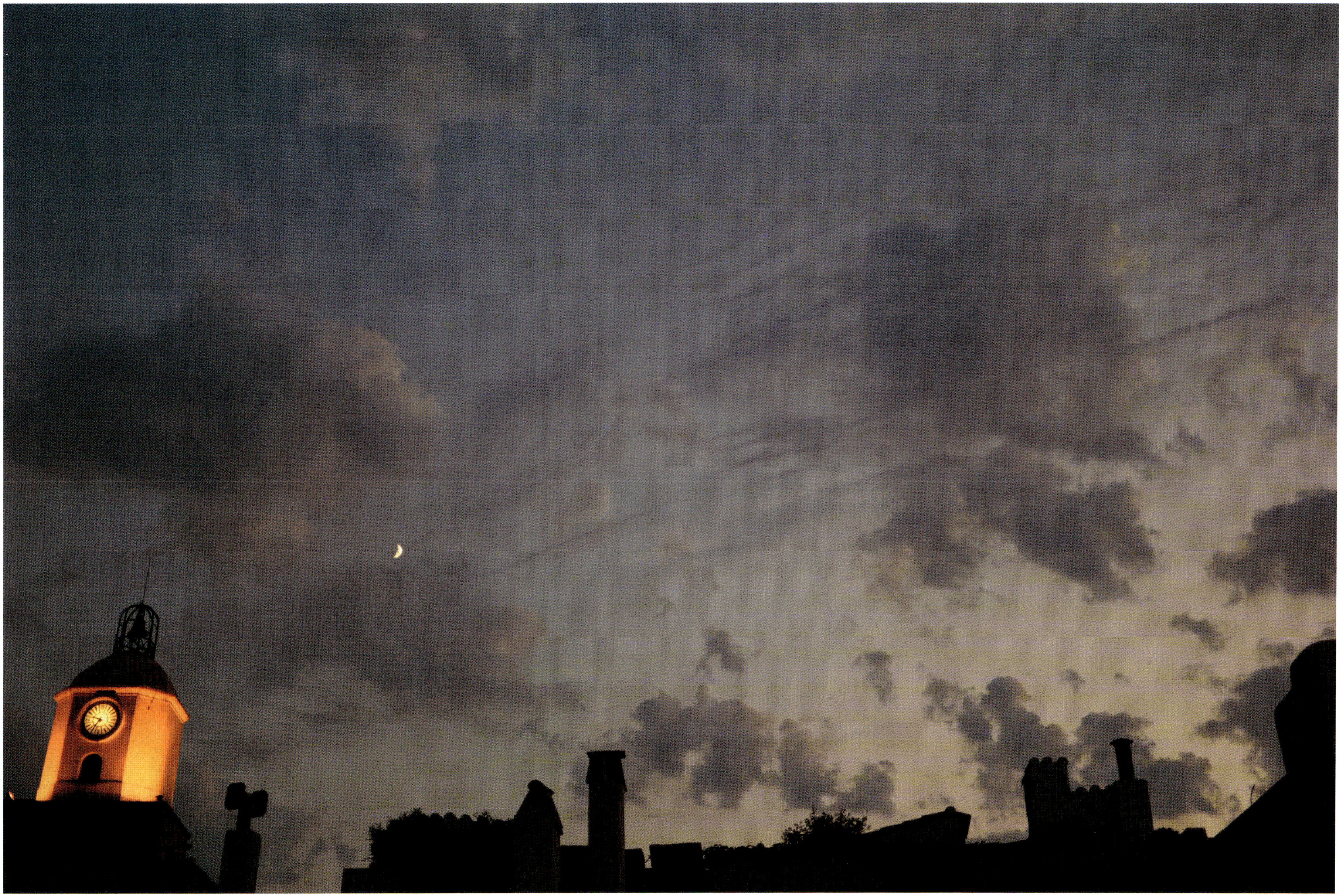

PLATE 68

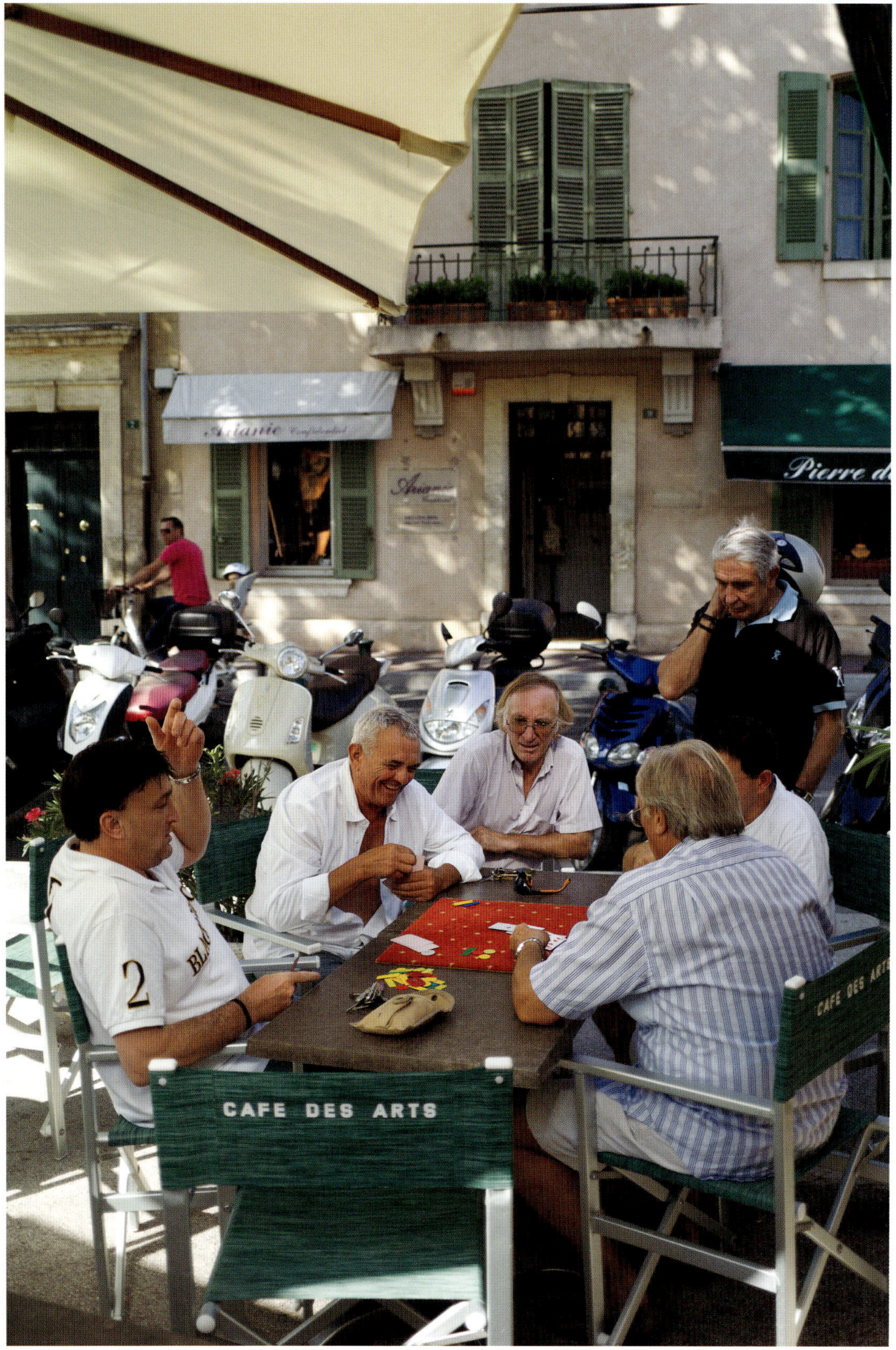

PLATE 69

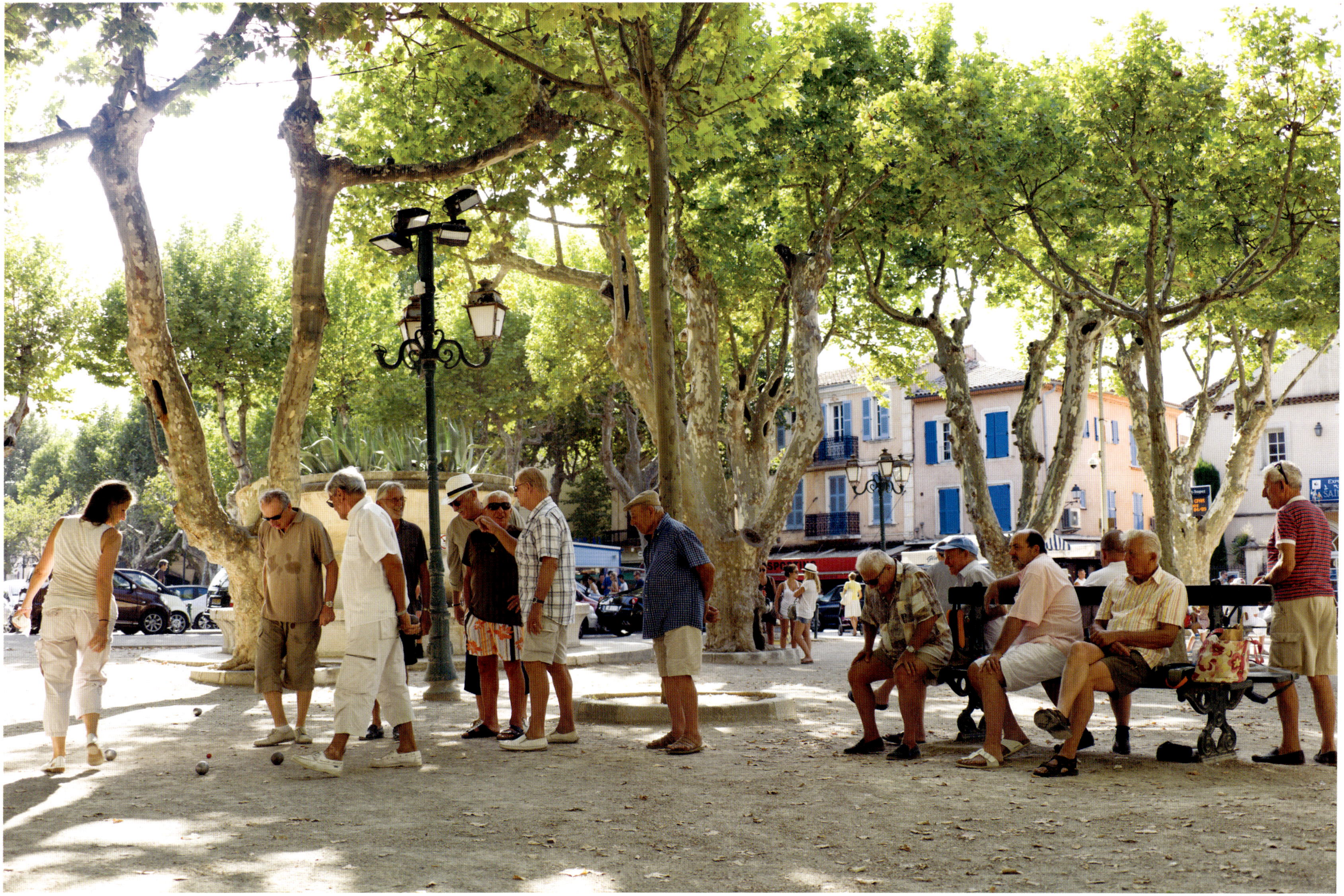

PLATE 70

THE LITTLE BEACH IN FRONT OF THE HOTEL, WHICH GAVE US SO MUCH PLEASURE WHEN VIEWED FROM THE terrace, gives us a different kind of pleasure up close. Unlike the commercial beaches, this one is Tropézienne. During our first afternoon there we are moved to tears by life at its tenderest. Two grandmothers watch over their toddler grandson. One of them calls to him when he strays too far, "Ici, mon coeur." Here, my heart.

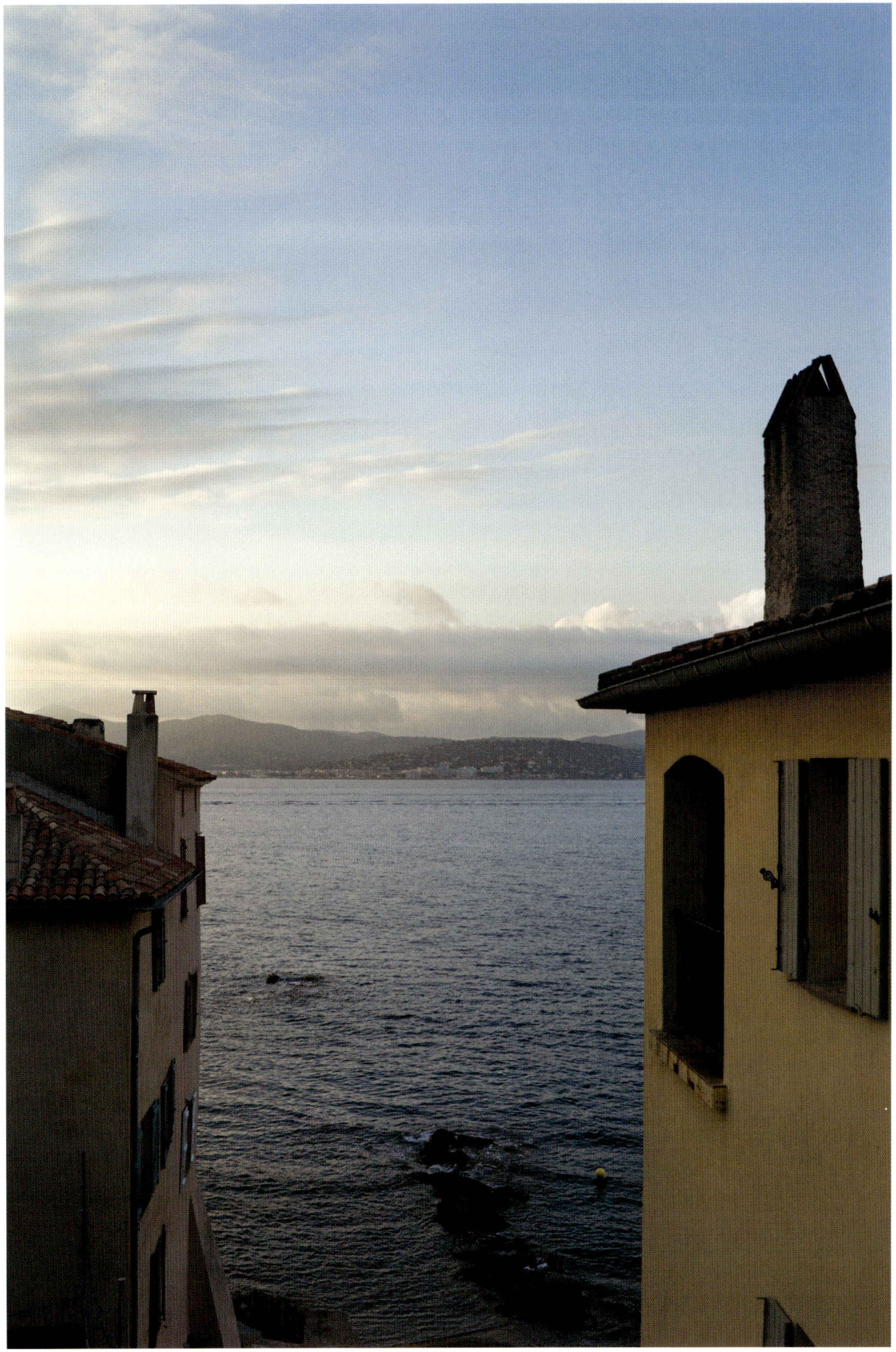

PLATE 71

AUTUMN

September

THE BIG WINDOW IS FLUNG OPEN AND LOOKS ACROSS THE VALLEY TO THE HILLSIDE WHERE, IN THE MIDST OF the vast forest, a field of lavender and seven cherry trees has been calling to us ever since we arrived in Bonnieux.

This evening we visit the field, driving along a tiny lane made for a horse-drawn cart some centuries ago, and when we enter—the soft-tilled earth giving like sand beneath our feet—the evening sunlight illuminates the low domes of clipped lavender plants. Seven cherry trees stand like sentinels along the far edge of the field, giving the whole place a sense of proportion and harmony, relating as they do, to the fourteen rows of lavender. We stop at the middle tree, which holds in its branches clusters of dried cherries as sweet and chewy as candy.

Although the lavender was harvested at least two months ago, the air in this square of lovingly tended land seems filled with a lavender mist. We walk the circumference slowly, and the word that comes to mind is: heaven.

I am not a religious person, but words exist and "heaven" is one of them, and therefore one cannot avoid having one's own visual and metaphoric interpretation of it. So, I suppose my interpretation of heaven is a place of serenity and ordered proportion, imbued with a sense of safety and mystery. A place where, like the lavender and cherry trees, one will be well tended and come to fruition year after year.

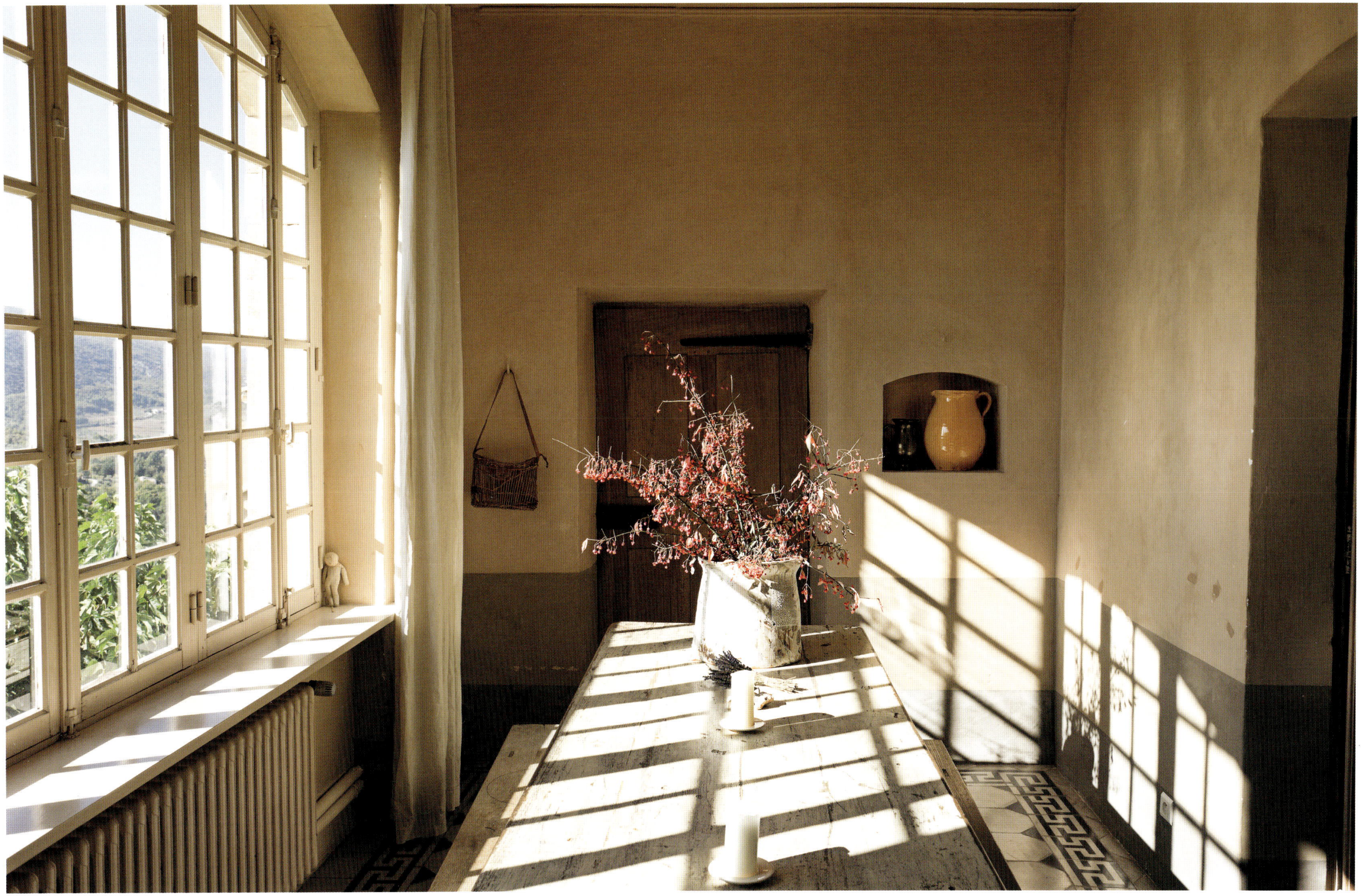

PLATE 72

PLATE 73

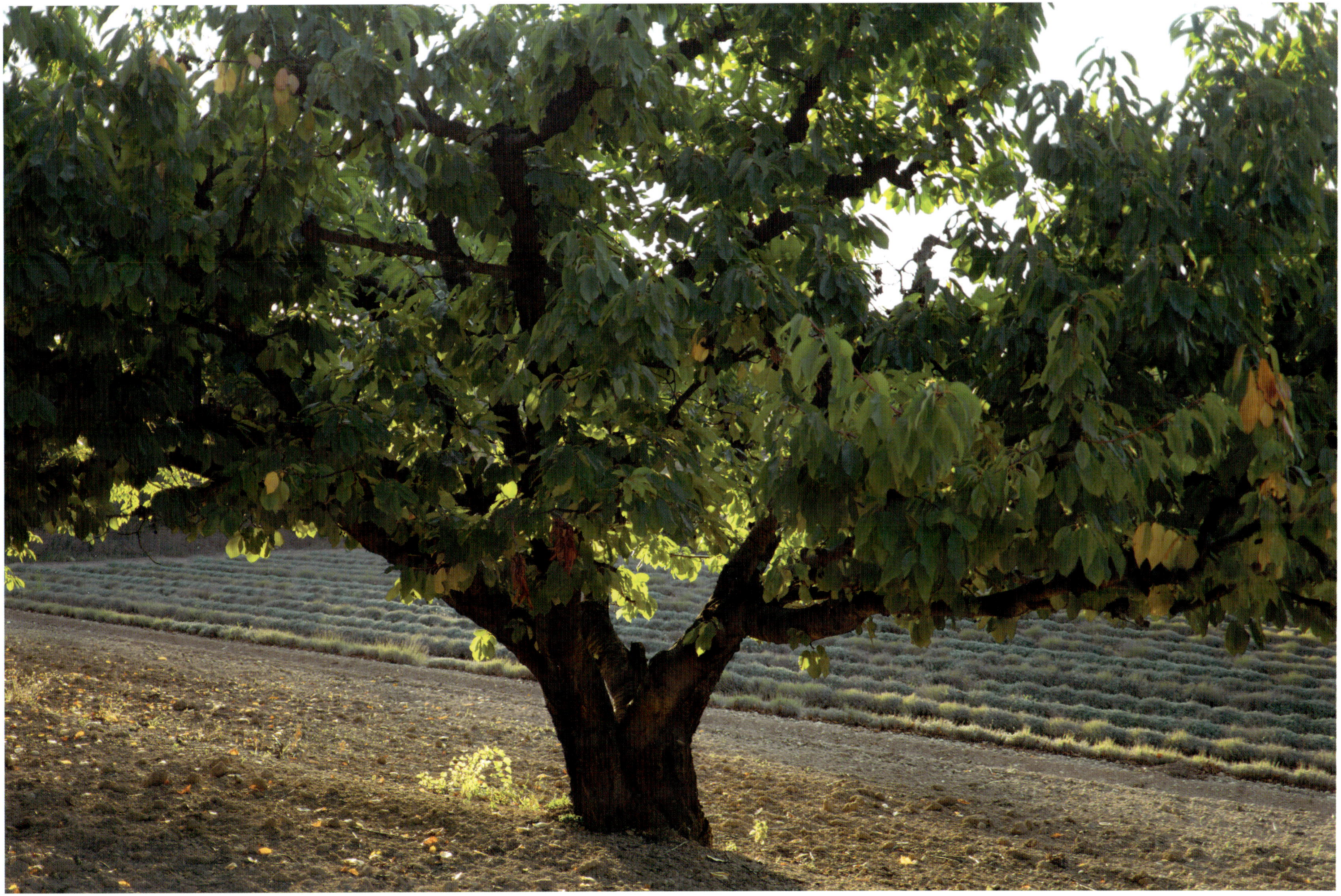

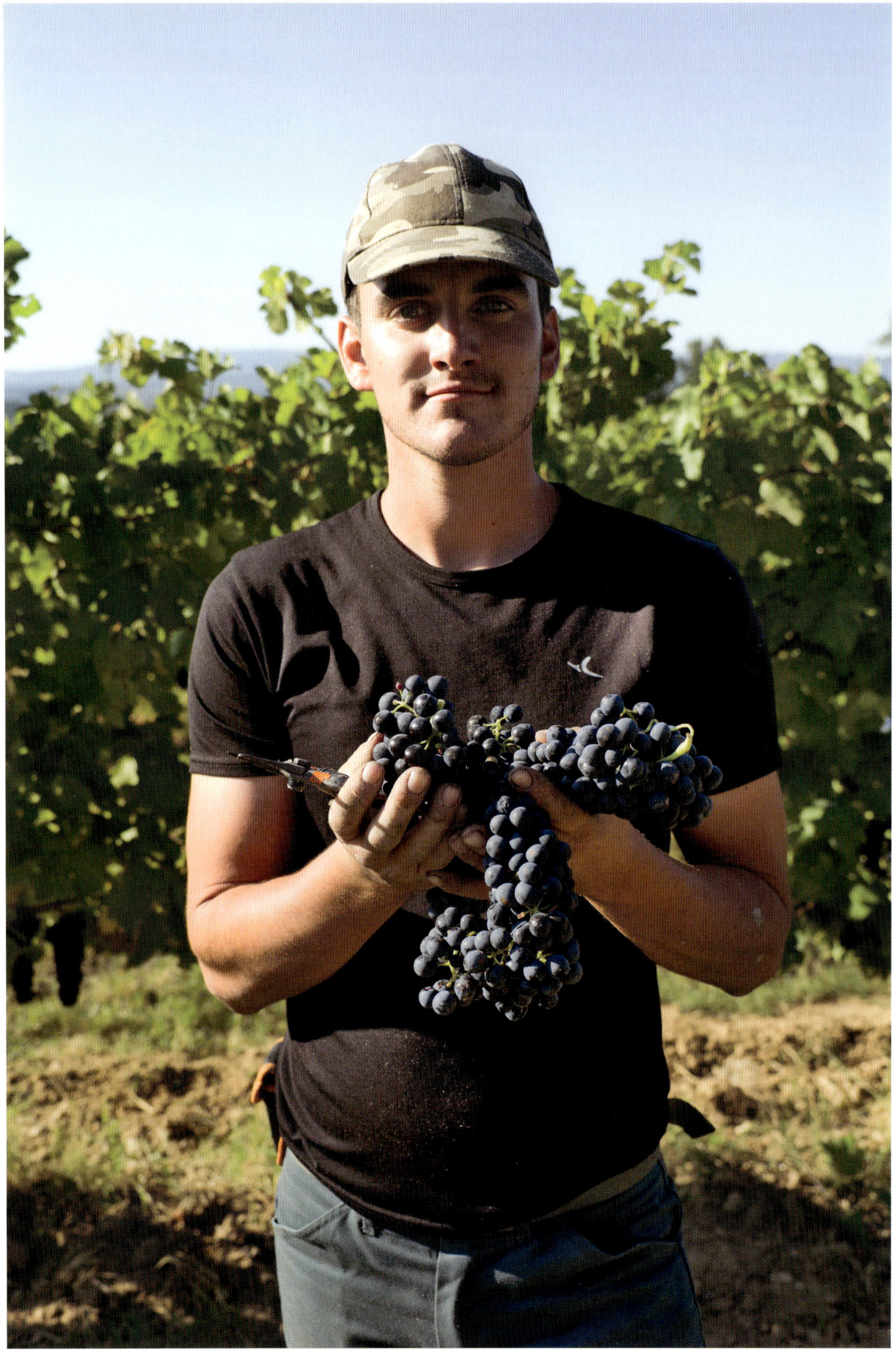

PLATE 74

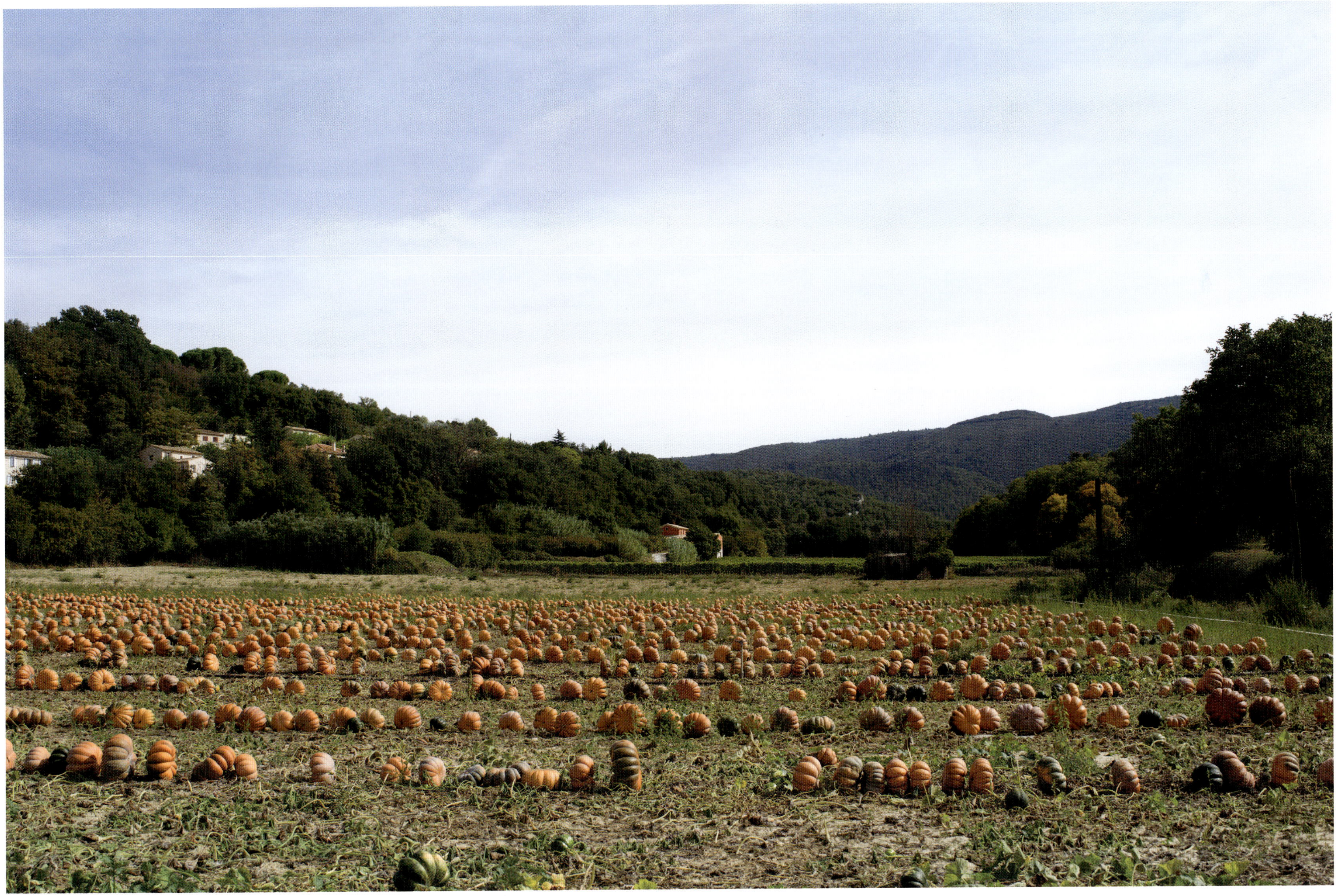

PLATE 75

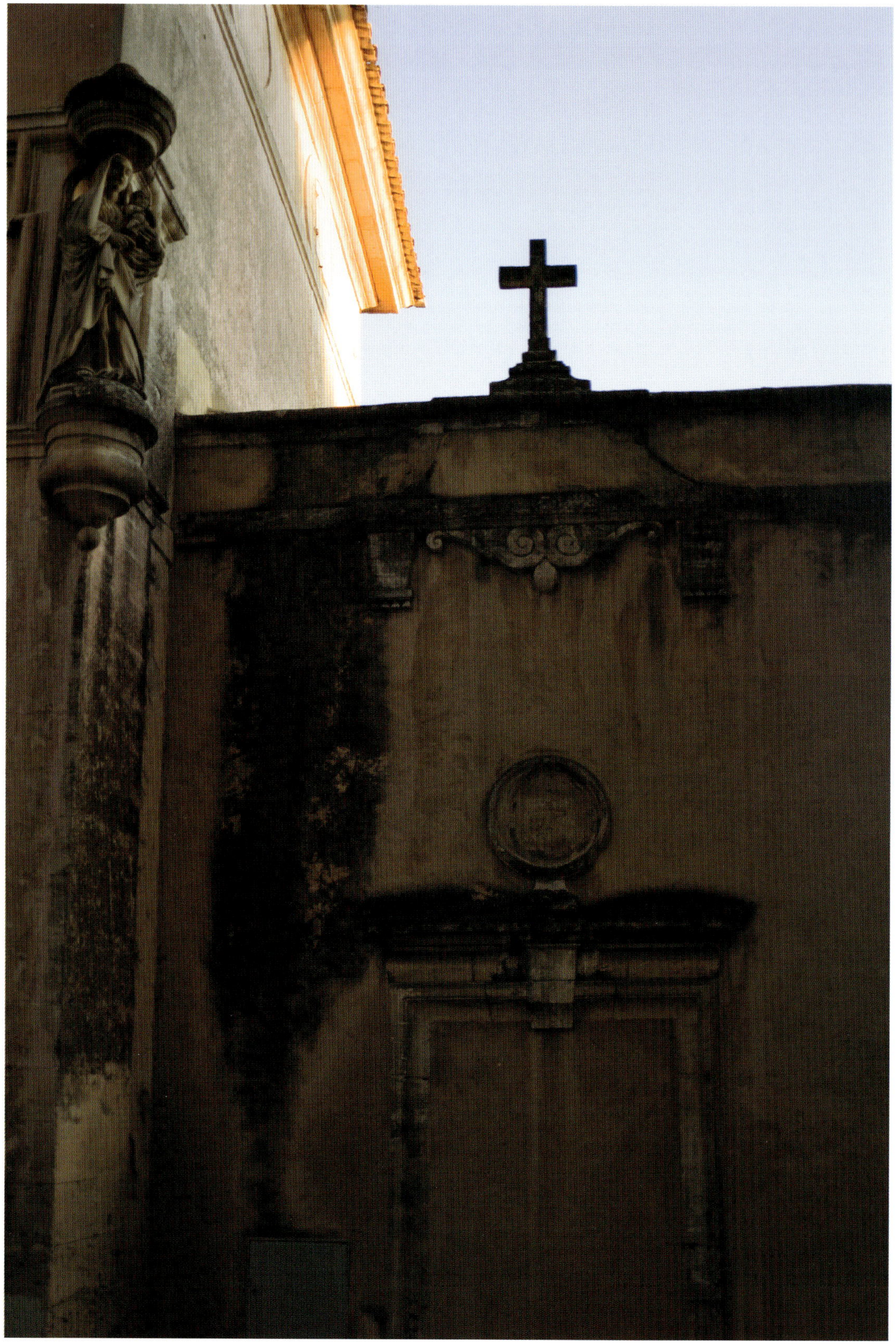

PLATE 76

PLATE 77

PLATE 78 (OVERLEAF)

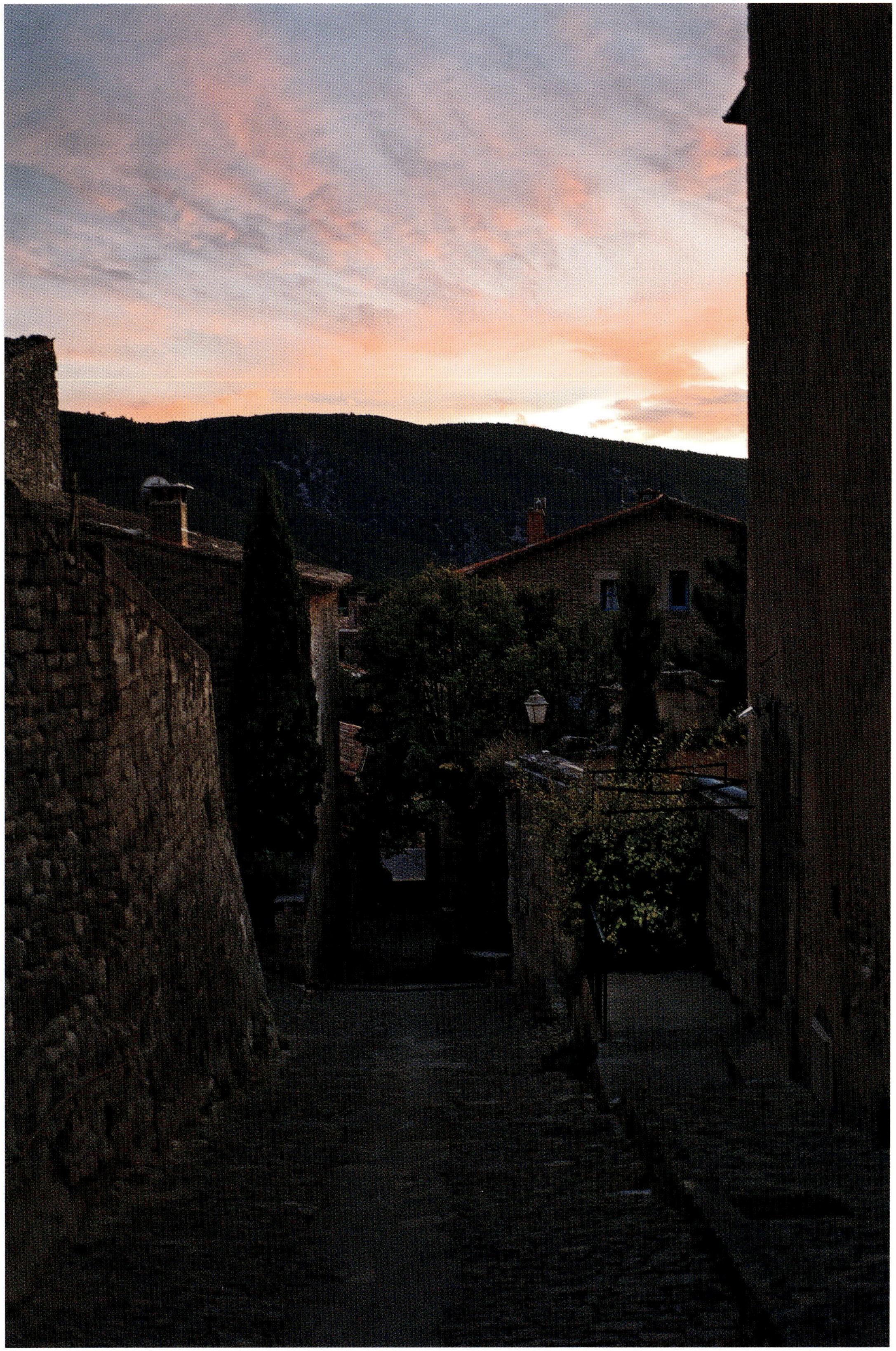

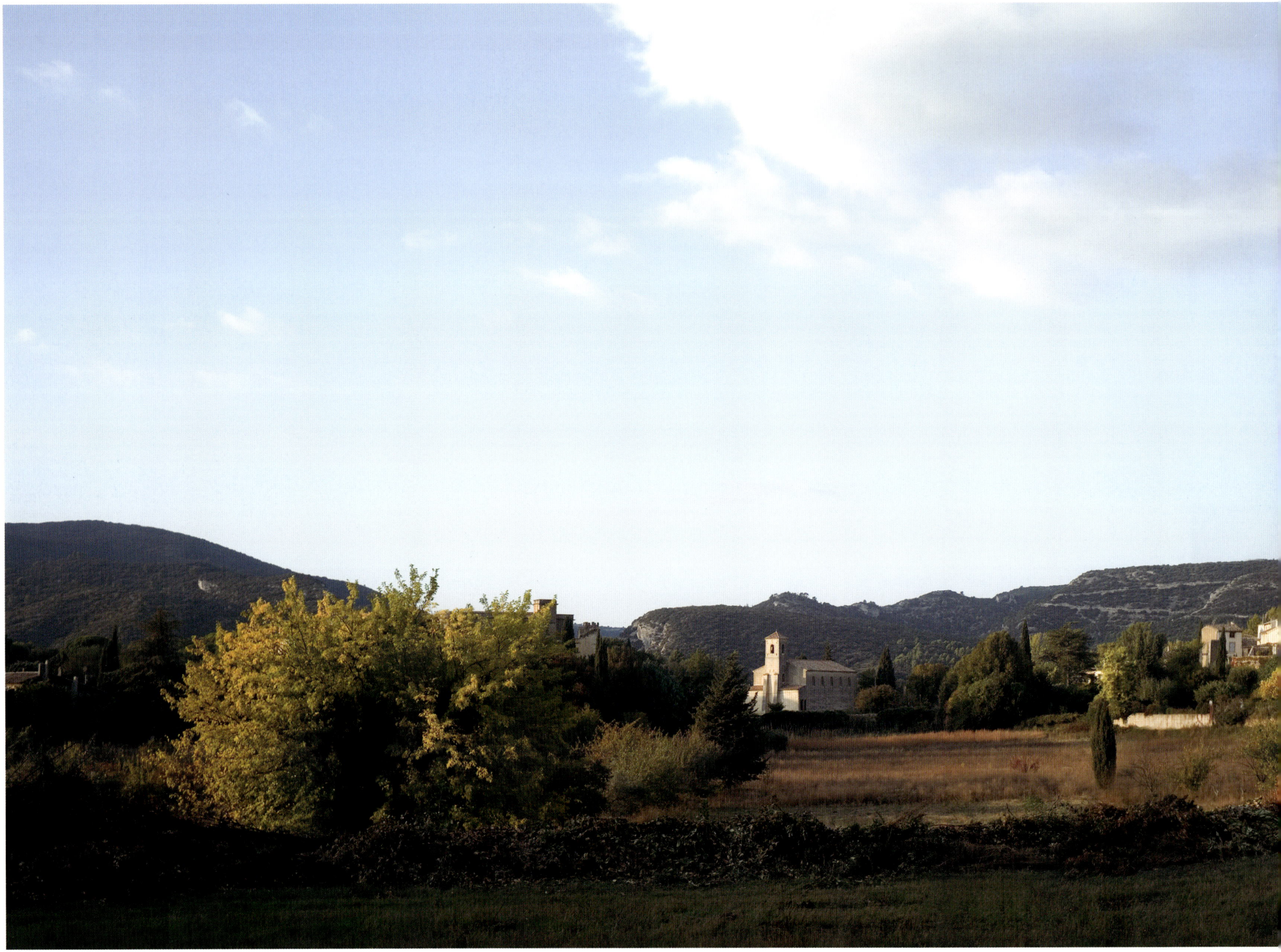

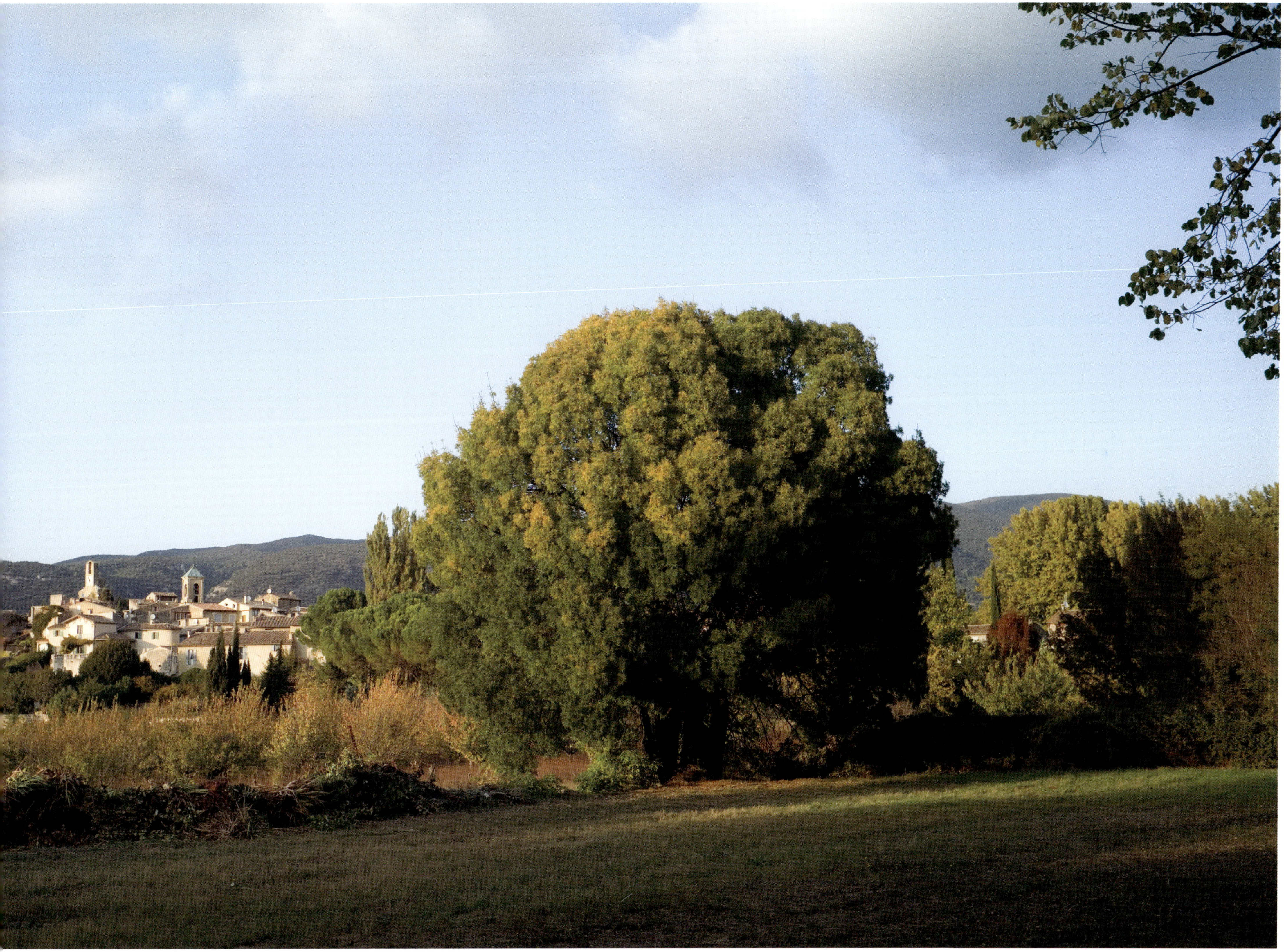

October

TODAY THE ROULETTE WHEEL STOPS ON NEITHER *ROUGE* NOR *NOIR* BUT ON *VERT*: THE GREEN OF FONTAINE-de-Vaucluse. Make that plural: greens. We don't recall ever seeing so many shades of green, not even in spring—perhaps not even in my native England.

The day is luscious, full sunshine with heat in it tempered by the mistral, which, in this village—because it is surrounded by cliffs on three sides—is more of a playful breeze. In fact, *vaucluse* means "closed valley" and *fontaine* means "spring," and the spring here is the largest in France and the fifth largest in Europe. It is also the source of the River Sorgue and a mighty river it is. Its lush underwater vegetation a virulent green so intense it looks Photoshopped.

We spend a couple of hours here, wandering, sitting, gazing. One can imagine that in the height of summer the pedestrian traffic is shoulder-to-shoulder, but on this Indian summer day, although there are some tourists, their number is few and the village has a relaxed and pleasant pace, as if the meander of we humans matches the meander of the river, our spirits lifted by the sheer beauty of nature.

On the way back to Bonnieux, we talk about the abundance of Provence: certainly its food and climate, but also the ceaseless supply of back roads, each one leading to a new discovery, many a mere jaunt away, none more than a day trip. Each of these little excursions serves up such a bounty of visual and physical pleasure that it is possible to feel satisfied to call it a full day and still be back at your hotel in thirty minutes.

Back in our rented apartment we sit by the fire and talk about the day, about Provence, about leaving home, about our kids, about what it's like to live in a foreign country where we know no one, to talk only with each other for days on end, to be this free and forgiving. While we no longer take the wild risks of youth, we're still willing to risk embracing the unknown. The former was life-threatening. The latter is life-affirming.

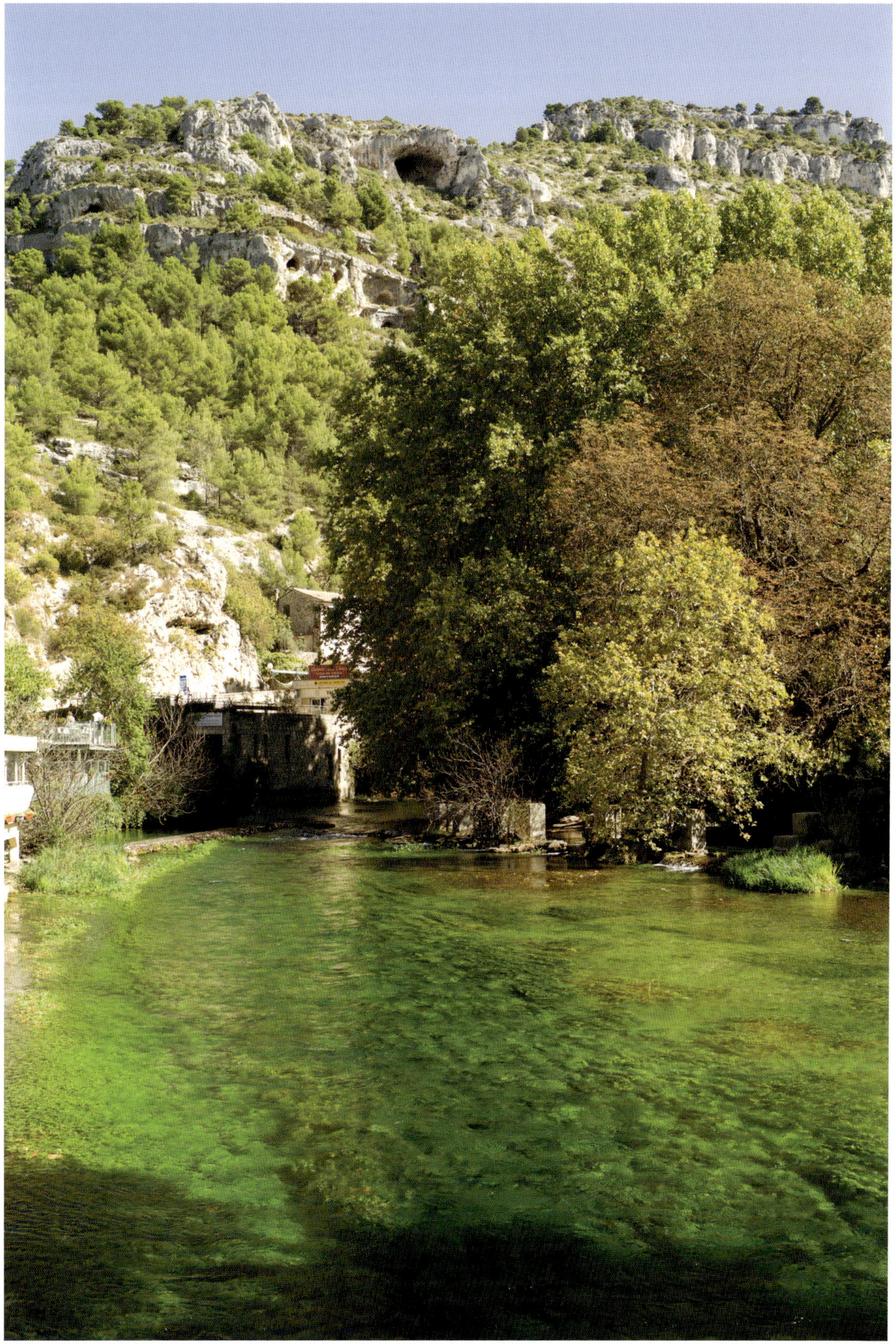

PLATE 79

PLATE 80

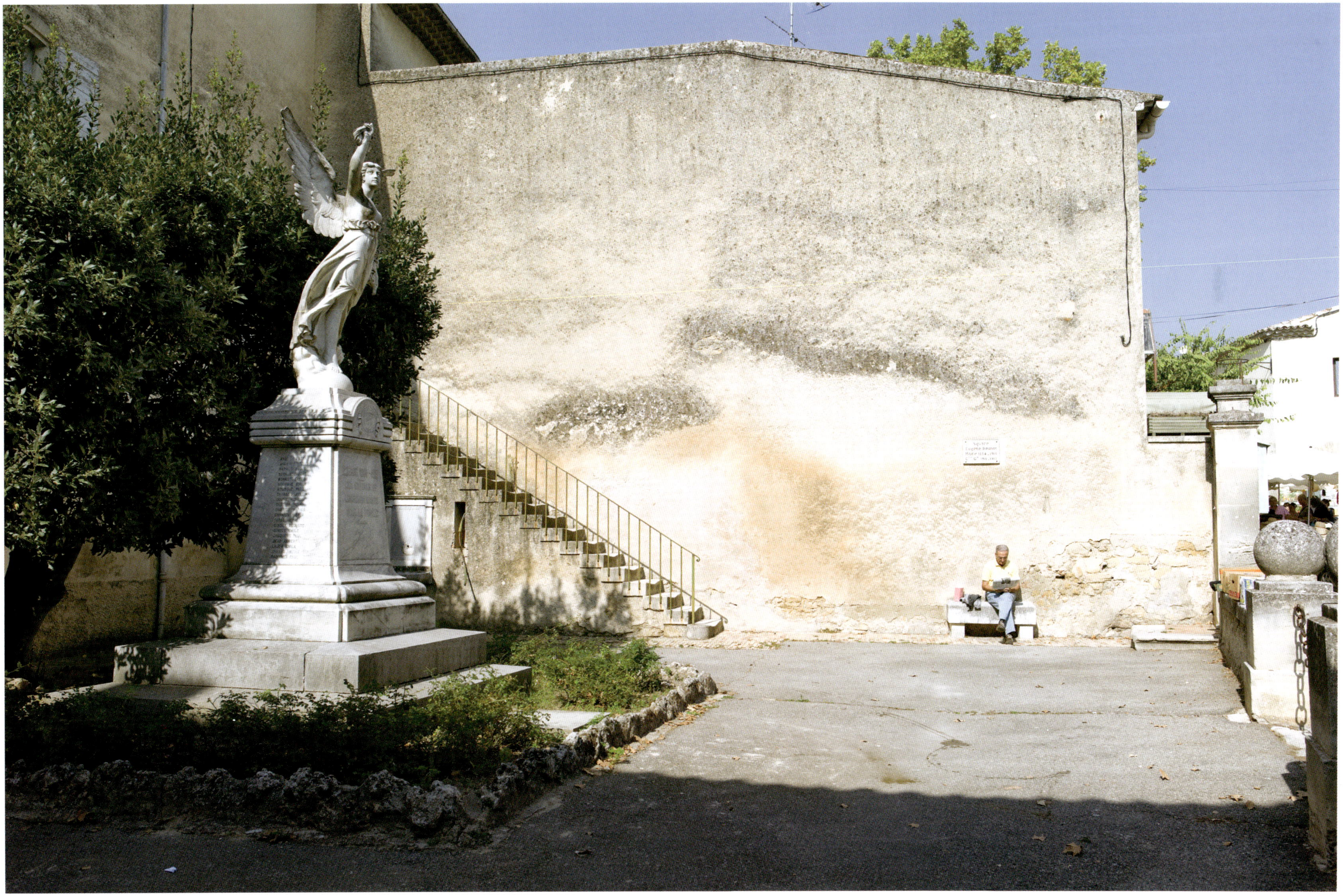

PLATE 81

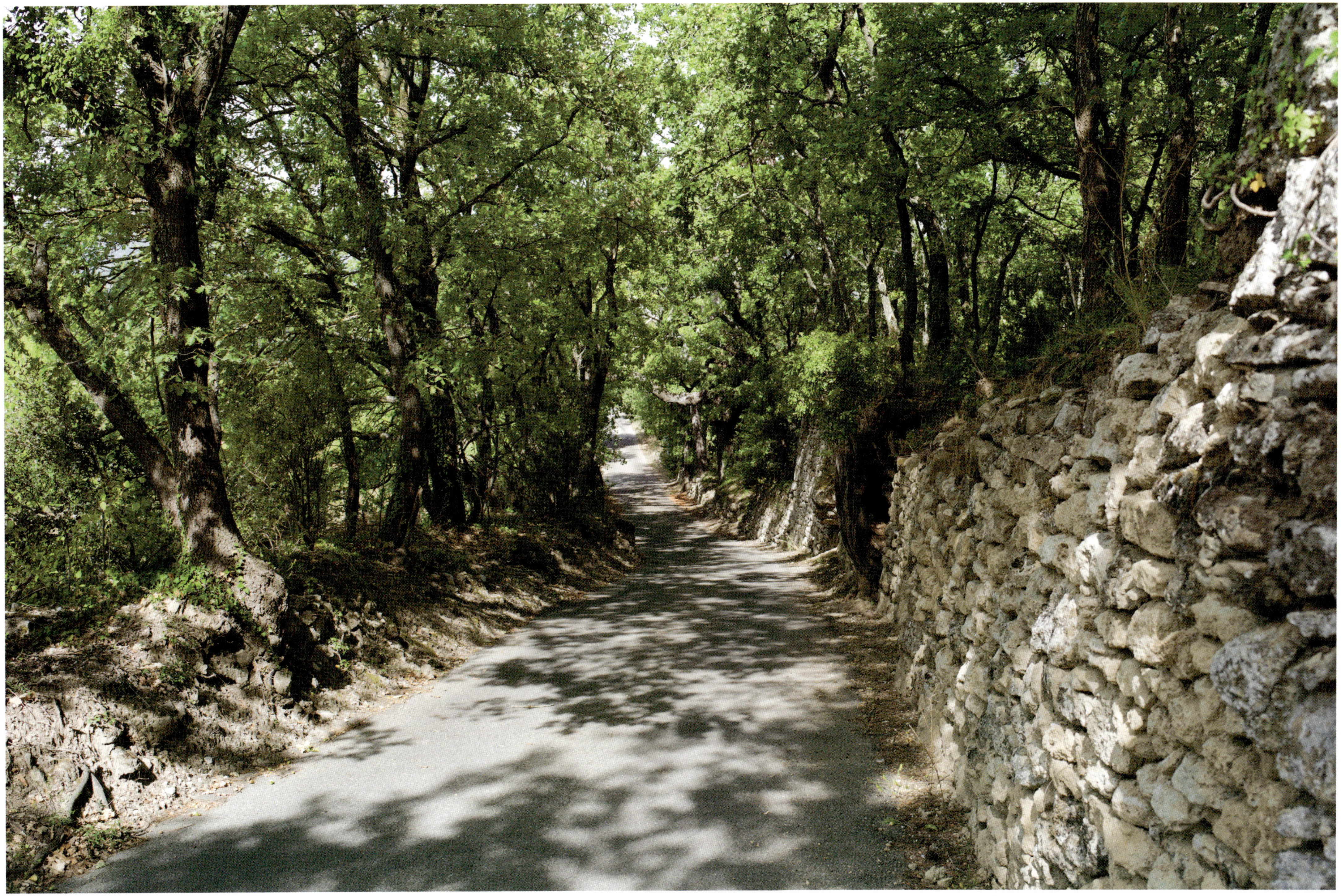

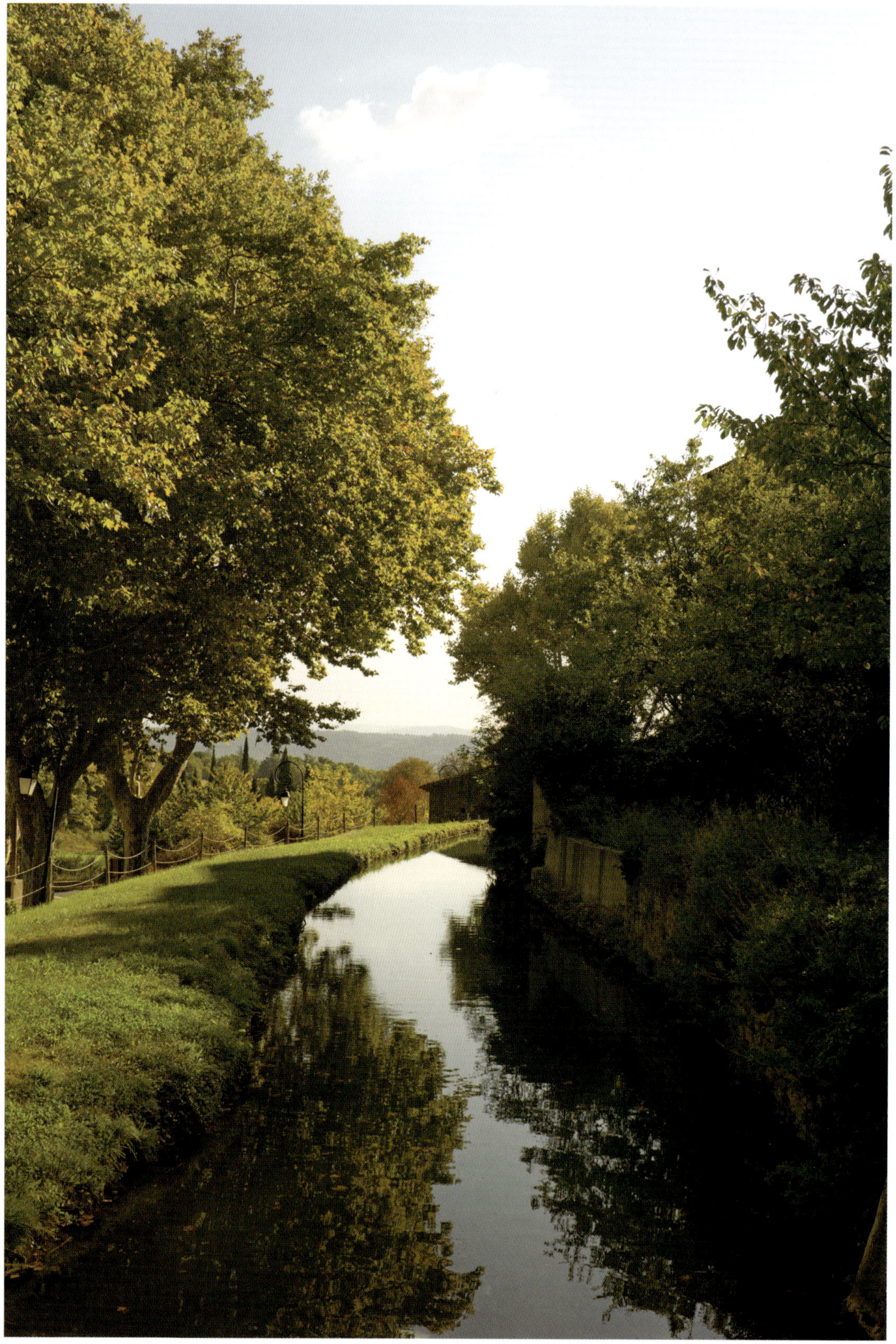

PLATE 82

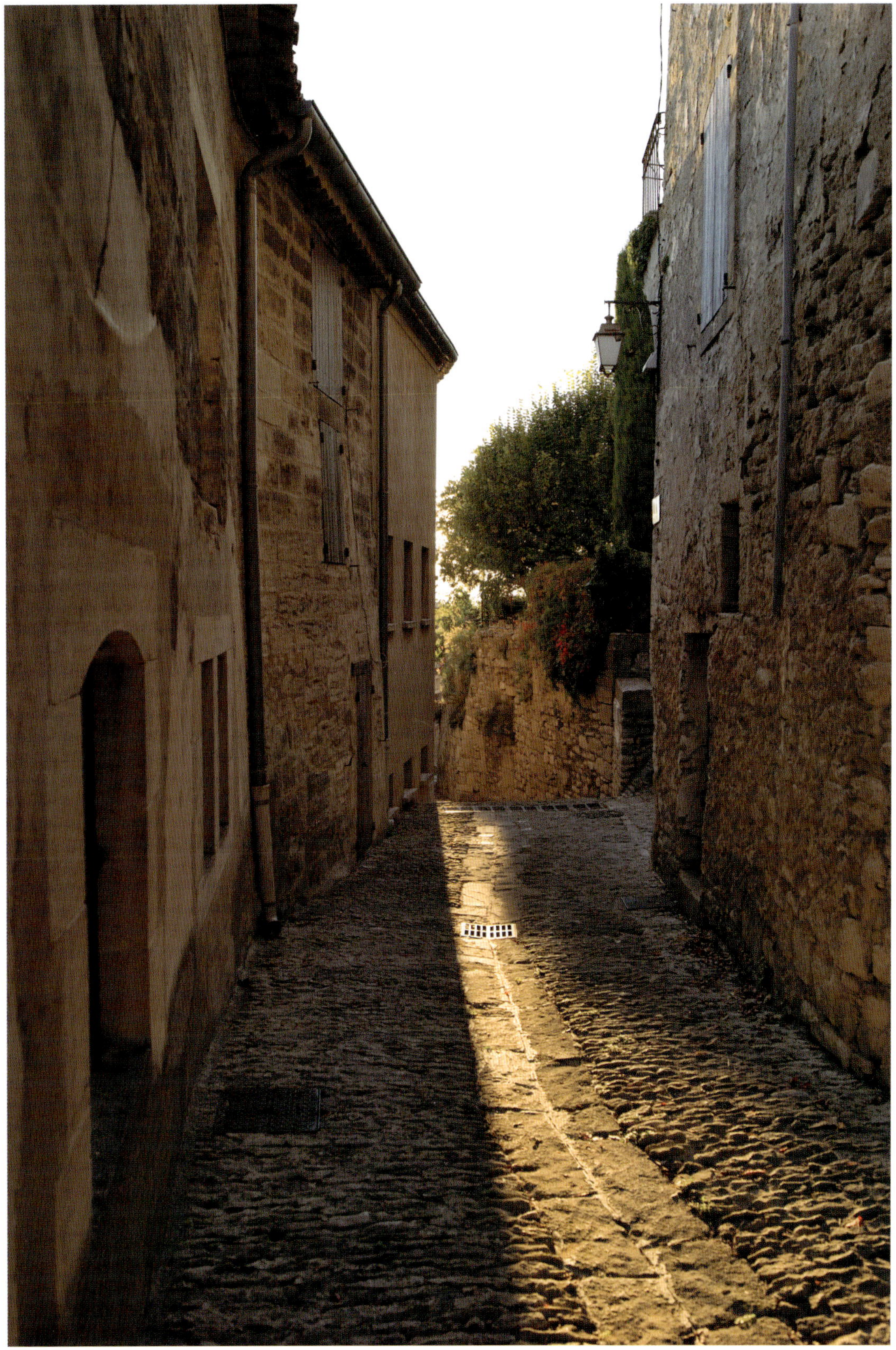

PLATE 83

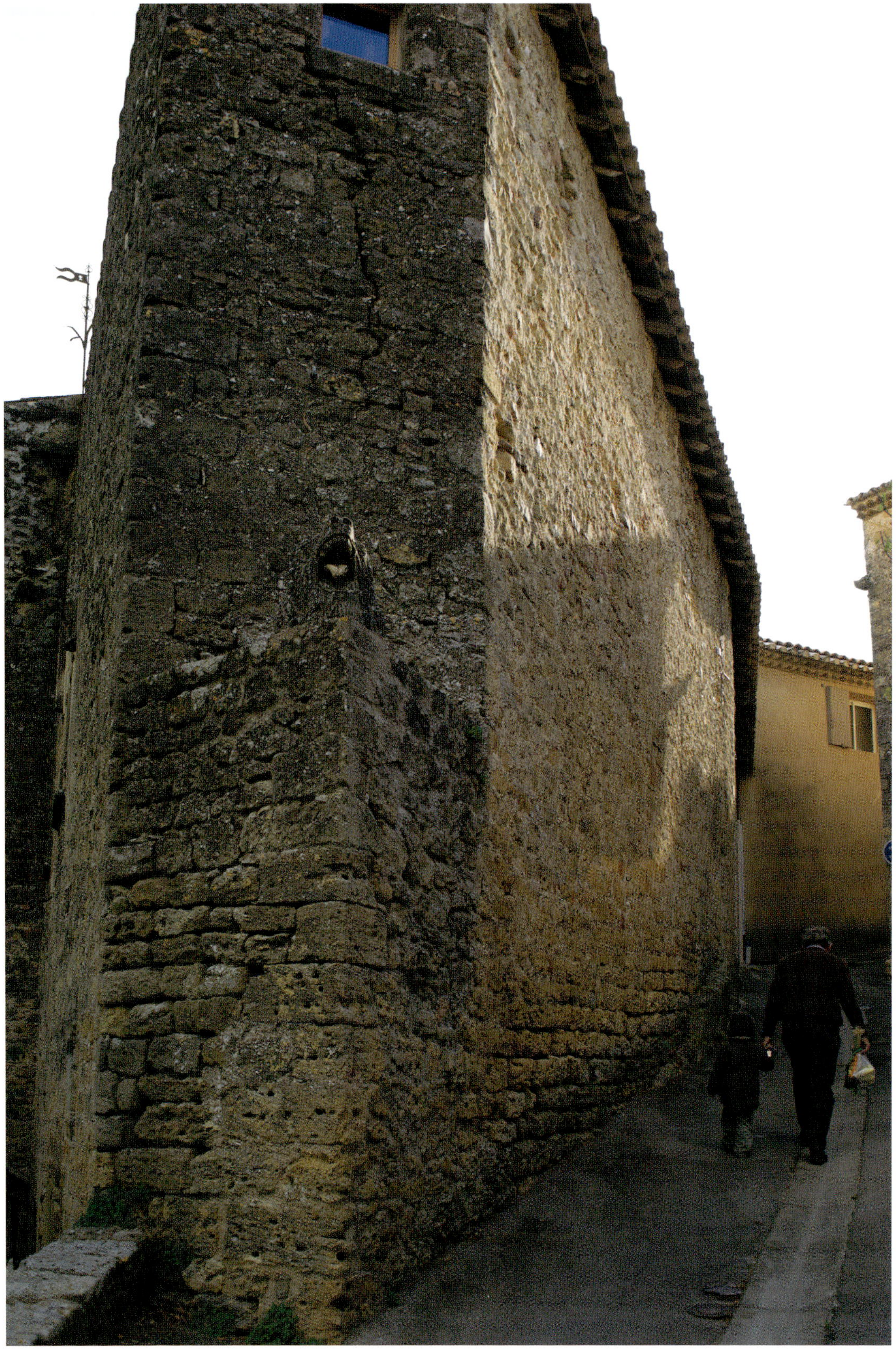

PLATE 84

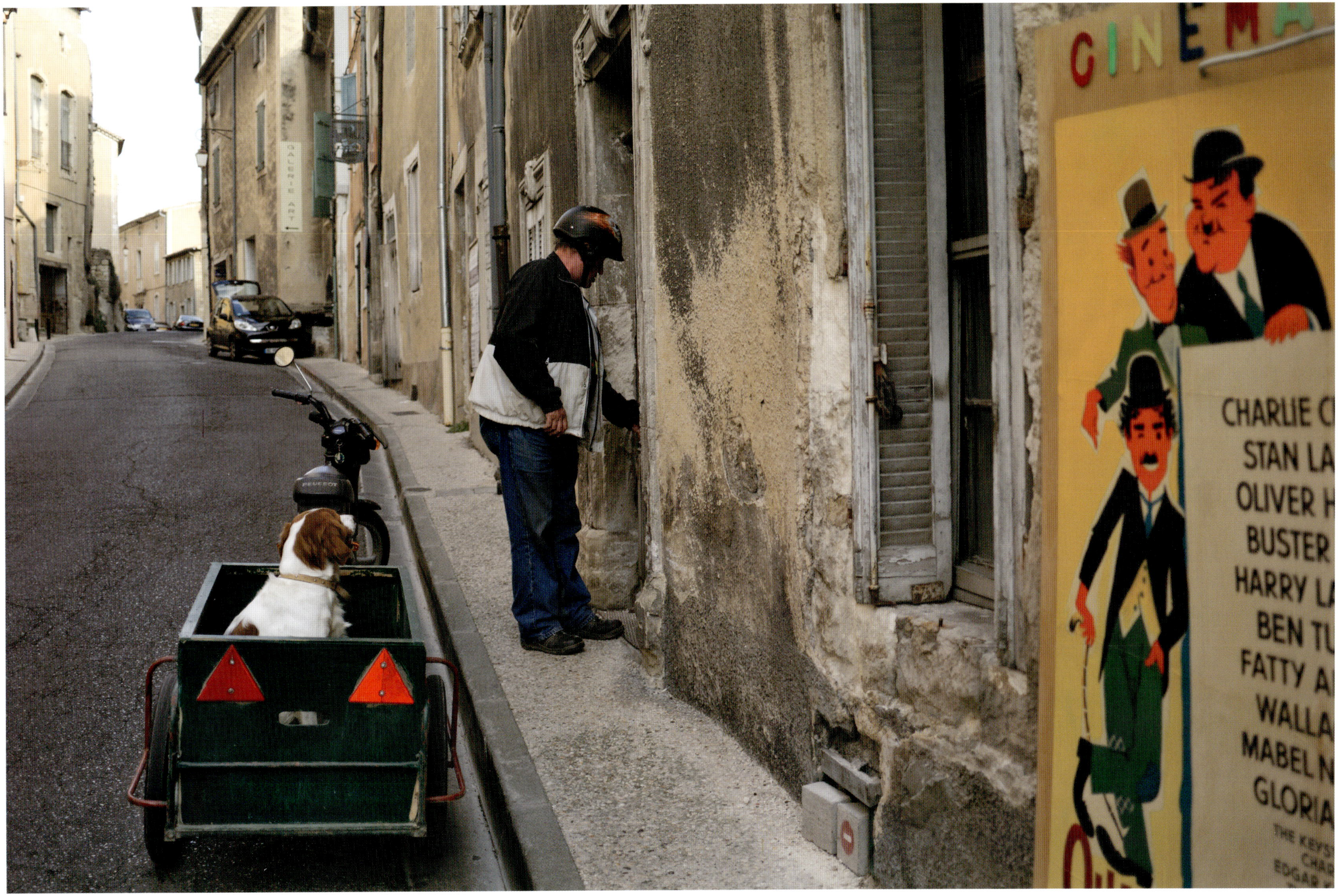

PLATE 85

PLATE 86 (OVERLEAF)

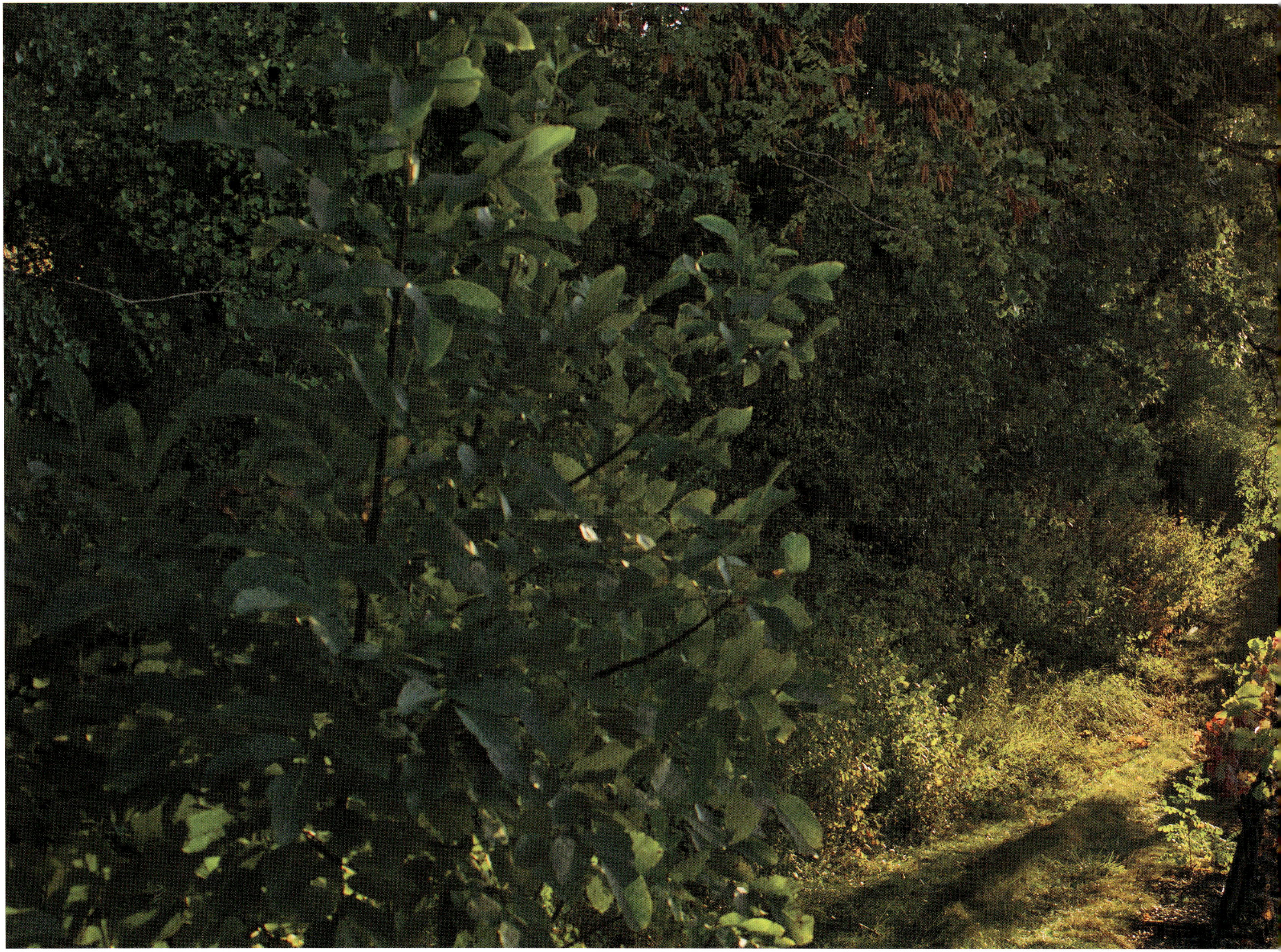

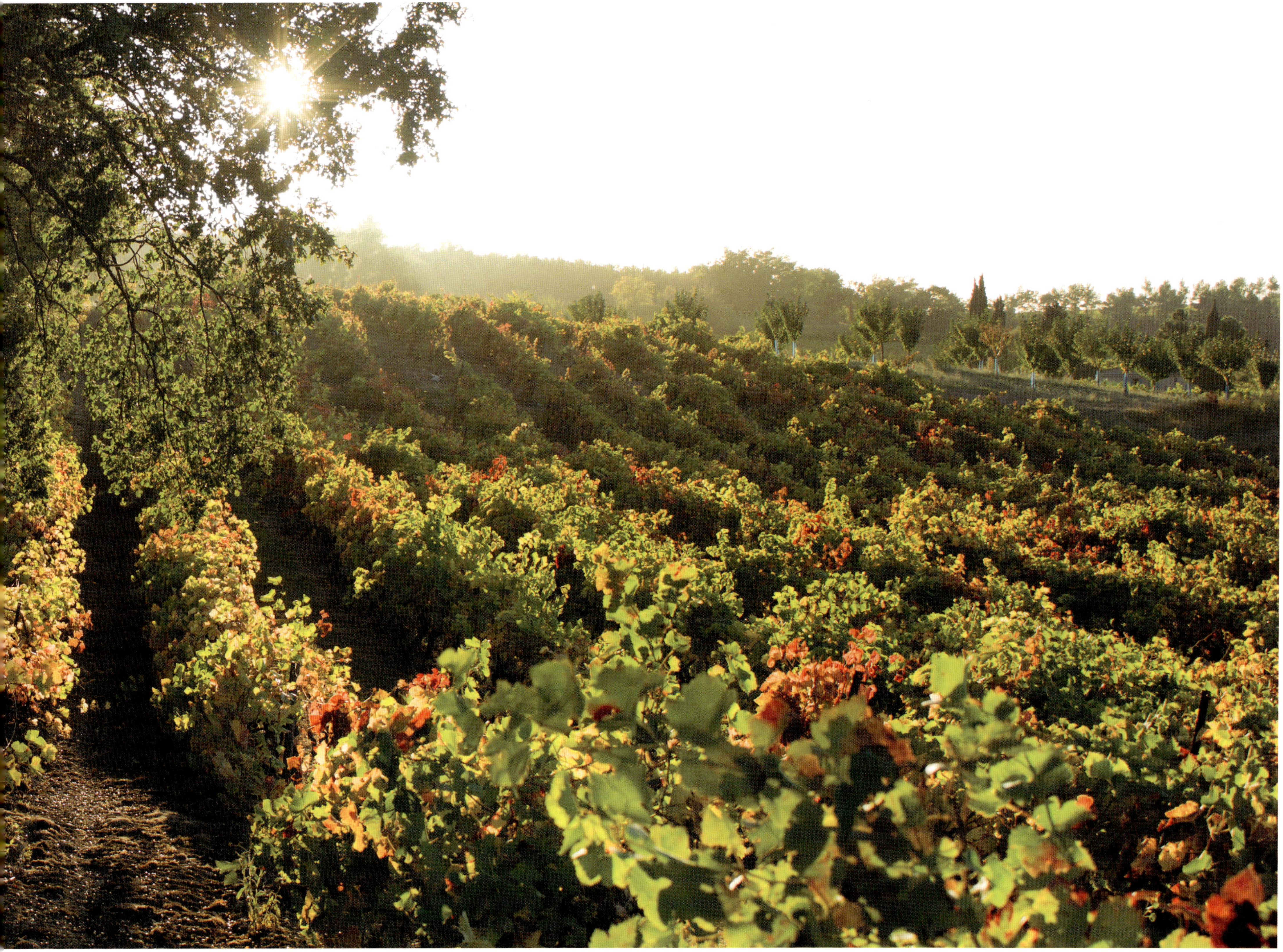

TODAY WE TRAVEL TO THE ENCLOS DE BORIES; BORIES ARE THE LITTLE, BEEHIVE-SHAPED STONE BUILDINGS dotted about the Luberon Valley. We were wondering what they were and recently found out they were huts dating back almost a thousand years, and were inhabited by Celtic nomads and shepherds. Each time I've seen one I've had an odd sensation close to goosebumps, followed by an almost visceral lurch, as if I've just woken up.

This sensation is intensified today when we enter the Enclos (Enclosure), which comprises perhaps twenty of these stone huts, many completely intact, some in partial ruin and a few returned to piles of stones. It's hard to describe what it's like to walk into these woods. I actually couldn't move at first. The energy vibrates between stones and trees, and if you let your focus go soft the entire scene seems to time-lapse into an overall woven scrim that, far from obscuring the scene, rather gives one a sense of time and perspective as infinite.

I want to stay here, rooted like this, for truly I feel as if I had been here centuries ago. I feel both a longing to live here and an unquestionable feeling that I have. We stay for two hours, barely speaking. Everything is quivering with light. The sun, low in the sky, comes through the woods at our height before falling to the ground in golden droplets. We wander in and out of low stone doorways, look up to ceilings as spiritual as any cathedral, see the niches where the woven straw was hung for the bees to deposit honey and wax. The moss is a still carpet, yet every thread is alive. And every leaf holds its breath.

In a trance, we walk to the edge of the woods and see, on the far hill, our village ablaze with the setting sun. We see our big window, see ourselves sitting there looking out to here, and then, looking down, see our beloved lavender field and its seven cherry trees.

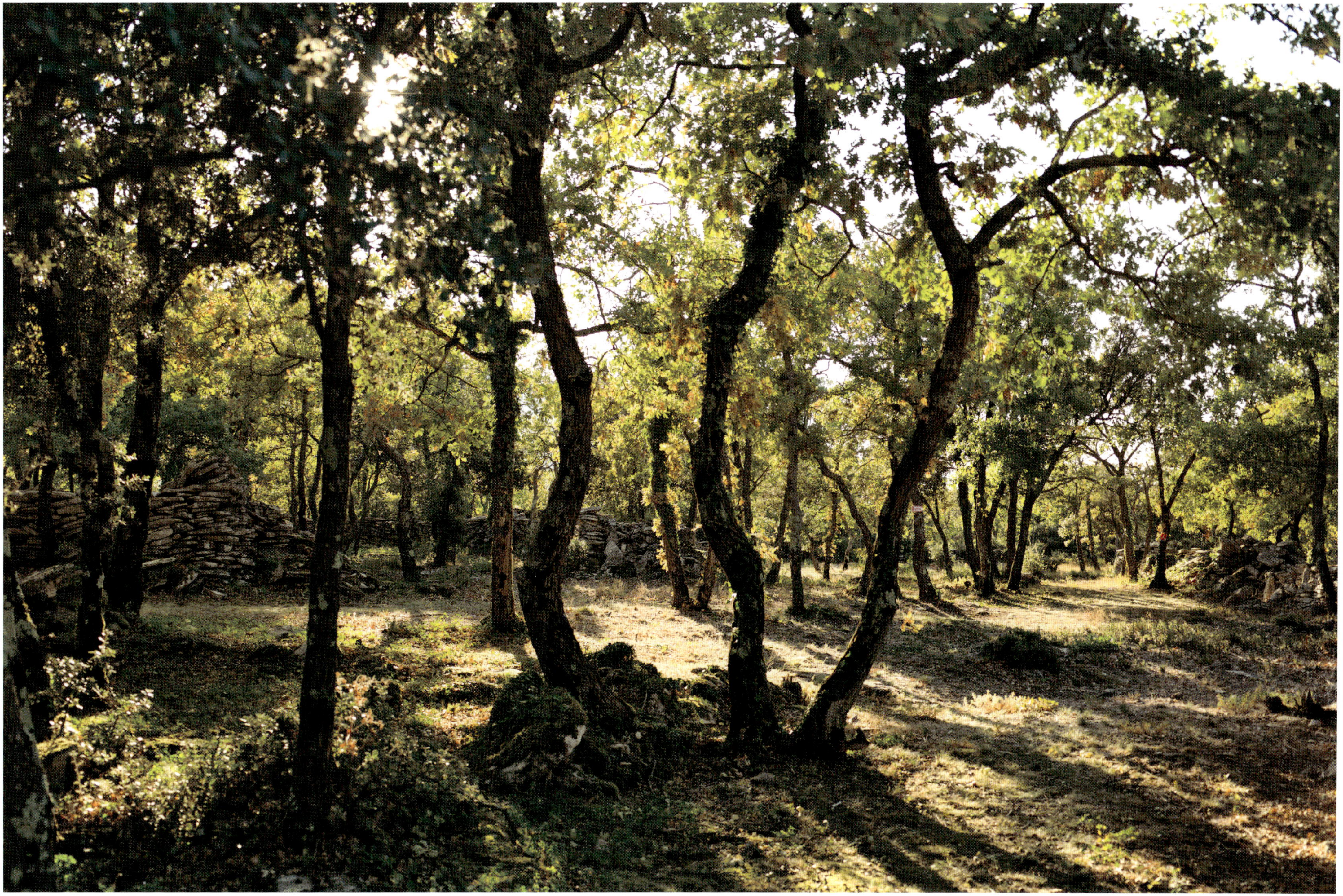

PLATE 87

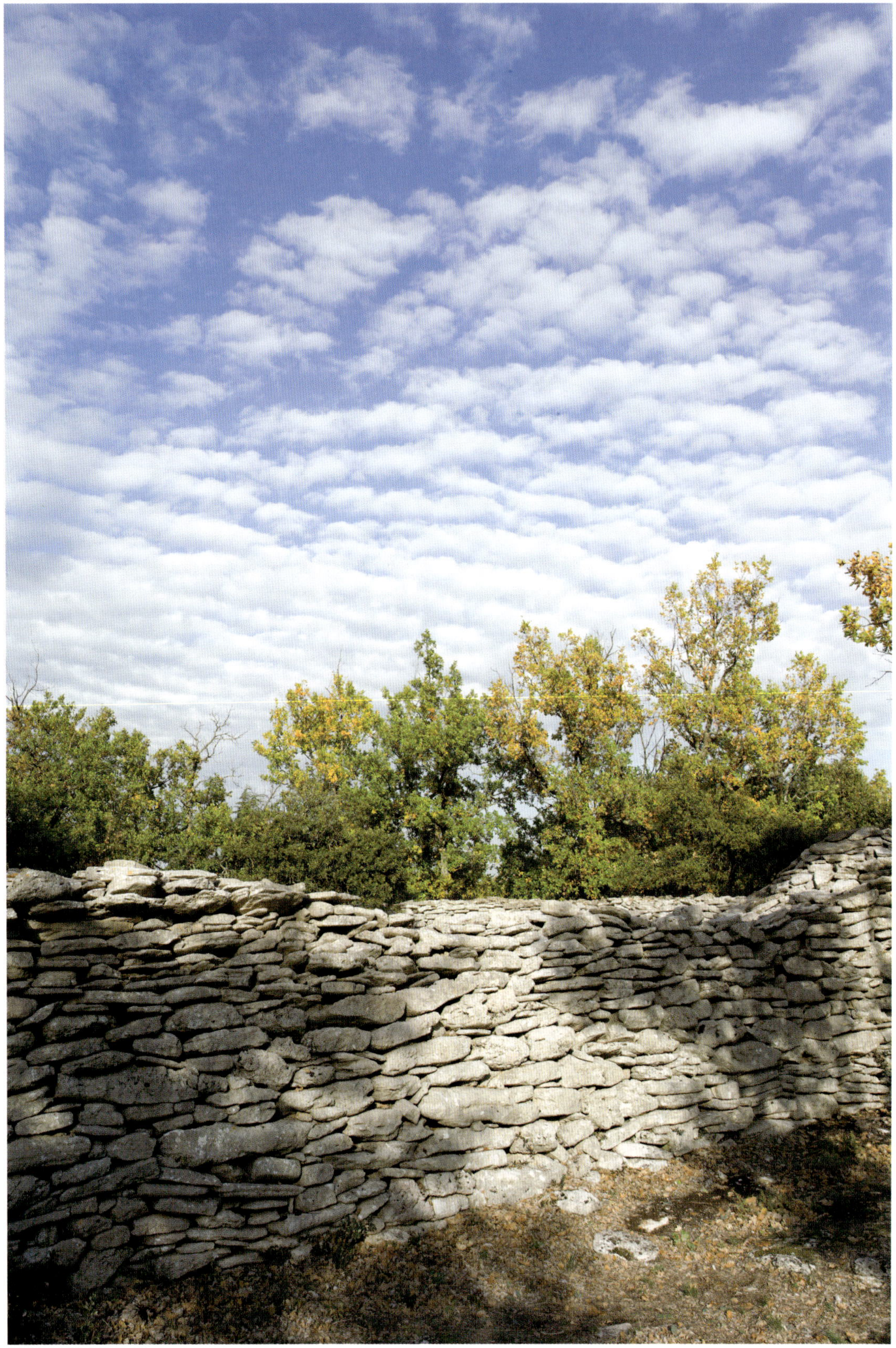

PLATE 88

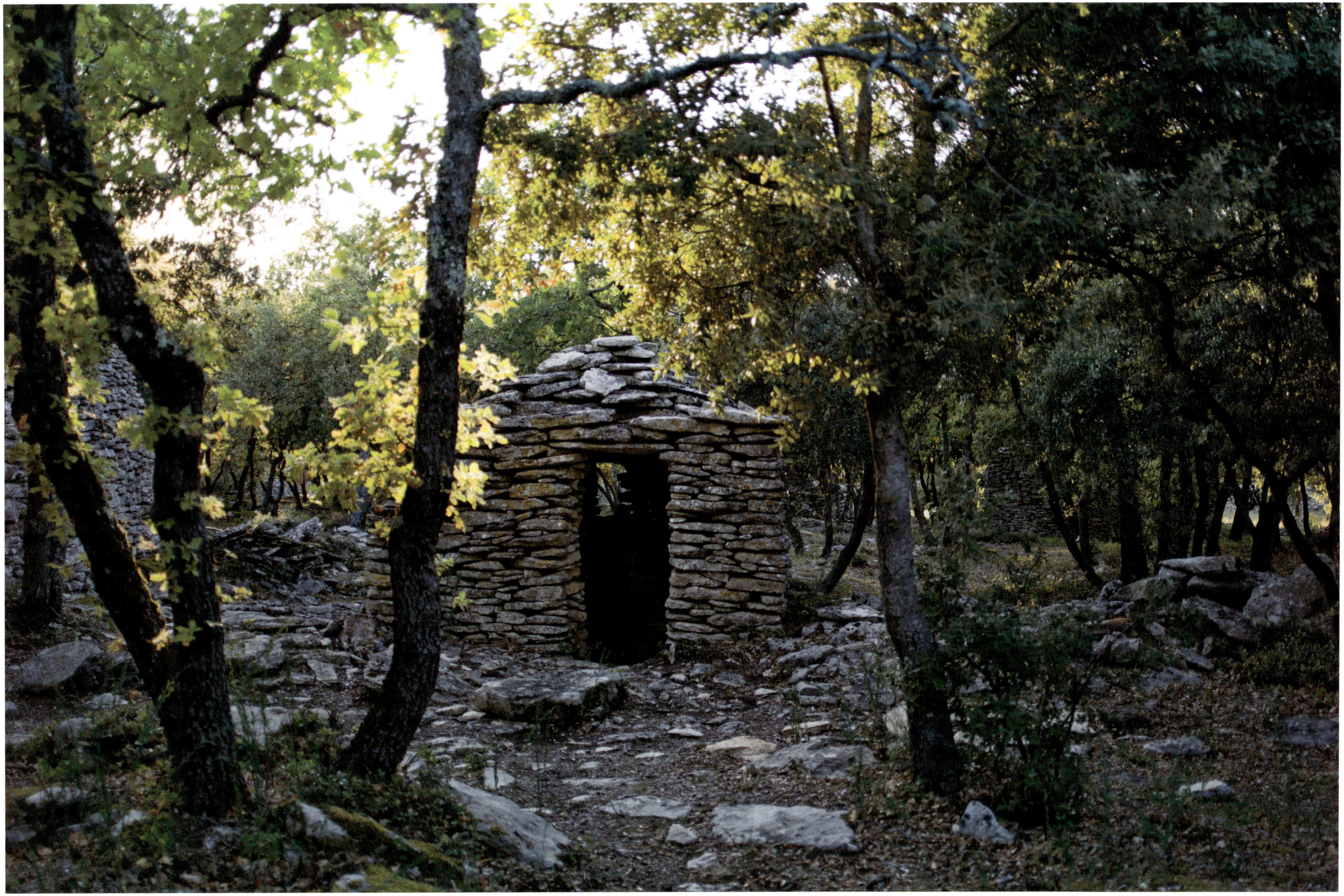

PLATE 89

PLATE 90 (OVERLEAF)

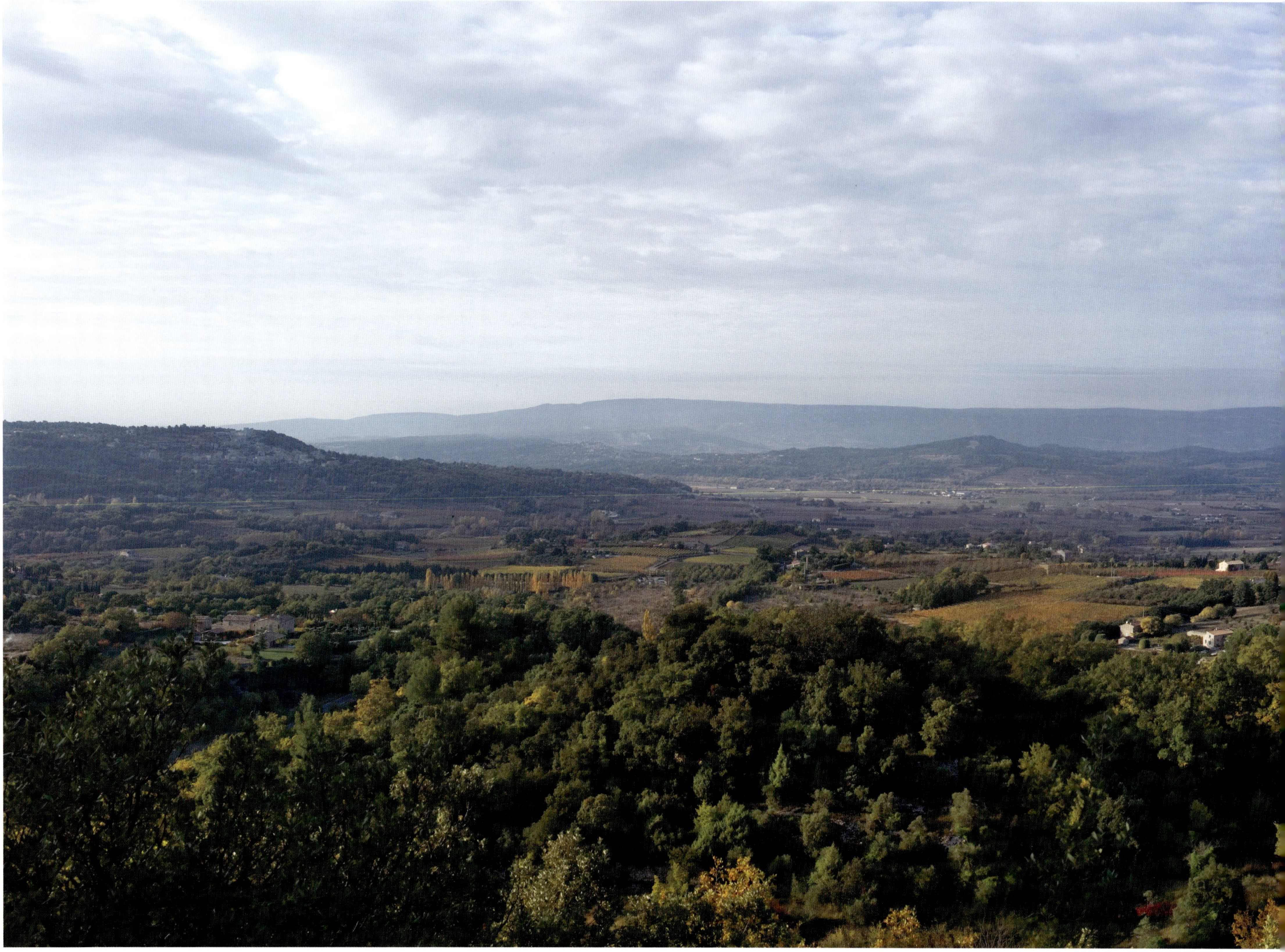

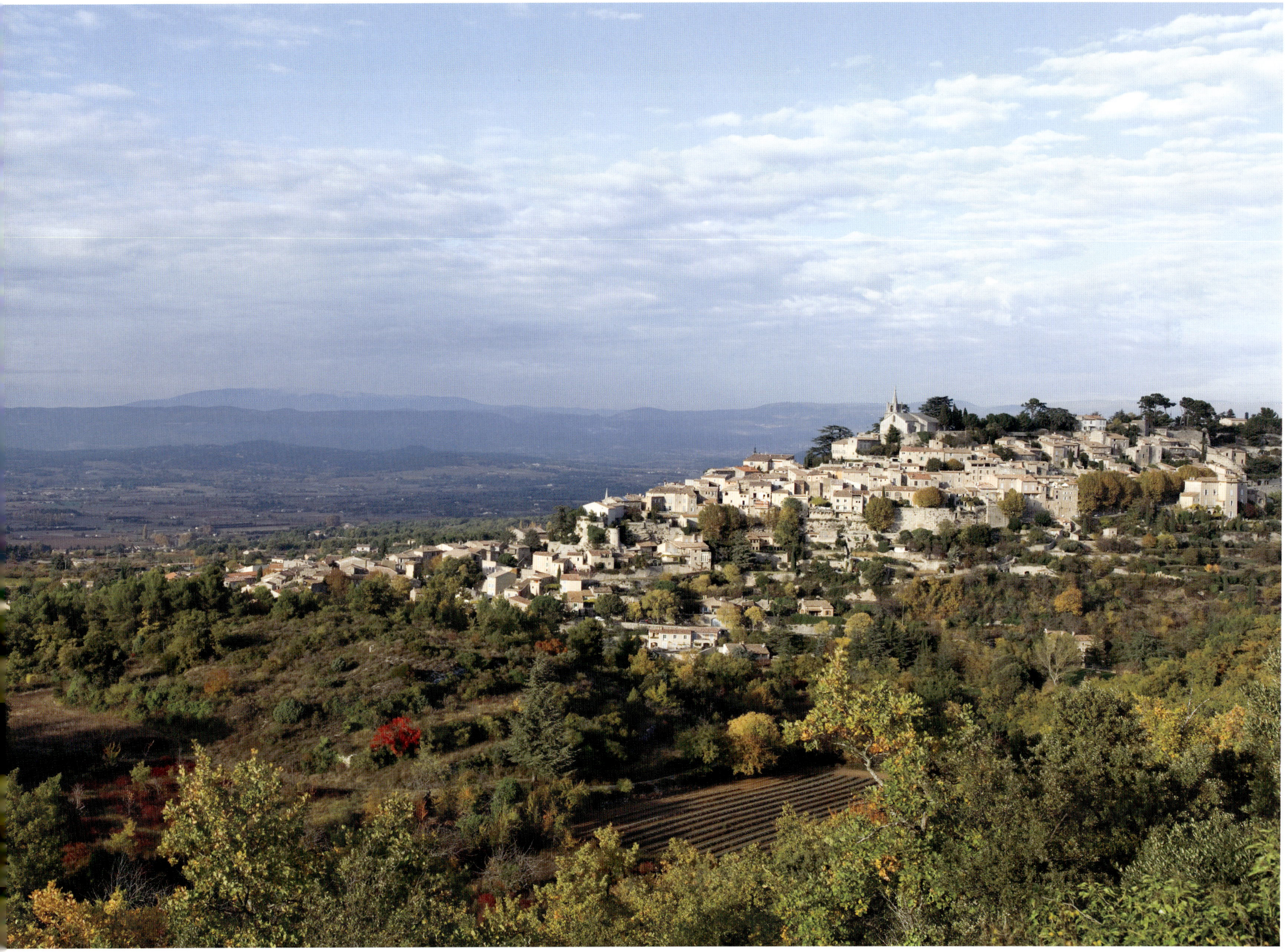

THE TALLEST SEA CLIFF IN FRANCE RISES OUT OF THE MEDITERRANEAN LIKE A GREAT WHITE WHALE, its stony face reflecting the spectrum of light, from pale dawn to the startling blush of sunset, before gradually disappearing into the dark of night. Cap Canaille: the chameleon of the Massif des Calanques.

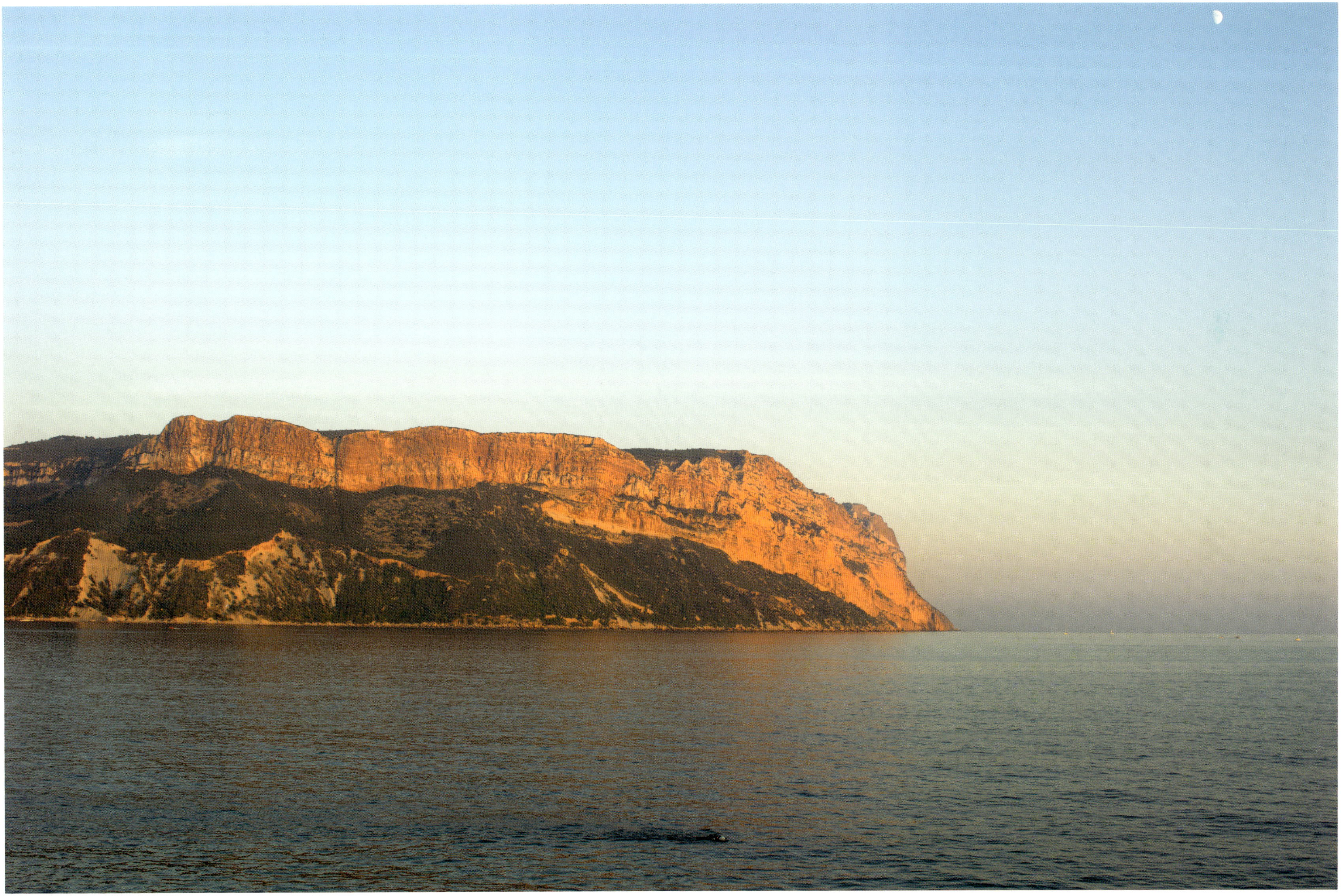

PLATE 91

PLATE 92

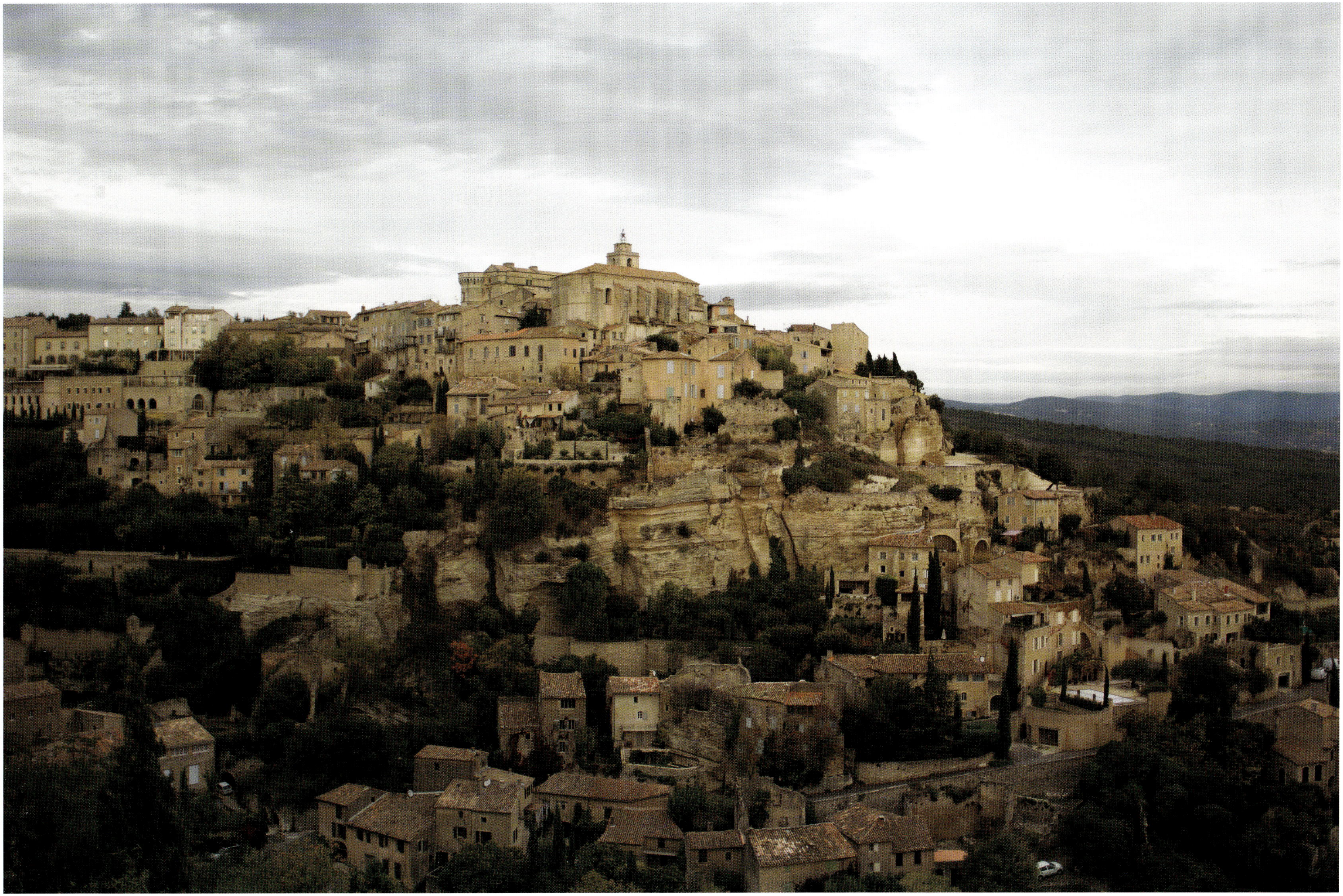

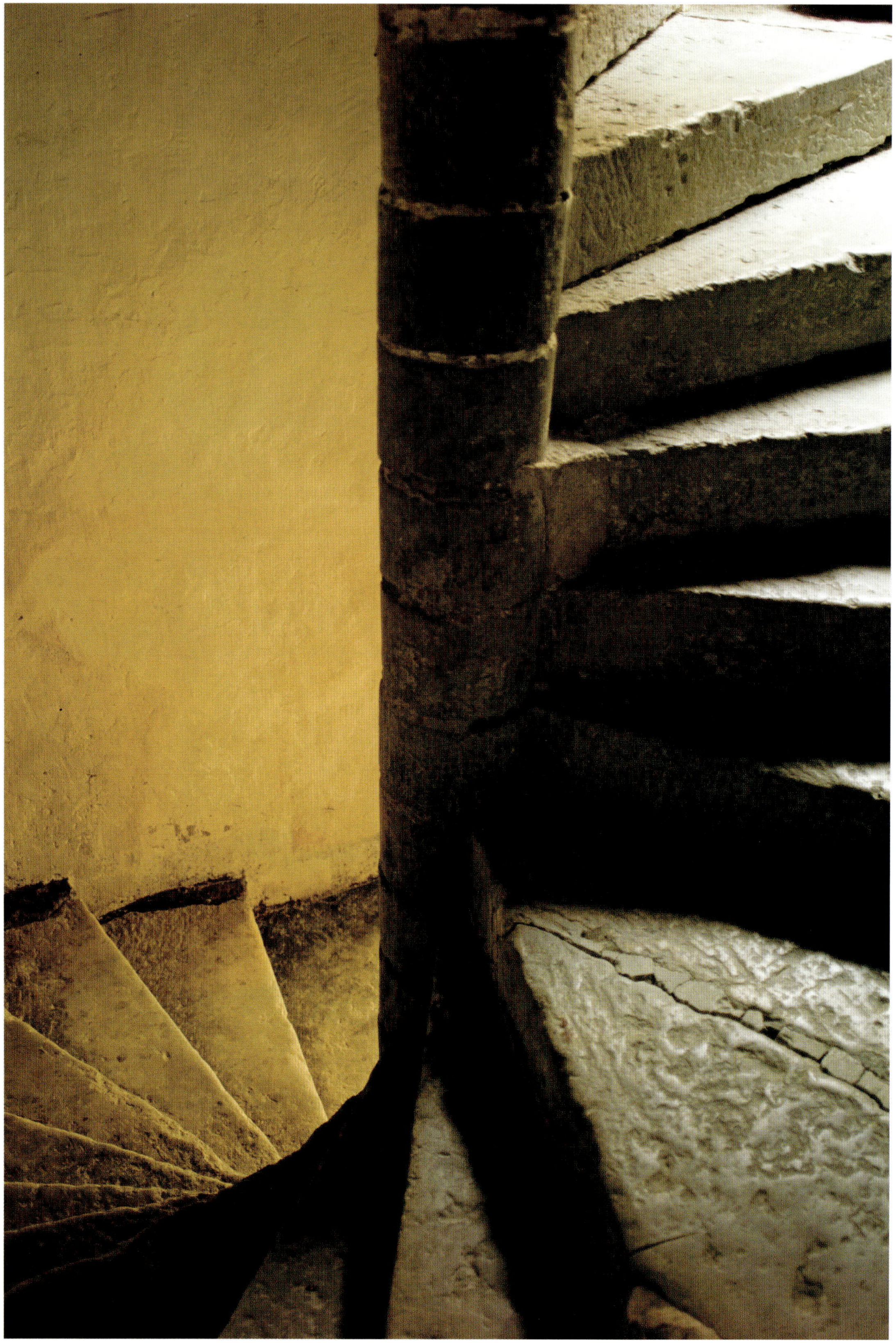

PLATE 93

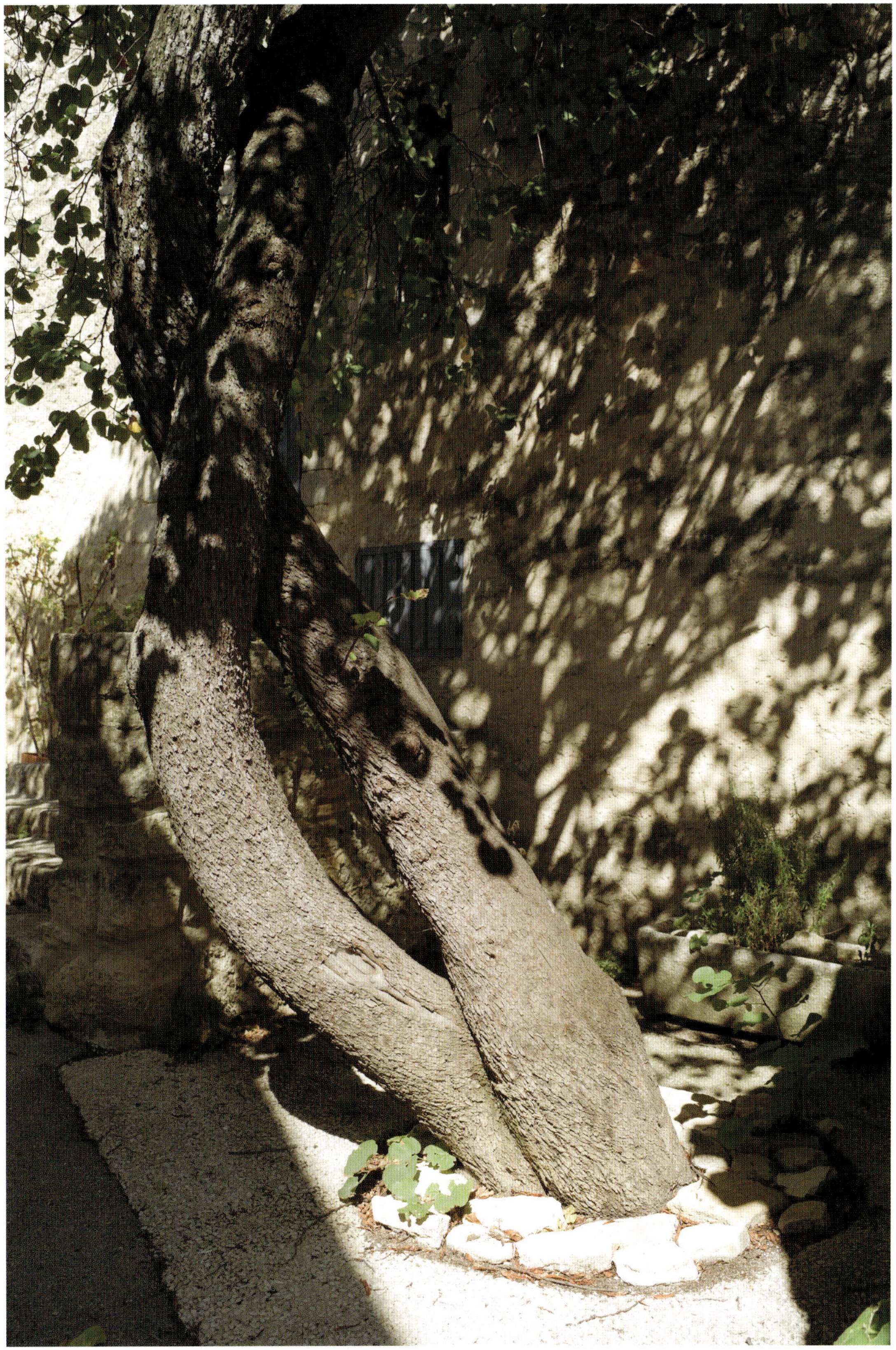

PLATE 94

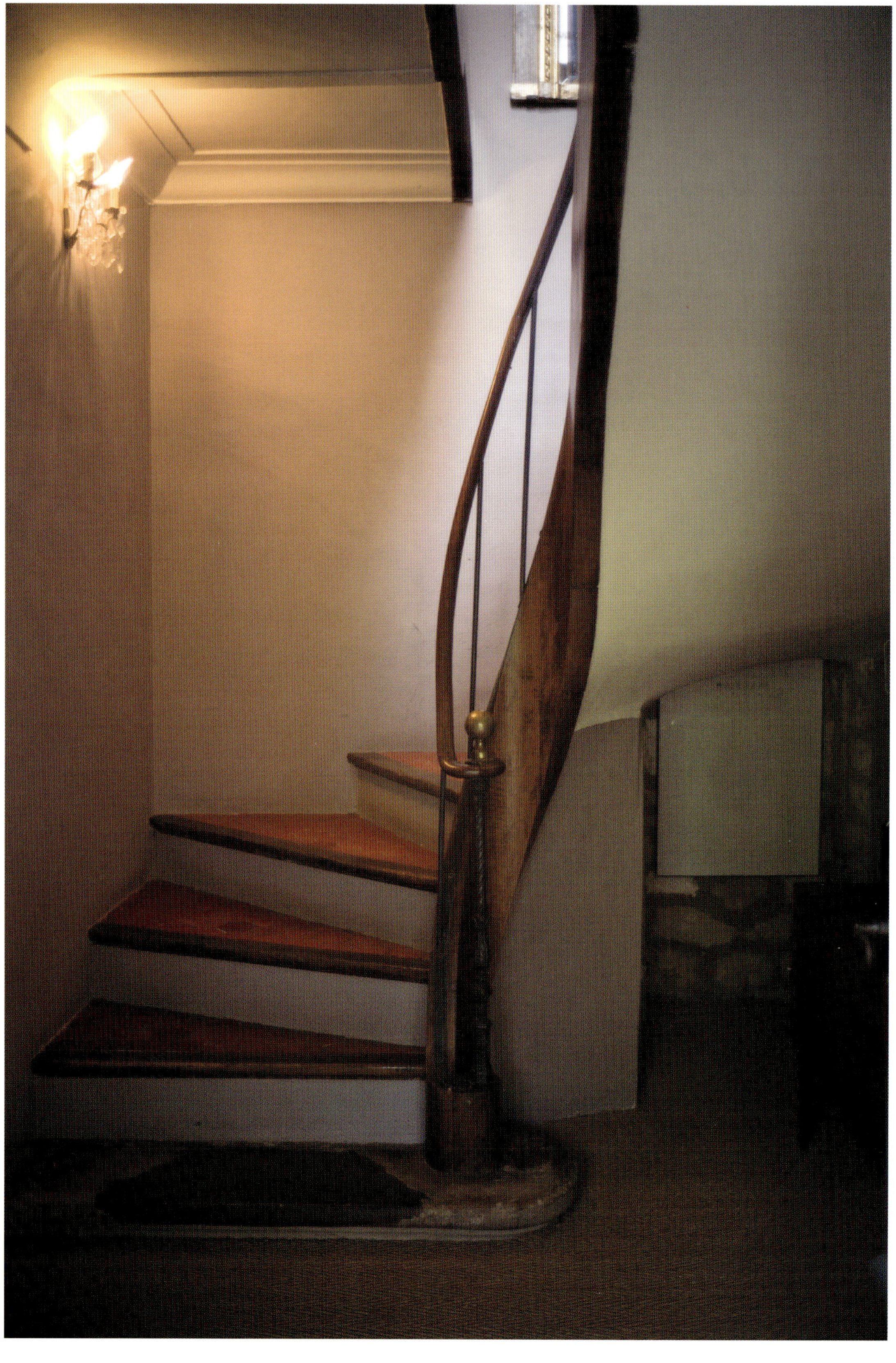

PLATE 95

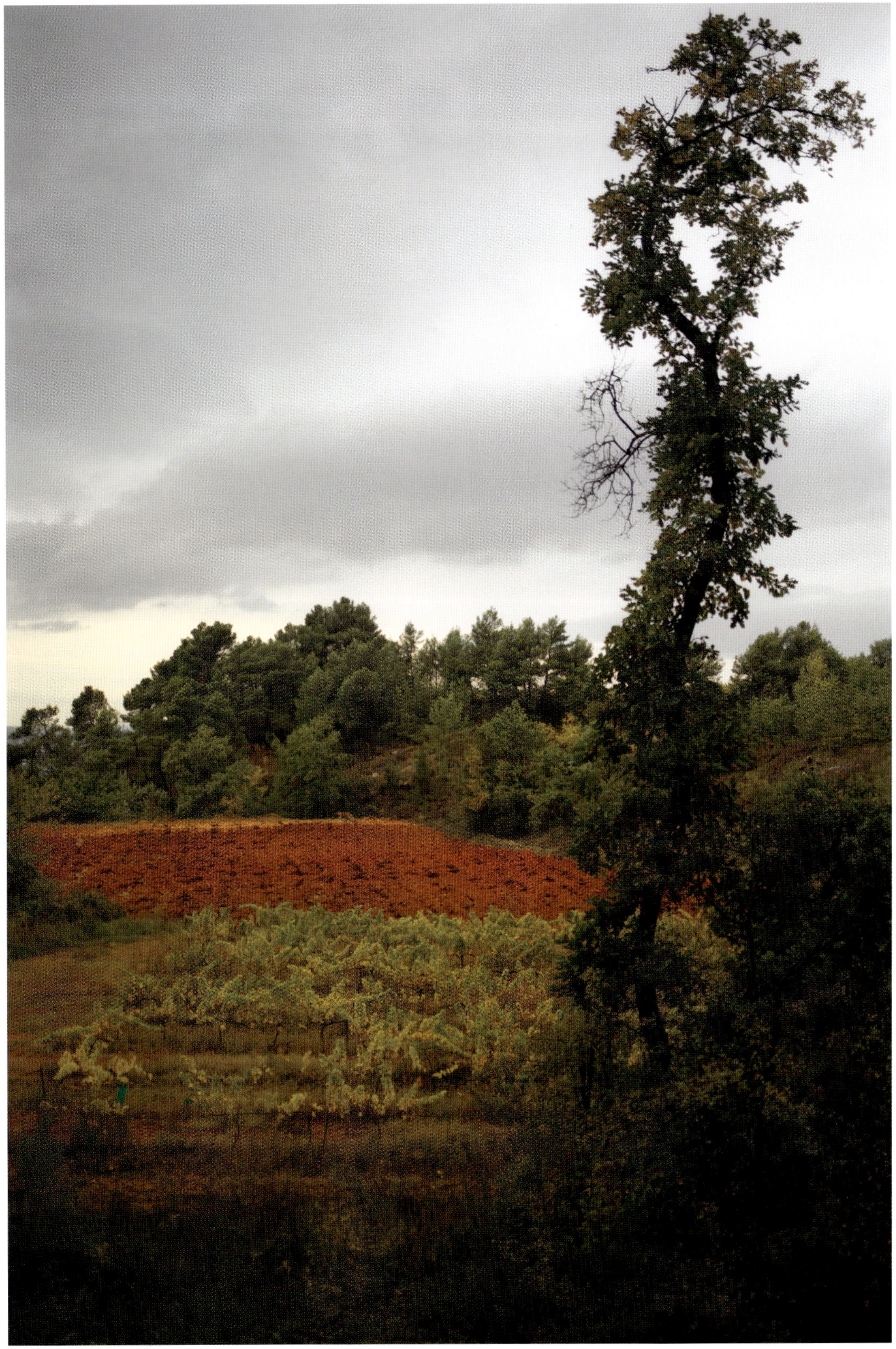

PLATE 96

WE HAVE REACHED A POINT IN OUR PROVENÇAL JOURNEY WHERE WE HAVE COME TO DISCOVER RECURRING themes in our understanding of this land. One of them is the sensation of glimpsing, and I think about how this ties in with another theme, which is the nature of the light.

To me, the glimpse is essential to seeing on a deeper level—it is a small shaft of seeing that is both narrow and deep: narrow in that it is not a panoramic vision; deep because one espies, for a brief moment, the heart of something, and based on that brief moment of seeing, one decides whether or not one wants to see more. There is also an element of surprise to the glimpse.

In the early weeks of being here, back in March and April, we had many glimpses into Provence and they were all surprising: the way a gorge abruptly rises out of a valley, the way the sea sparkles in the far distance, the way one suddenly catches a glimpse of something ancient in the midst of urban sprawl.

Today, after stopping in Isle–sur-la-Sorgue for a quick perusal of its renowned antique market, we look at the map to see which nearby towns we haven't yet visited and which might interest. We choose two. The first doesn't call to us so we drive on to Saint-Didier. On approach it seems that it, too, might disappoint, but as we have learned over and over here, sometimes you have to persevere. In other words, there is a difference between a cursory glance and a glimpse. The former is something you cast; the latter is something you reap.

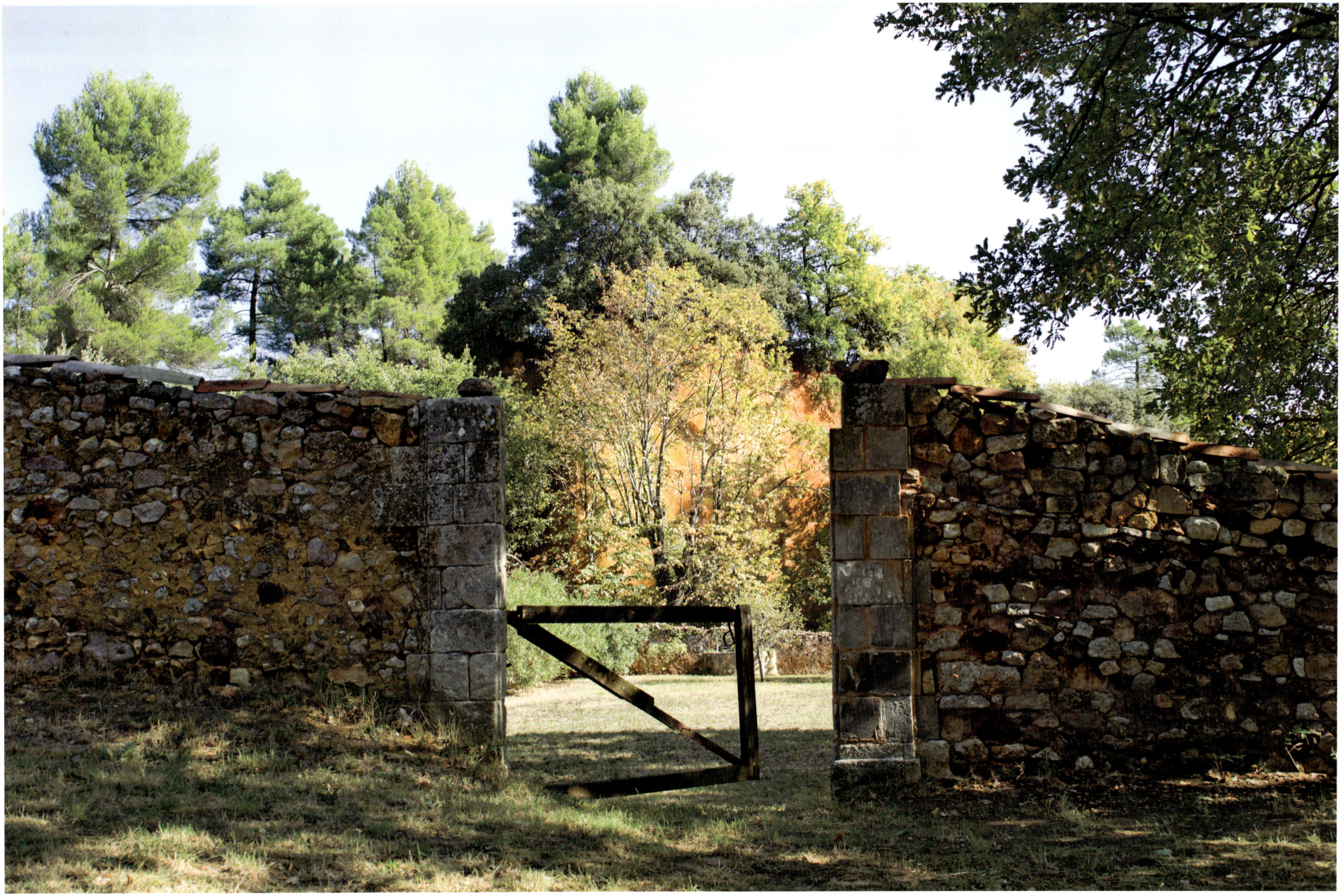

PLATE 97

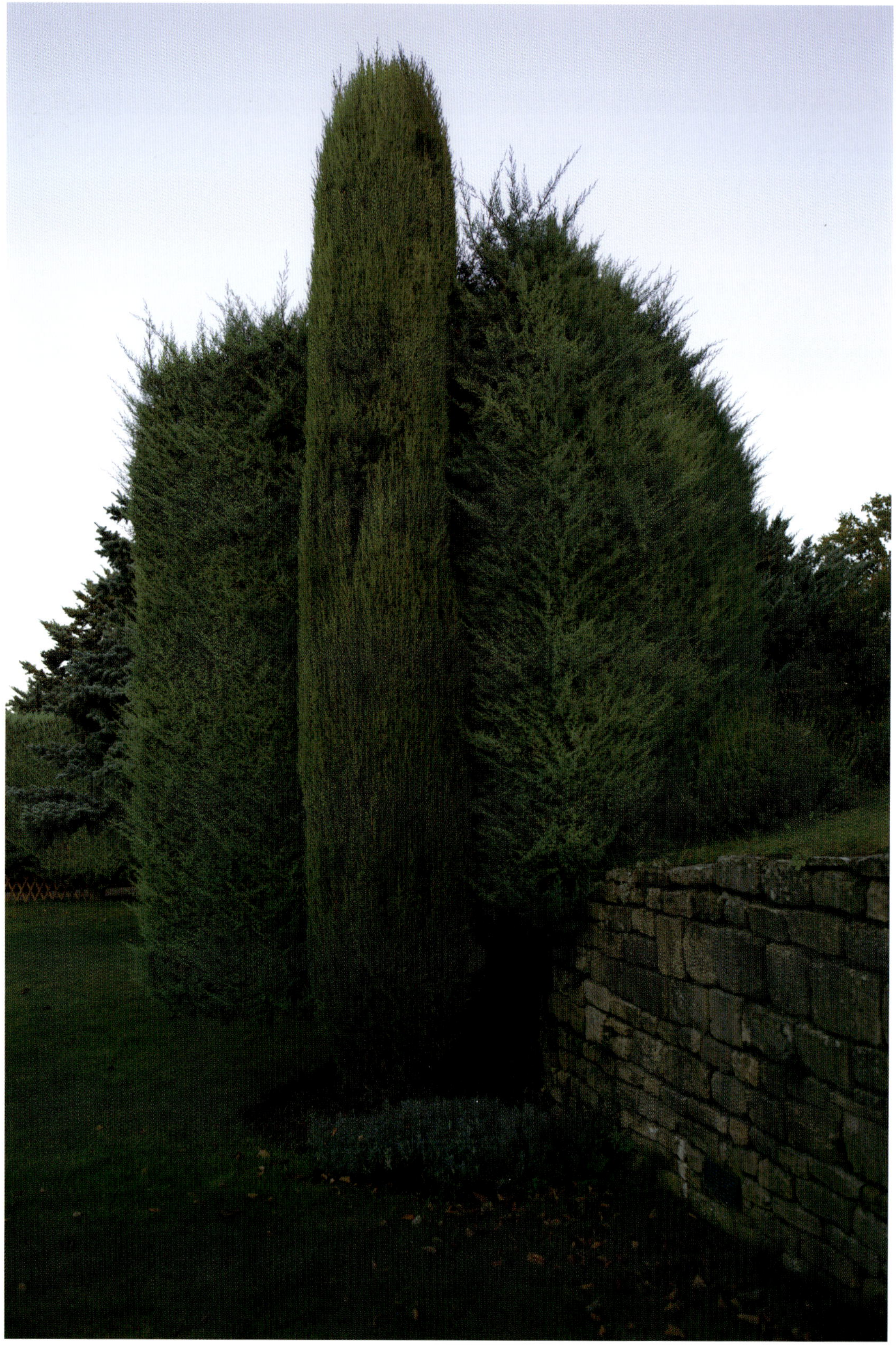

PLATE 98

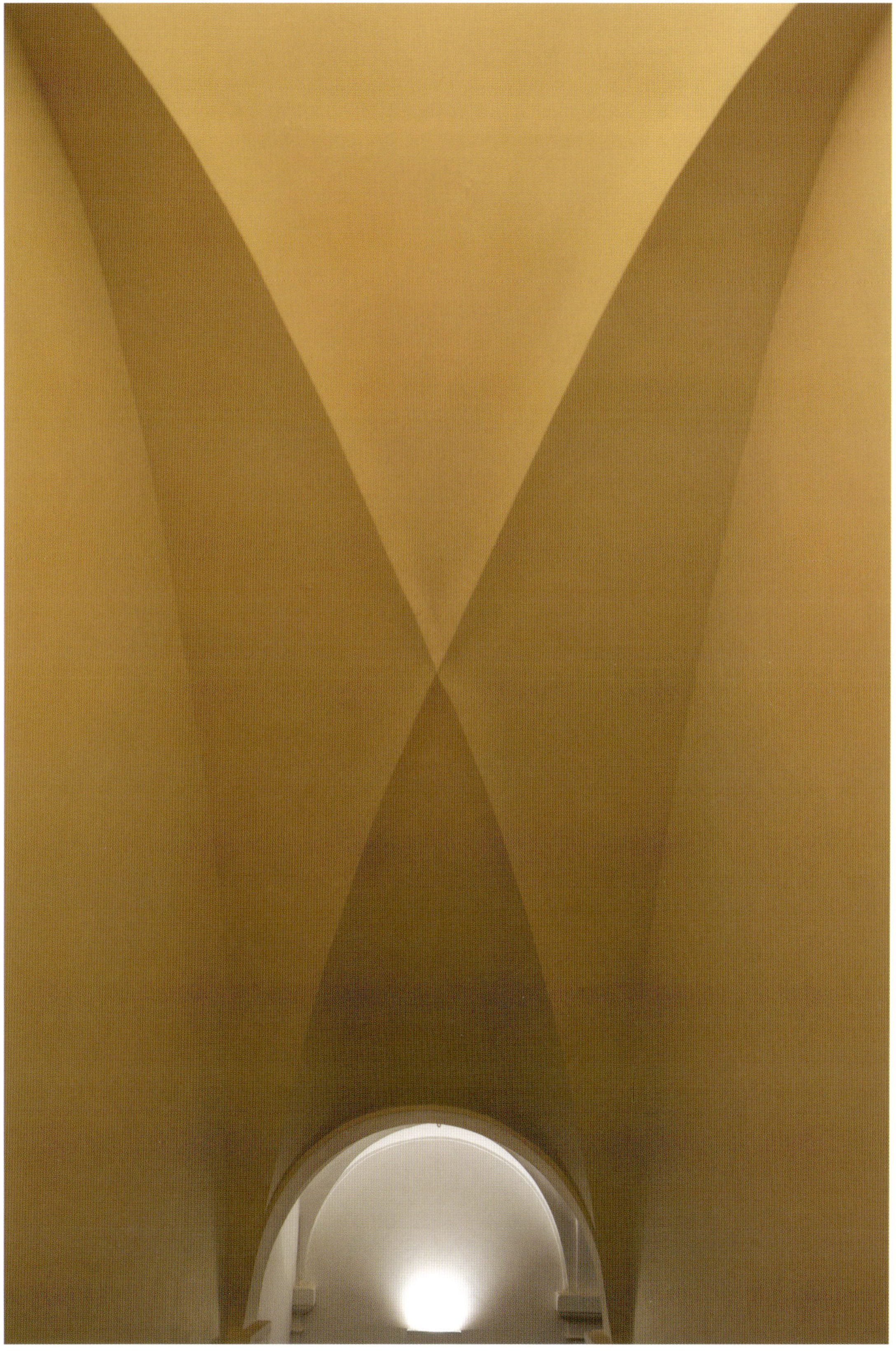

PLATE 99

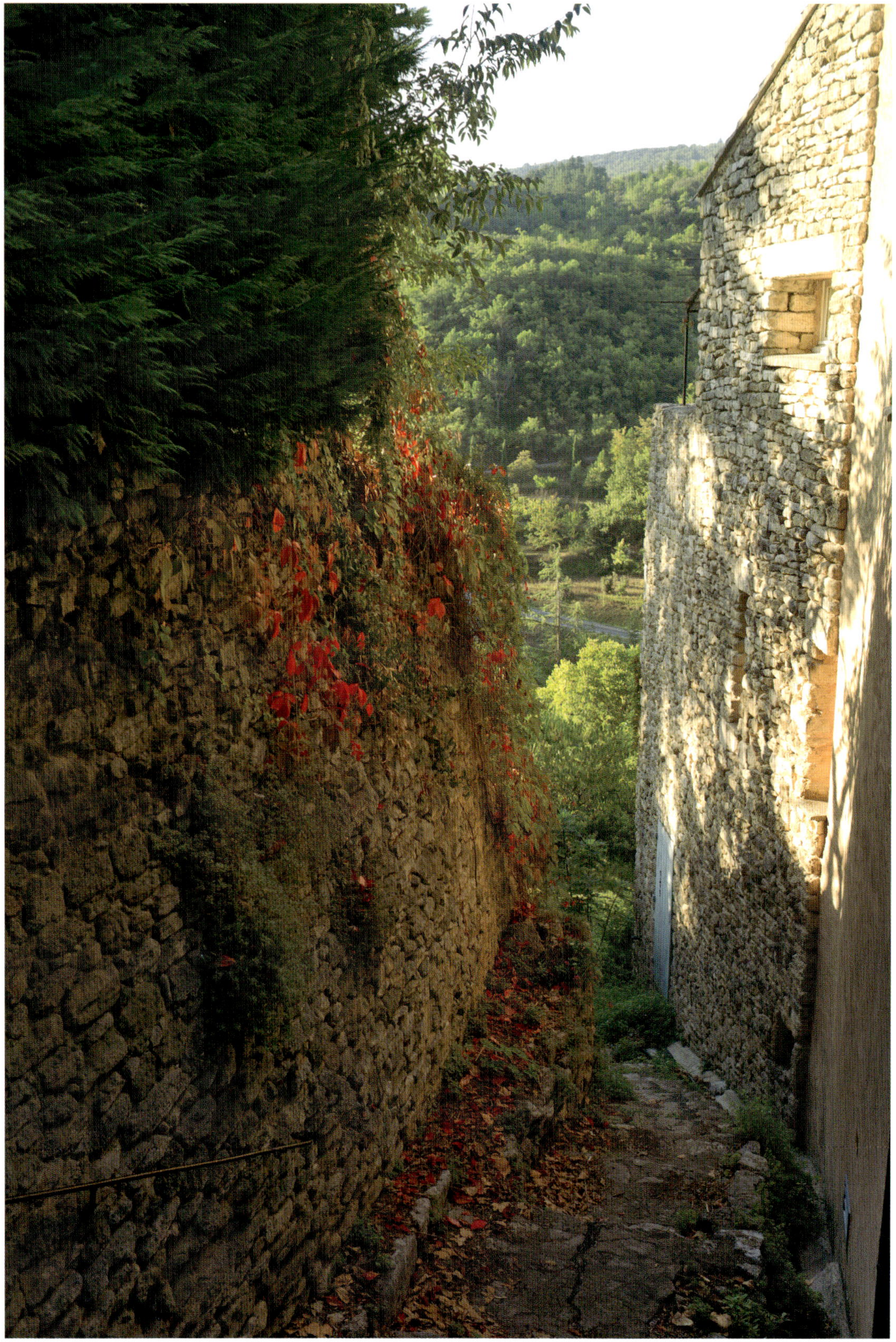

PLATE 100

PLATE 101

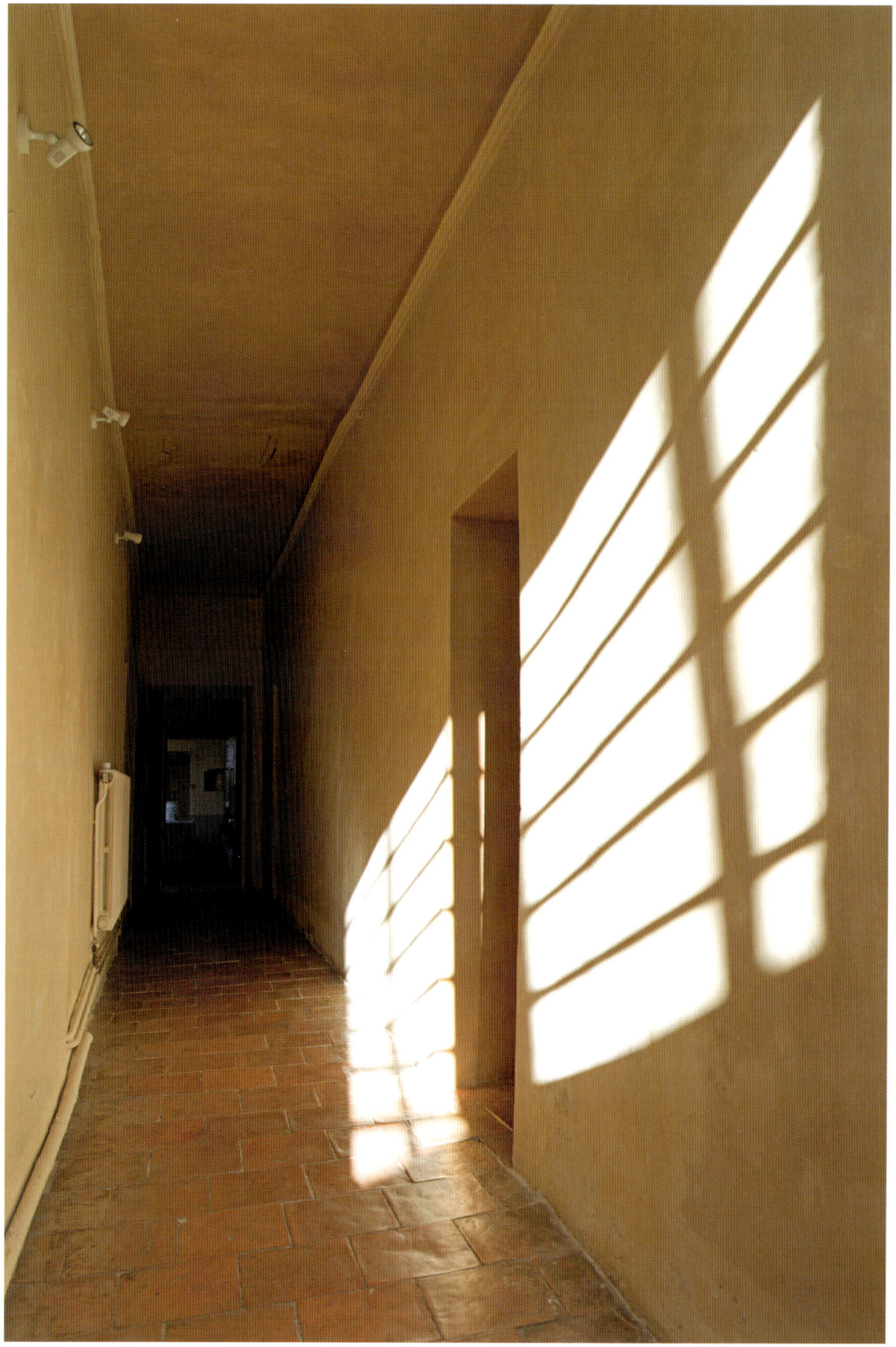

OUR FIRST GLIMPSE OF SAINT-DIDIER IS ONE OF THOSE OUTDOOR CAFÉS YOU'VE SEEN IN A THOUSAND French films. The patrons are straight out of central casting: mainly older, local men, sitting around arguing. Then we spot another outdoor café that is also very French but of a different clientele—the sort of solitary people who like to enjoy a glass of wine or an espresso while reading. It is the end of the lunch hour, but we can see in the garden of another restaurant yet a third, quintessentially French scene: the remains of a three-course lunch, with empty wine glasses and cloth napkins.

These three cafés provide three different glimpses into French life, life in a real French country village, and it makes us want to look further. We park and began our amble, turning down a couple of cul-de-sacs that beckon, poking our noses over garden fences and into courtyards.

During the one and a half hours we spend here we do not see one tourist. We do see a large boules court and a community center. And there are all the necessary yet simple amenities: a charcuterie, a boulangerie, a patisserie, a tiny supermarket, a florist, a hairdresser, the post office, and the aforementioned cafés. We pass a small public garden. We see a man barefoot in his garden lounger, reading, a boy playing in a tree, a young couple cleaning their backyard. All of these glimpses add up to a larger picture, illustrating a simple, less-frenzied way of life.

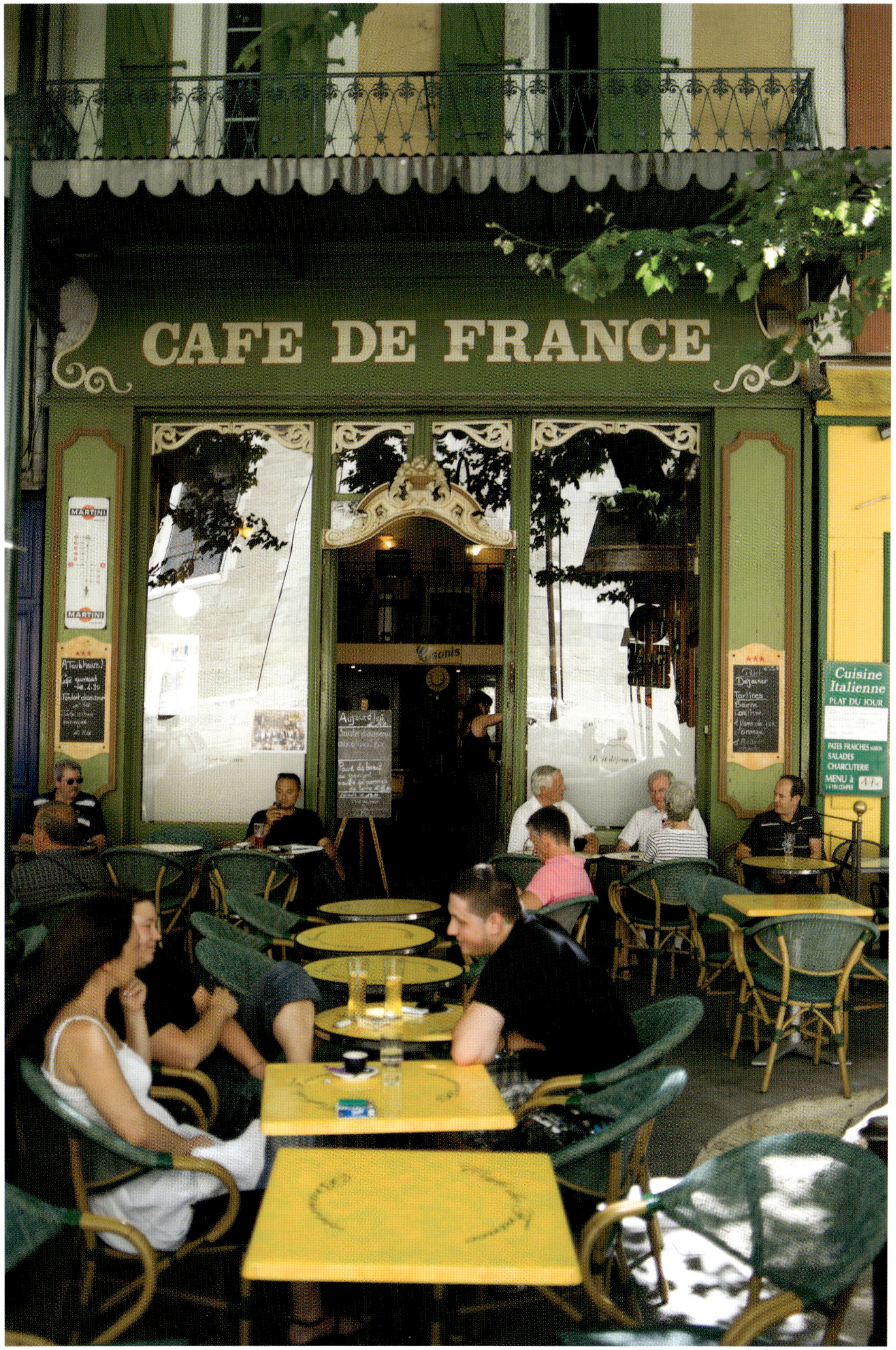
CAFE DE FRANCE
MARTINI
Cuisine Italienne
PLAT DU JOUR
SALADES
CHARCUTERIE

PLATE 102

ON THE WAY BACK TO THE CAR, WE PASS THE SECOND CAFÉ AND NOTICE A LONG ZINC BAR, AND BEYOND it a garden with tables. On the small terrace above the garden we meet Olivia. We tell her what we are doing in Provence and what appeals to us about her town. Yes, she says, it's real here. She takes us inside to the zinc bar, perhaps twenty-four-feet long, immaculate, old, and proudly trucked down from a bar in Paris by her mother. The real thing, she says as she pulls two lemonades on tap for us.

Now, having glimpsed the real thing, we head home. Pulling out of the town we are immediately deep in the country. Just like that. The village ends, the valley begins. And just as suddenly, the valley ends and we find ourselves in one of the most spectacular gorges we have yet seen. And now the gorge ends and we are in another village. And so the afternoon goes: villages, fields, valleys, gorges, villages, fields.

And then, there is the light, which in this season is scintillating. It wasn't until the end of our first trip here in the spring that we came to understand the quality of the light. I described it then as piercing, and in fact the longer I am here the more it strikes me that the light is like an épée, the French sword with the long, glancing blade. It is a light that is perfect for glimpsing in that it is swift and piercing and goes to the heart of everything, and once there it illuminates everything from within.

In Tuscany we experience the light as all-encompassing: a warm embrace that seems to gather us into the center of everything. Here, in Provence, the light individuates everything up close, while in the far distance the light dissolves into mist, keeping the world at a remove.

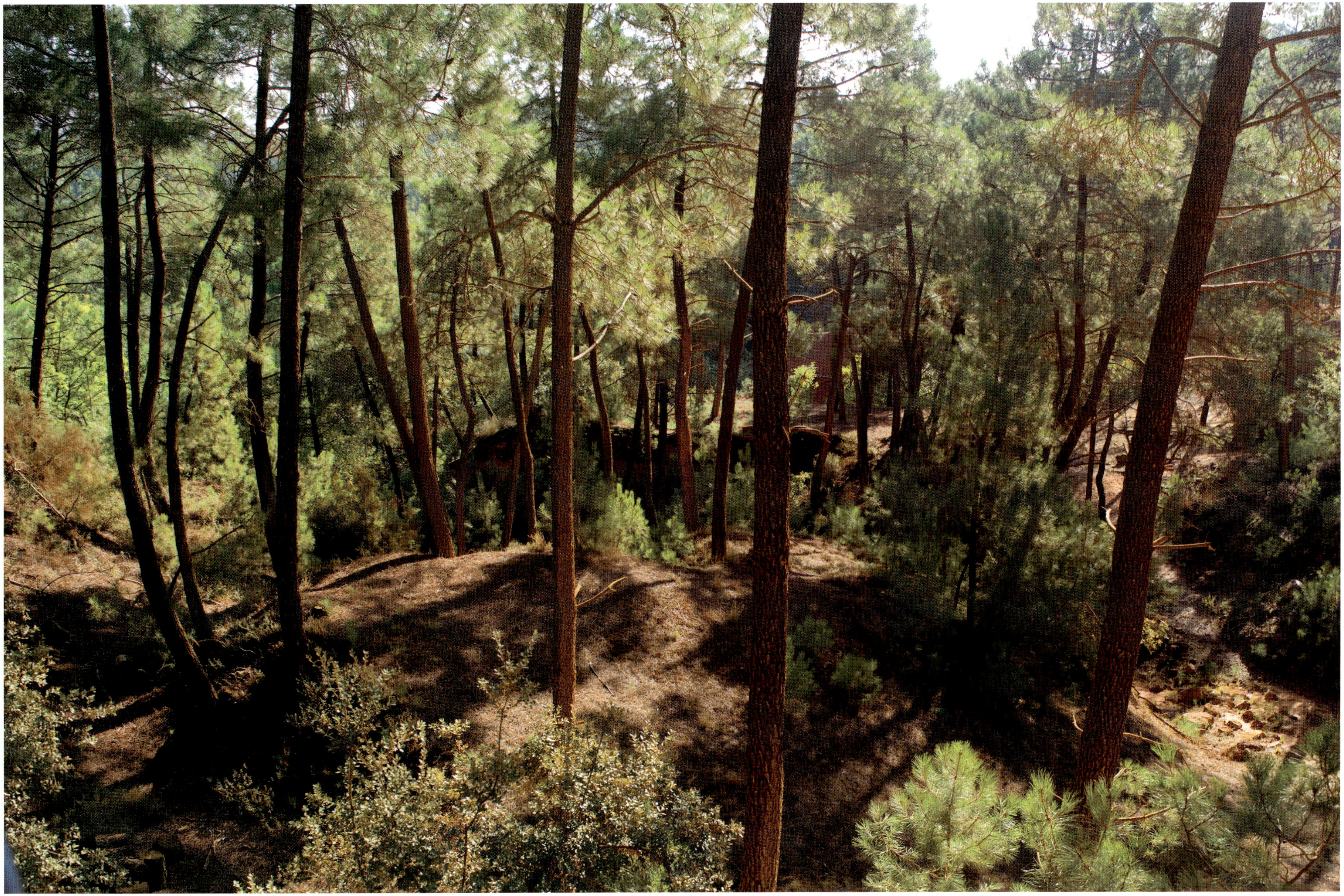

PLATE 103

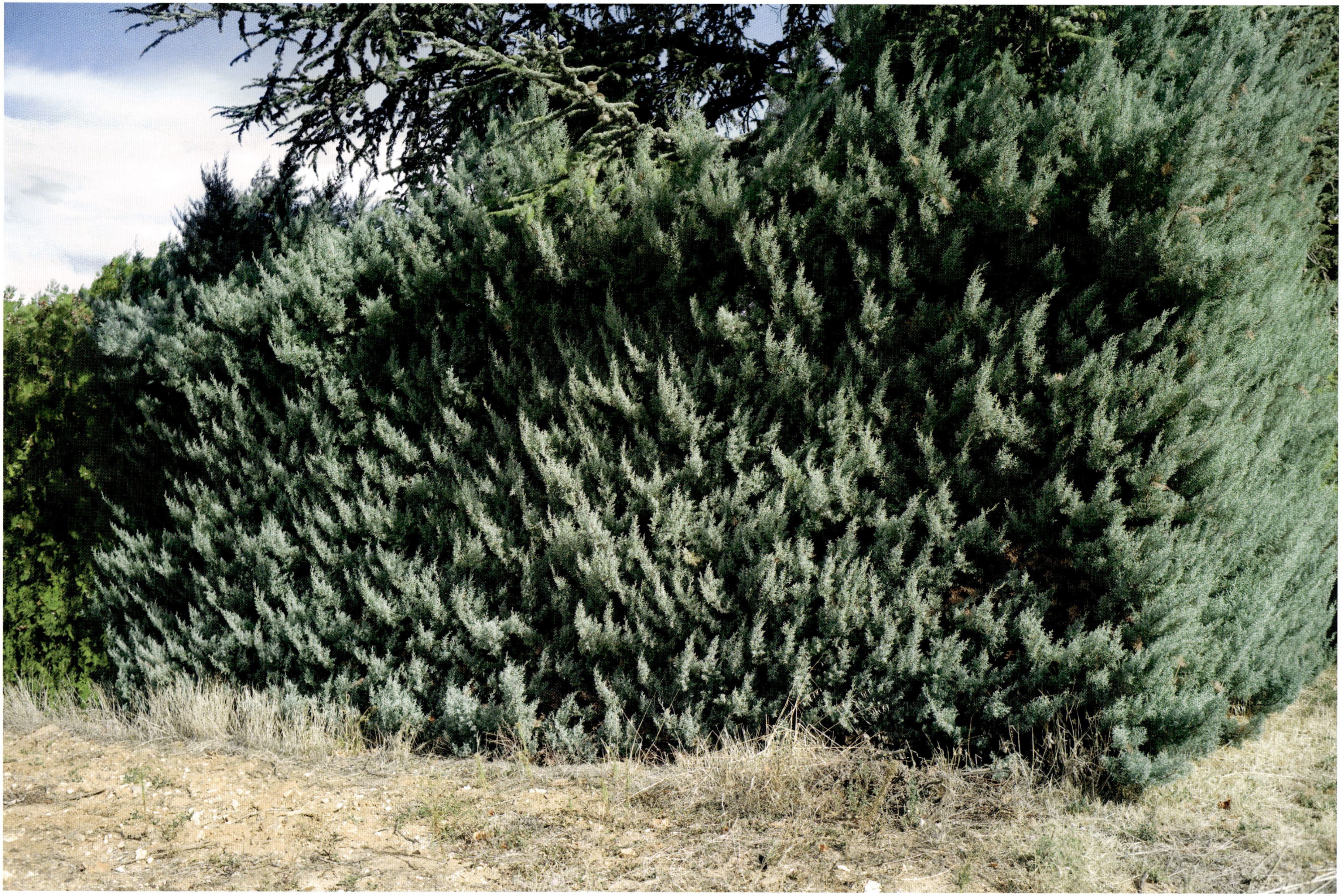

PLATE 104

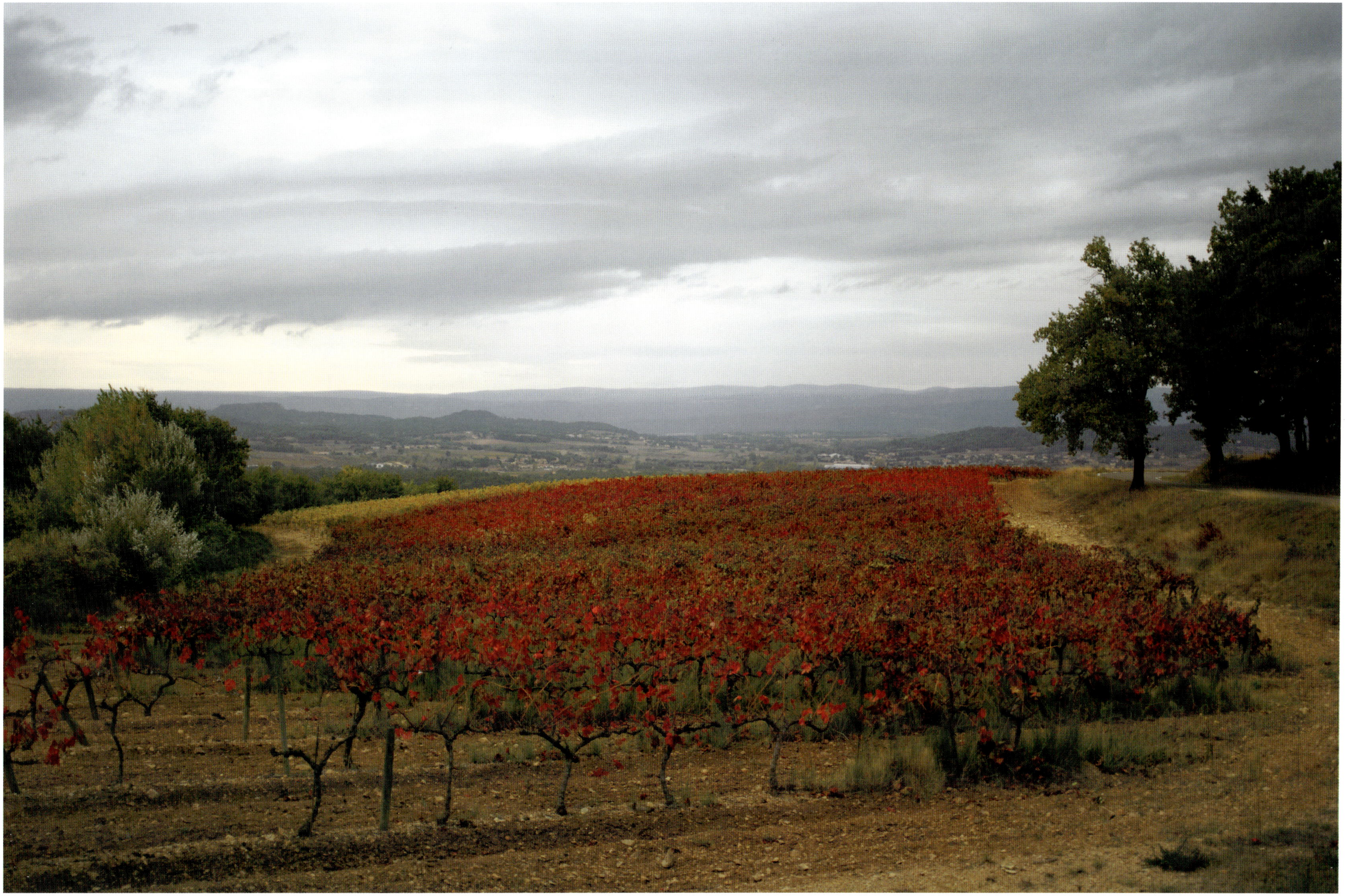

PLATE 105

IT'S MARKET DAY IN LOURMARIN, AND WE PAY A BRIEF VISIT JUST FOR THE PLEASURE OF LOOKING AT THE stalls, the sellers, and the shoppers. This market life is one of Provence's greatest gifts. There's something really comforting about being able to count on this form of shopping which, because every village has its own market day, means you can shop for just what you need that day and therefore always buy the freshest produce in season. But it's also the sense of community that is heartening. Getting to know the fishmongers, the poultry purveyors, the vegetable farmers, the mushroom man, the pastry makers and so on. Here, twenty types of olives and oils, over there pottery, scarves, the ubiquitous market baskets, olive wood. The hat man is there and next to him, Robert, a man of constant motion as he spreads assorted tapenades on morsels of baguette, seducing the crowd to sample.

We are staying at La Feniere hotel for two days. The sun has come out and we retire to an outdoor divan to read under a canopy of ocher canvas. The sky is a rich blue with an occasional white puff of merry cloud. Every once in a while we look up and see what we so often see here: a complexity of layered landscape, each plant and shrub and tree a thing unto itself and yet seemingly woven into the surrounding flora. It's a slightly dizzying experience that interferes with one's depth perception, and today it is matched by an equally complex layering of birdsong. Provence is a land that has its own mysterious, syncopated rhythm, which one must first feel before one can begin to hear the melody and beyond, the harmony.

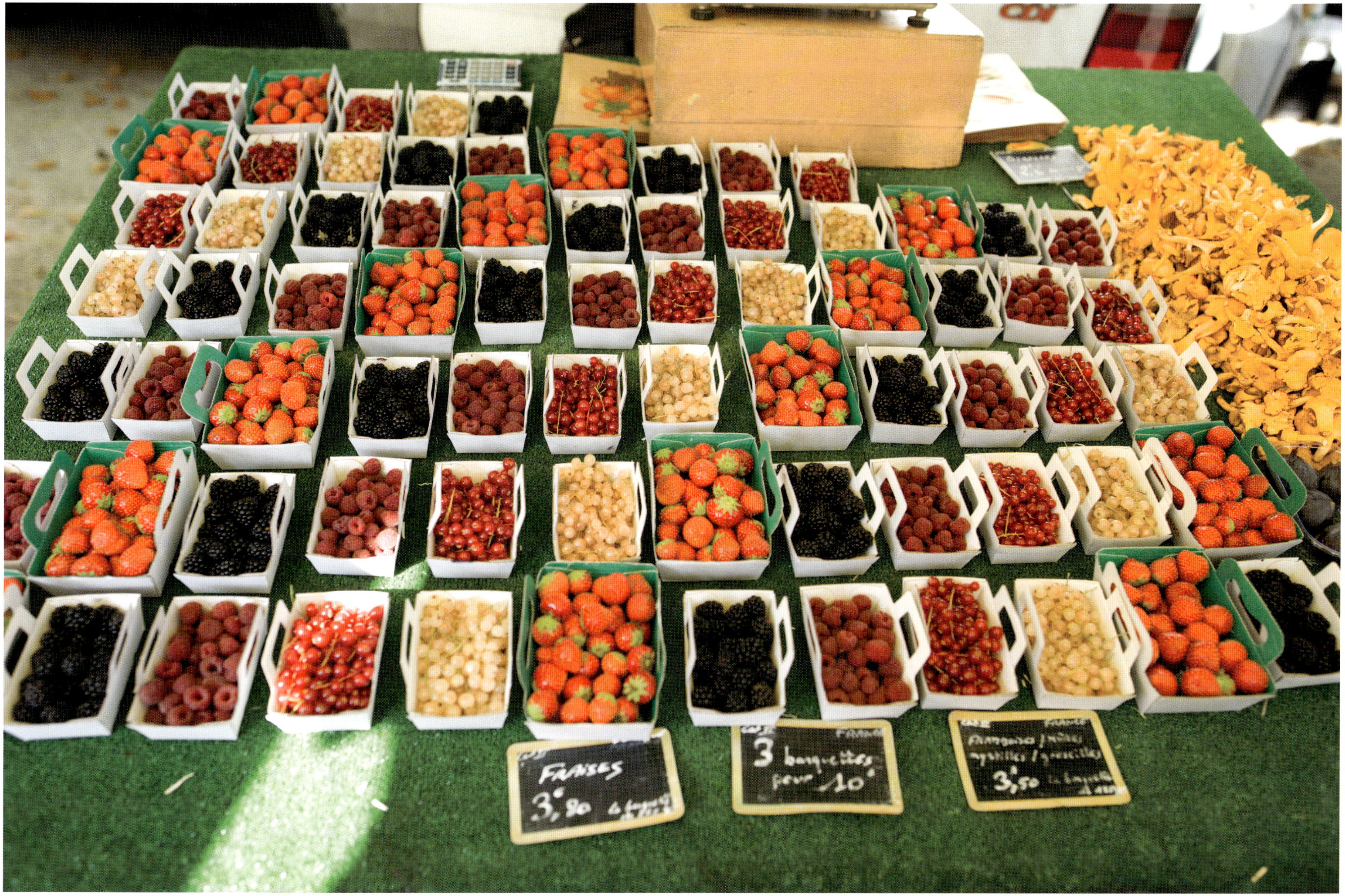

PLATE 106

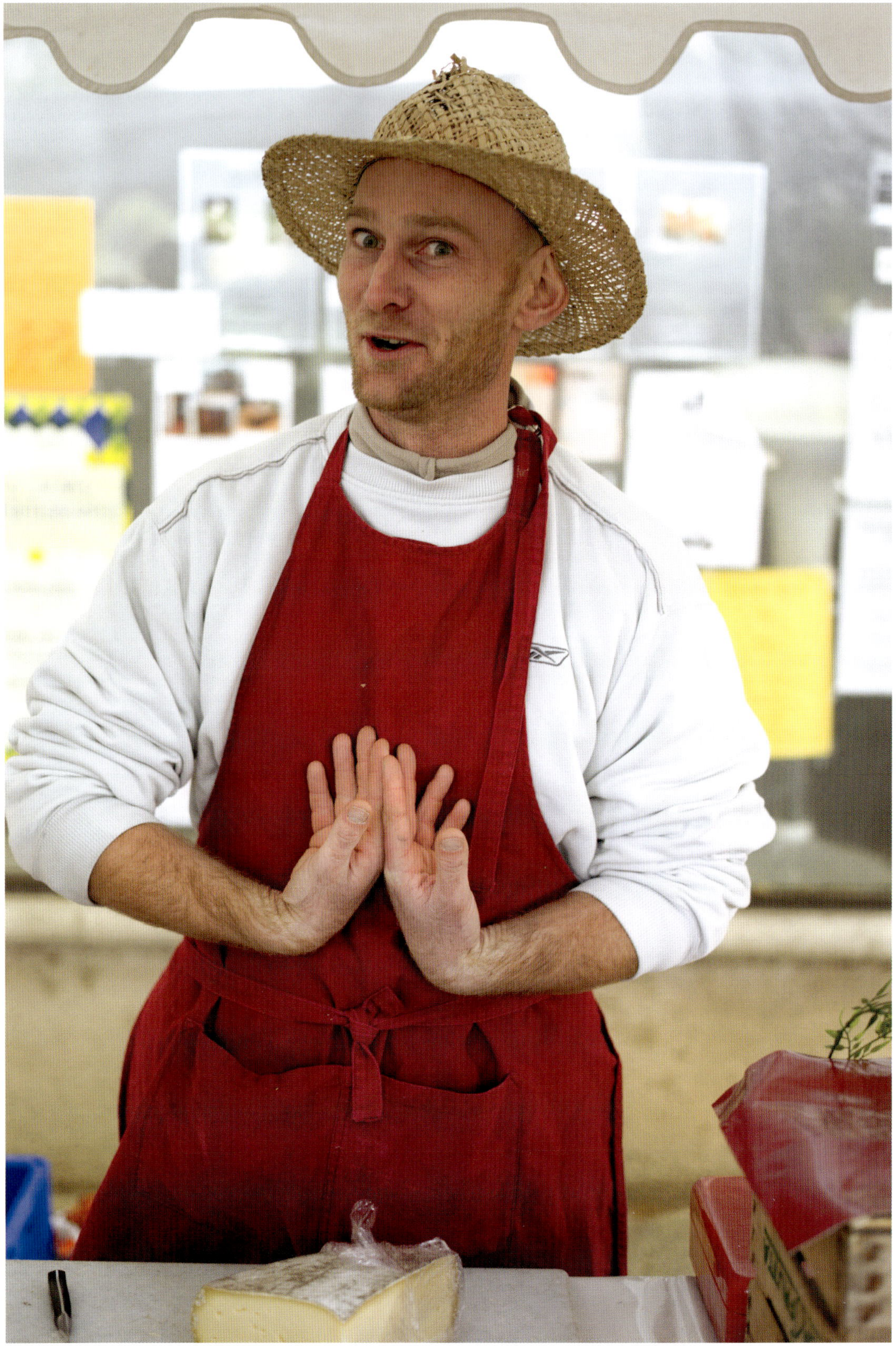

PLATE 107

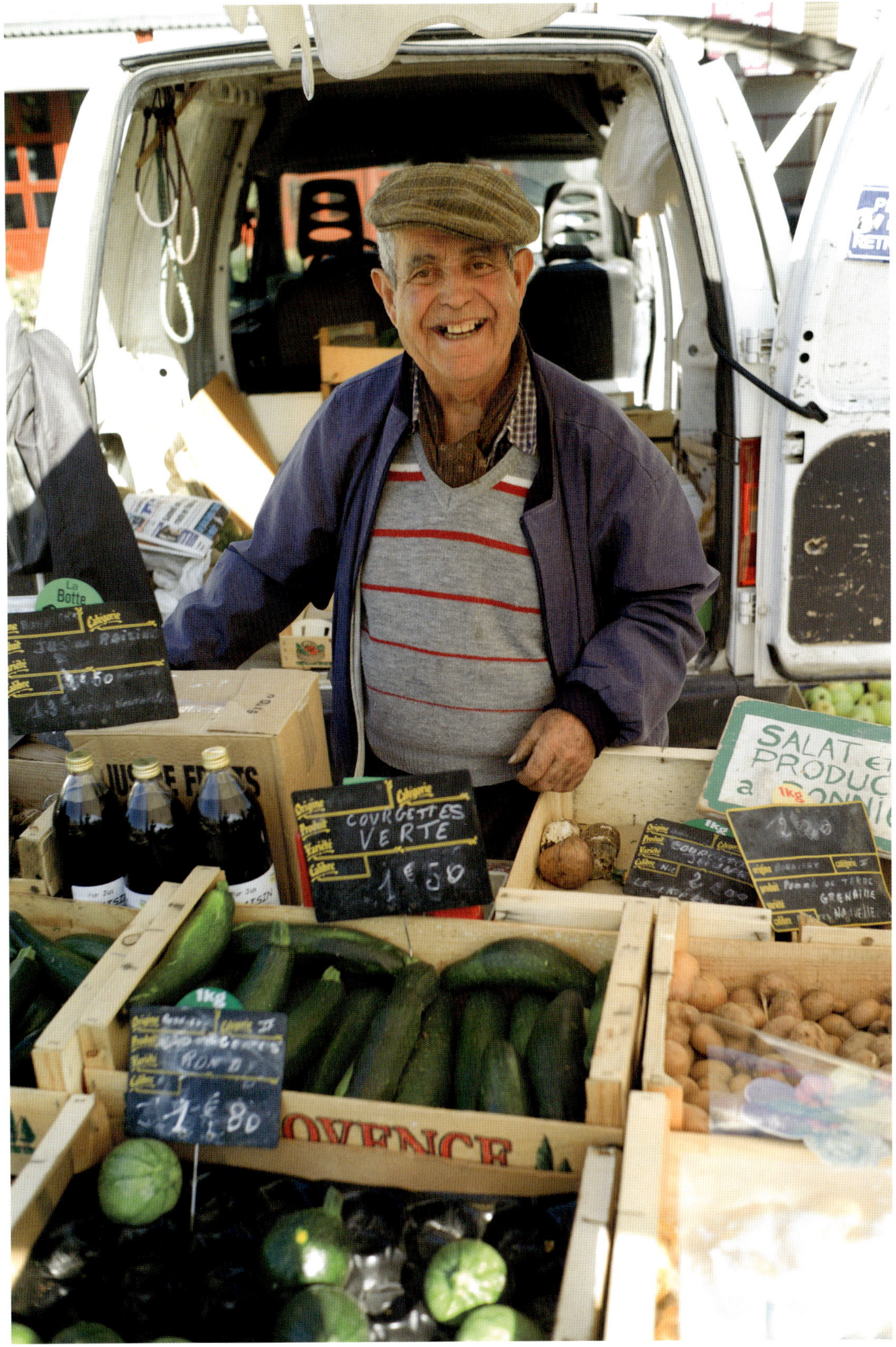

PLATE 108

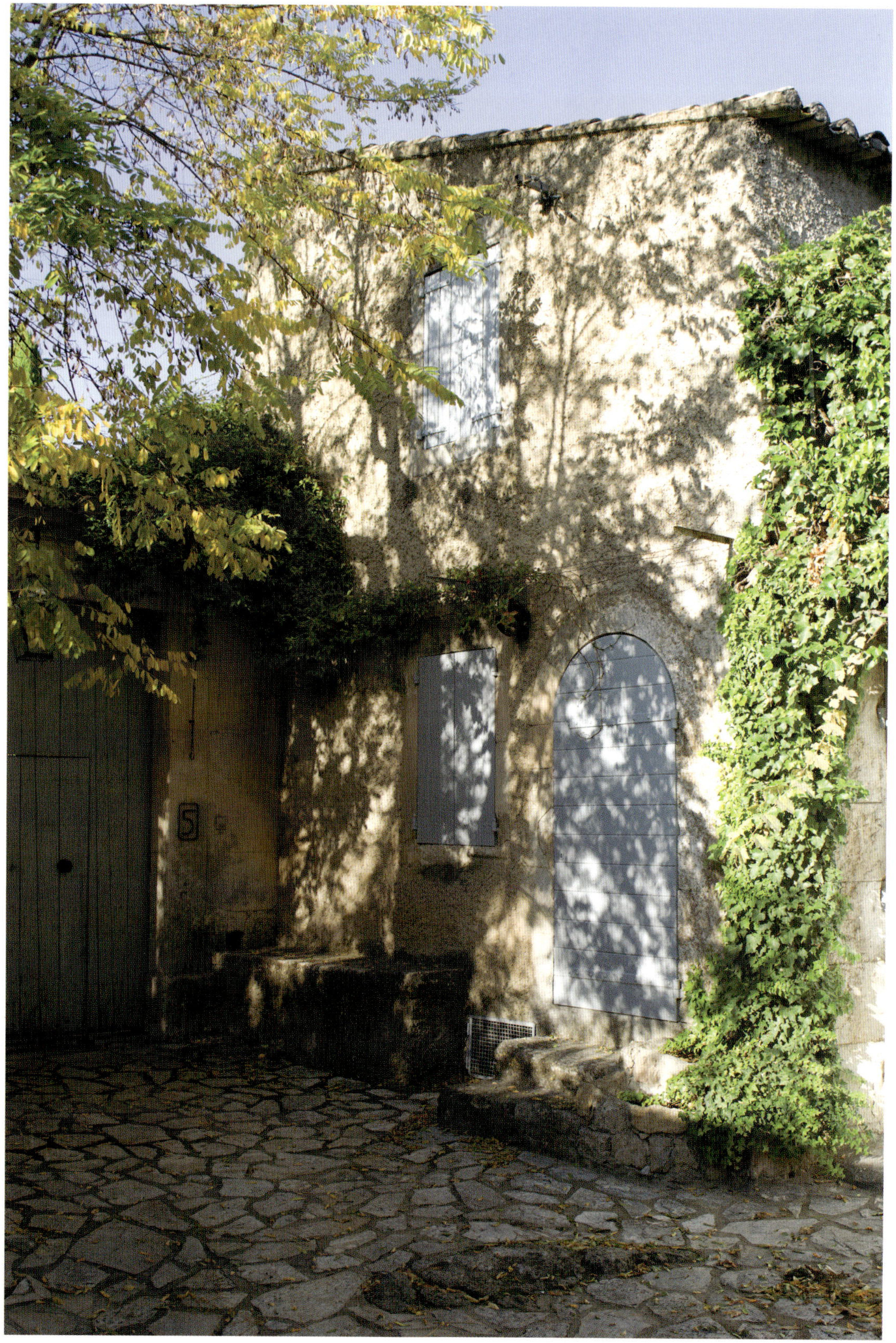

PLATE 109

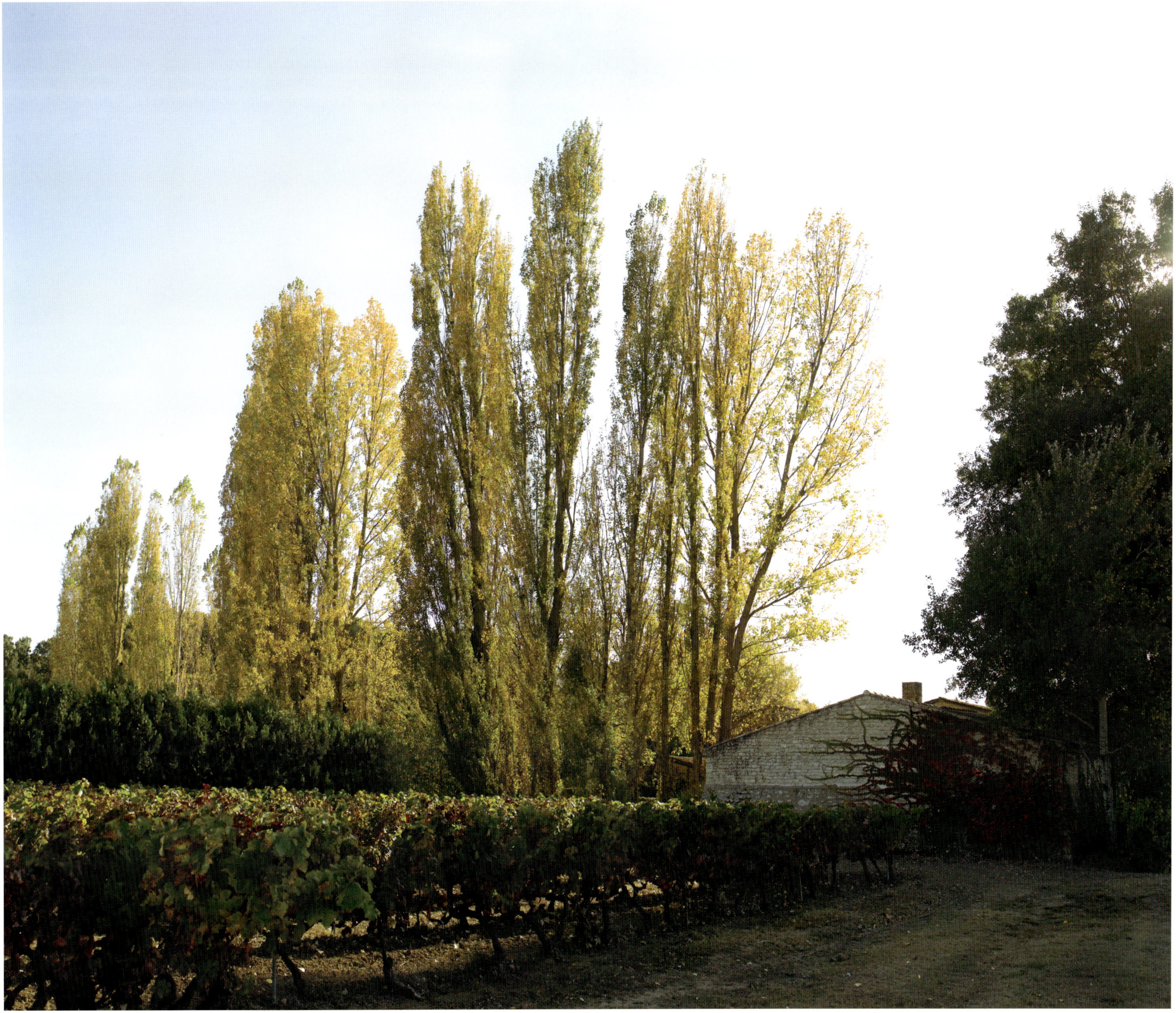

PLATE 110

AFTER TWO HOURS OF RELAXING IN THE SUN WITH OUR BOOKS, WE ARE BOTH READY TO GET TO WORK. Cucuron is a nearby village we haven't yet explored so we head in that direction. Within a mile, a patch of landscape beckons: a patch consisting of perhaps an acre's worth of random, untended land bordering tilled fields. Apart from the fact that it is bristling with autumn color and texture, and as such is vibrantly alive, perhaps what excites us is the sheer, defiant, forward energy of nature. It is willfully determined to spring up in the face of human negligence. It doesn't care if it's by the road or for how long it will get to exist before man once again asserts his will. It is this irrepressible energy, so evident here, that fills me with glee. In its adolescent growth and garish attire this patch of land has a sort of "look Ma, no hands" attitude. And in a way, it reflects what we are doing at this moment in our lives. We're springing up in defiance for as long as we have left, flinging ourselves along roadsides and into strange places, bursting with vigor. This is our autumn.

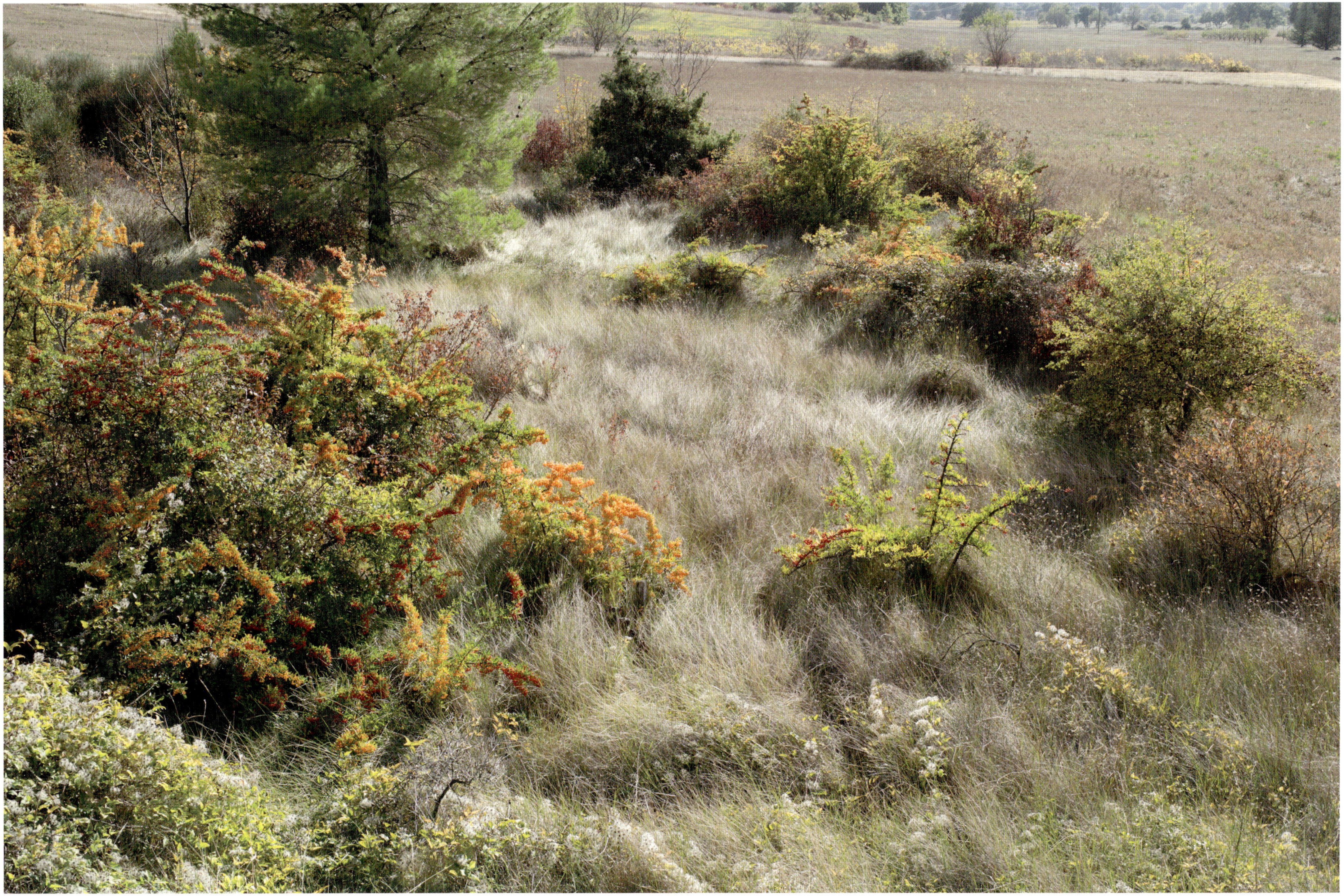

PLATE 111

PLATE 112 (OVERLEAF)

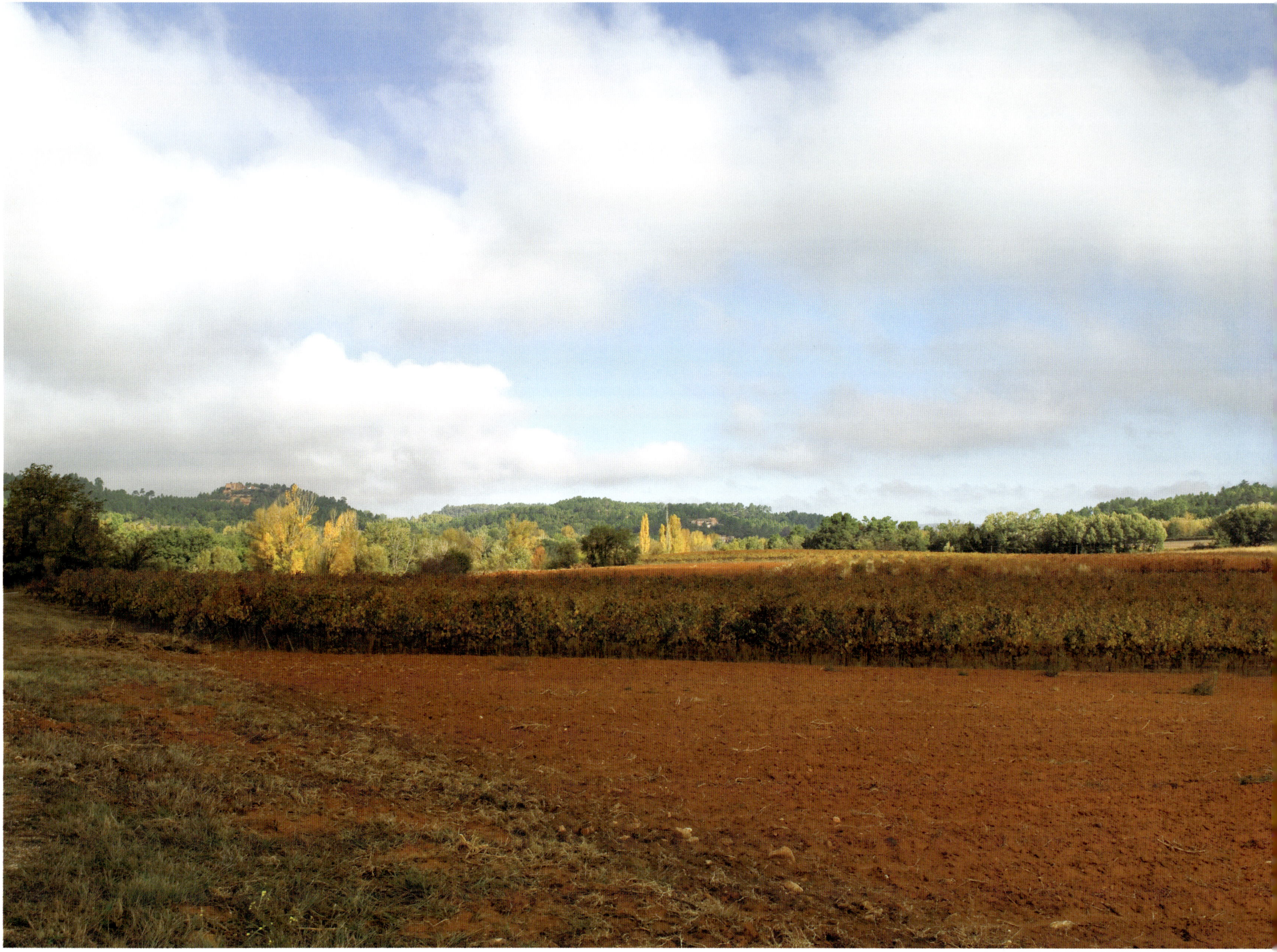

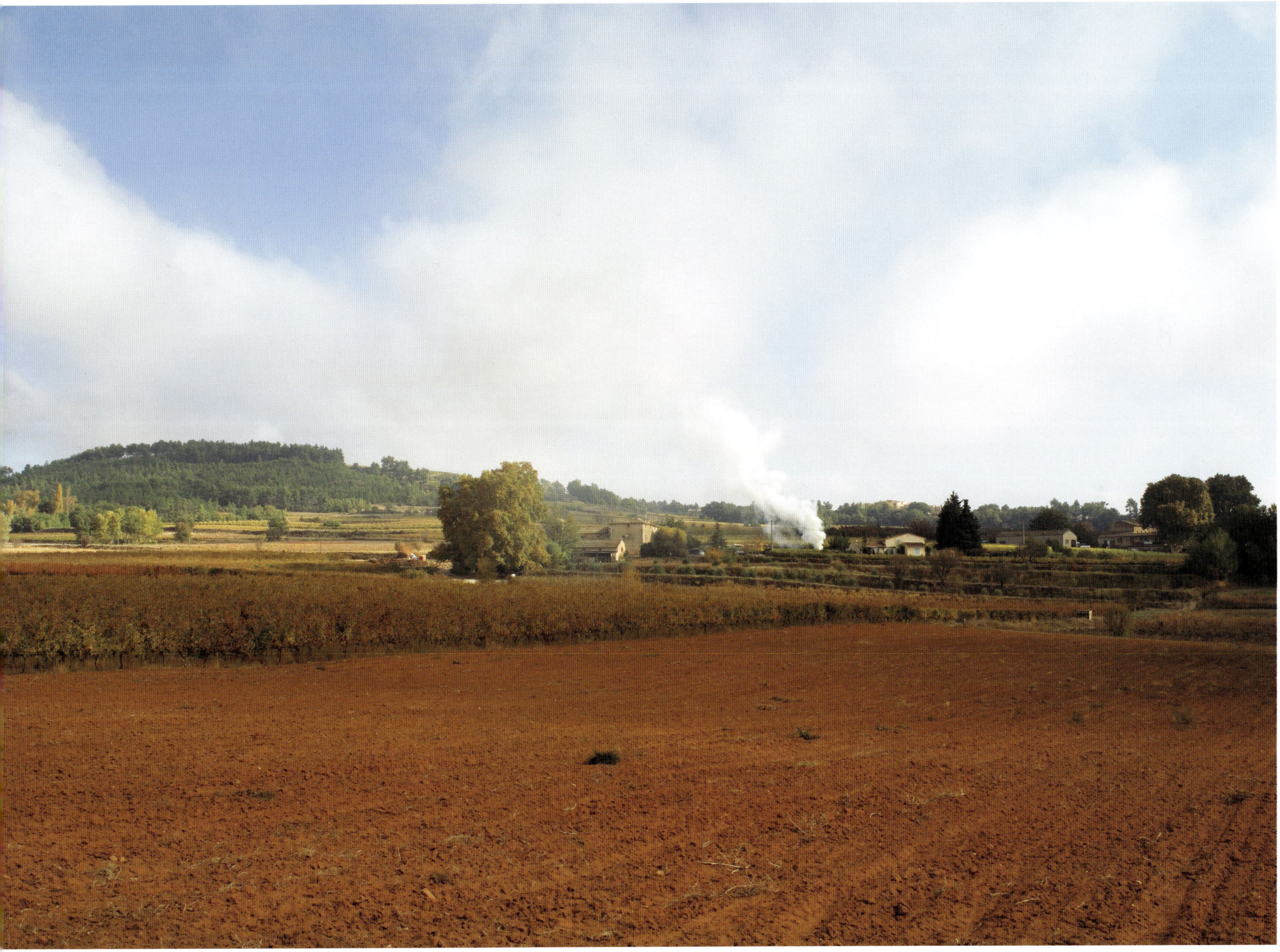

November

VIBRANT POPS AND SPLASHES OF ORANGE FOLIAGE AGAINST A SMOKE-GRAY SKY; THE ASSORTMENT OF REDS, browns, yellows, and greens of the grape vines are as varied as the wines themselves. The extraordinary sunlit canyons of Roussillon, their ochers and oranges stippled with boysenberry, the colors soaked by a day of pouring rain—colors so intense that they almost sear the retina. After a few minutes here, it feels as if the air itself is saturated with color. We, along with the few off-season tourists, are all aglow from the reflection and this glow takes on an almost spiritual aura, rendering us speechless.

A gorge we drove through a mere three days before was then a textured landscape of gray rock and green trees. Now, this same gorge is lit with the whole spectrum of color one associates with a New England fall, and yet here it seems even more remarkable. Not to diminish those vast sweeps of maples on fire, the sight of which takes your breath away. But here, the color seems even more intense because it isn't the entire landscape but, rather, individual trees and bushes standing out against the gray of cliff and sky, as if someone has chosen which of them should be torched.

The épée of Provencal light strikes once again, calling you to attention with its piercing stroke. One can see the call to impressionism and pointillism and, for me, Van Gogh is ever-present in the wind, which whips and whorls trees and foliage with twisted energy and garish color. And then there is the sadness inherent in late autumn, made more poignant by the contrast of the color against the slate sky—an urgent need to burn bright even as winter closes in.

These first few days of November remind us of the first few days here in March. Then, winter was loathe to leave, greeting us with a week of cold, wet days before making way for spring. Now it feels like winter is in a hurry to get here. The mistral is back and with it days of rain, sometimes in sheets that seep through the windows before trickling down the walls.

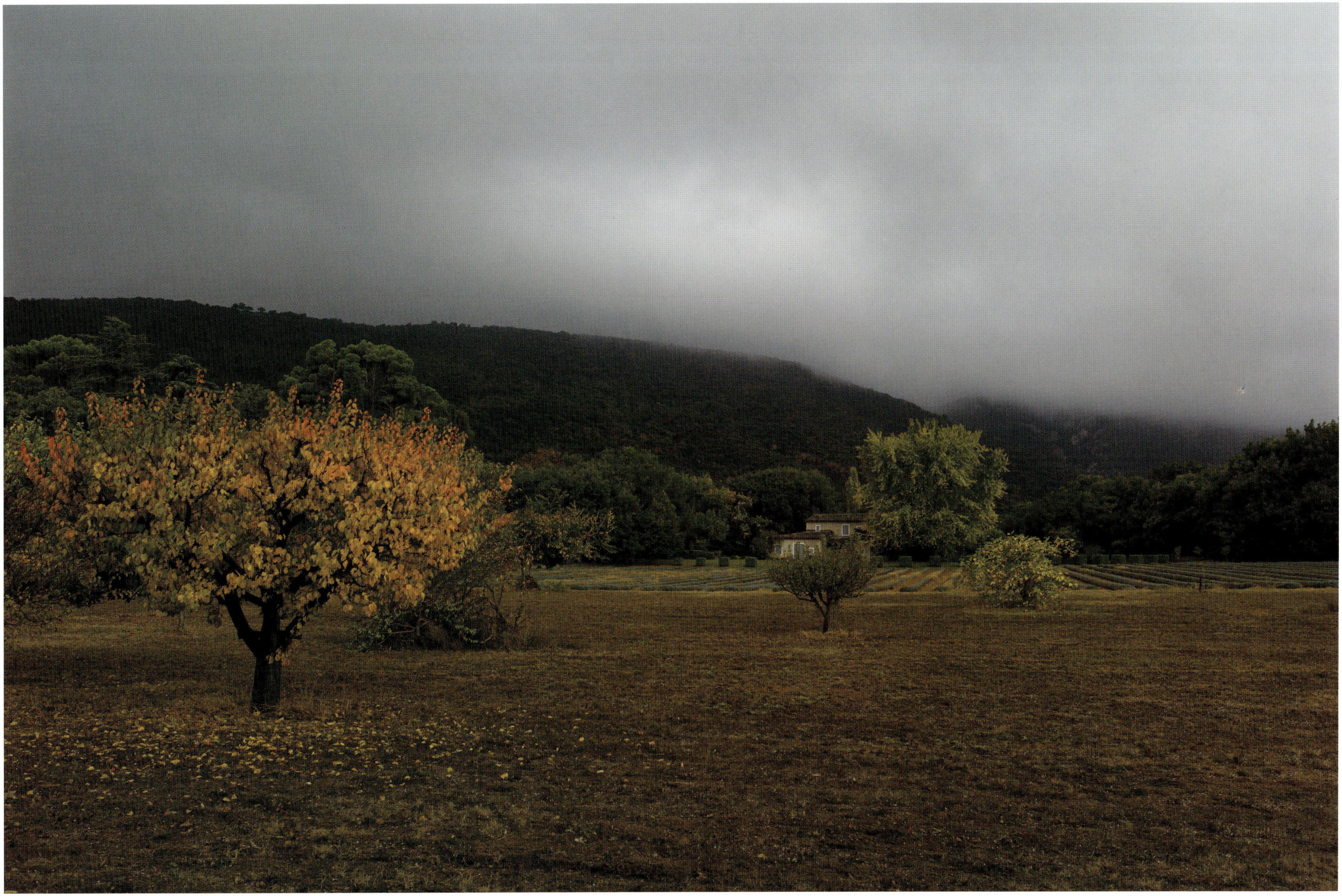

PLATE 113

IN THE VINEYARDS, WHOLE SWATHS ARE LIT BY A SUDDEN YELLOWING, WITH A VIBRANCY ONE ASSOCIATES with summer fields of mustard and sunflowers. It is as if the sun has fallen from the rain-soaked sky and spread itself on the earth in defiance. Yet winter will not be stayed. The poplars are already bereft of leaves, their whispery skeletons shivering in the wind.

In between rain showers we return to a series of allées Joel had captured in the spring when they were flaunting their new greenery. I watch him at play, looking for a break in the traffic then leaping into the middle of the road, turning this way and that, the camera and he inseparable, scanning, focusing, snapping. It's a joy to watch him in his element, where he, like all of us when we are "in" ourselves, becomes ageless.

We drive back roads in silence, soaking up this glorious land, alive to the gaiety of color, the madness of the mistral, the harsh rocks and gnarled trees, the insistence of nature and the endurance of humanity. Provence is tough in its beauty and one wonders at the centuries of backbreaking toil that made it possible, just barely, to survive here. We are in awe of the French spirit that fought its way through wars and famine and hard labor. You can feel how these souls have soaked into the land, much like the falling leaves.

Provence is both spiritual and pragmatic, and after these few months here we can feel both the celebration of the land and an understanding of life. The people here have a deeply ingrained acceptance of the temporary nature of existence, and as a result, live it to the hilt.

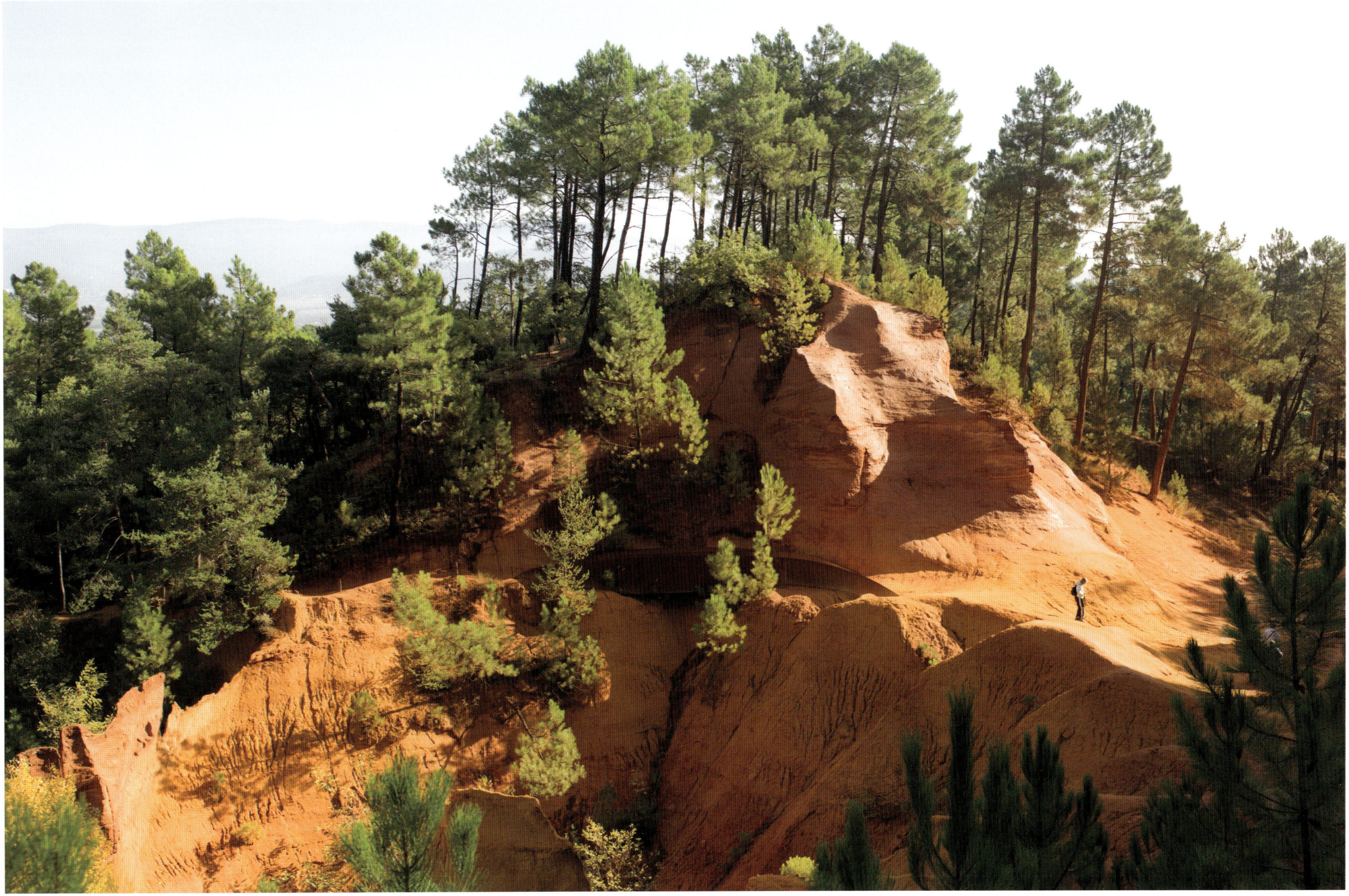

PLATE 114

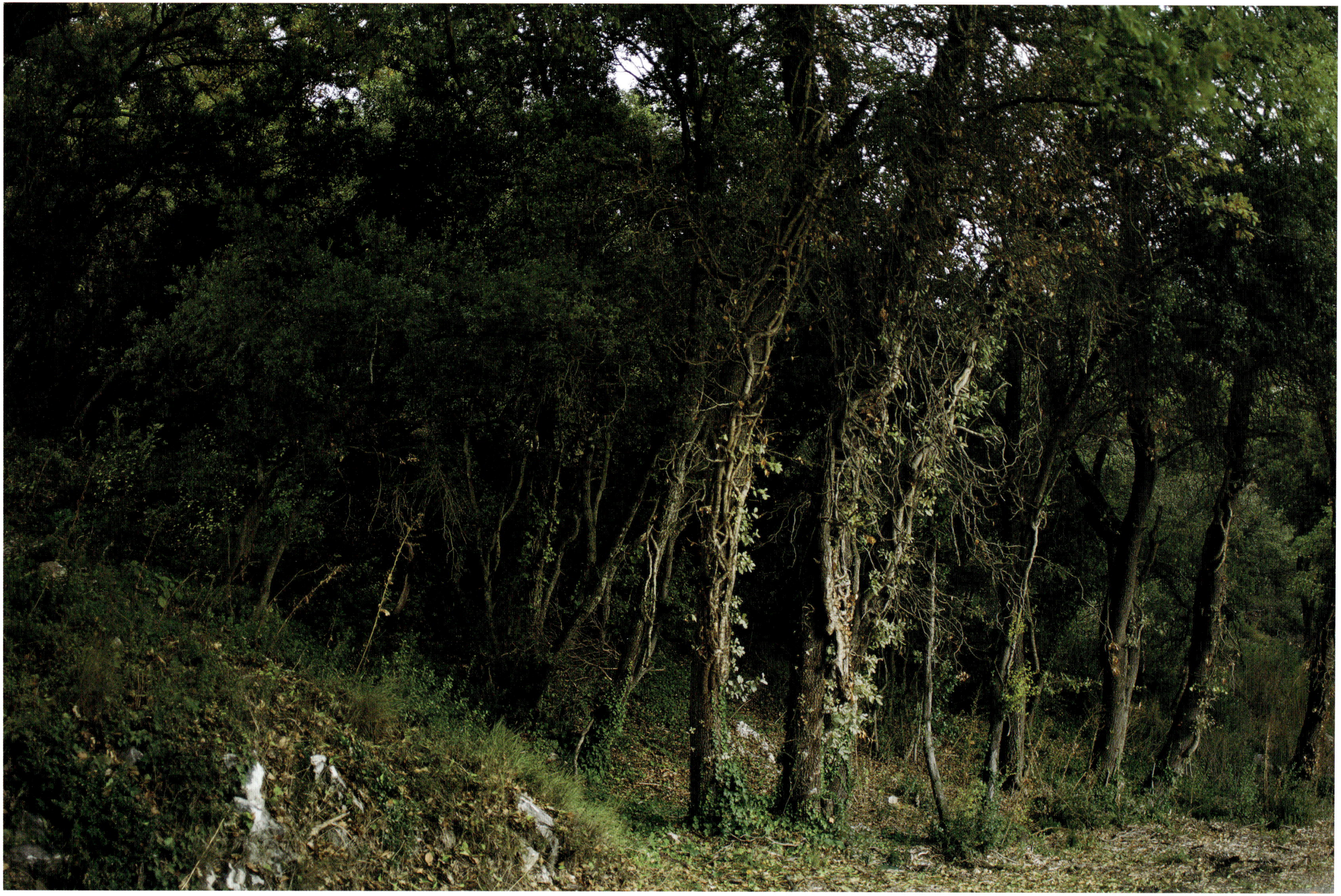

PLATE 115

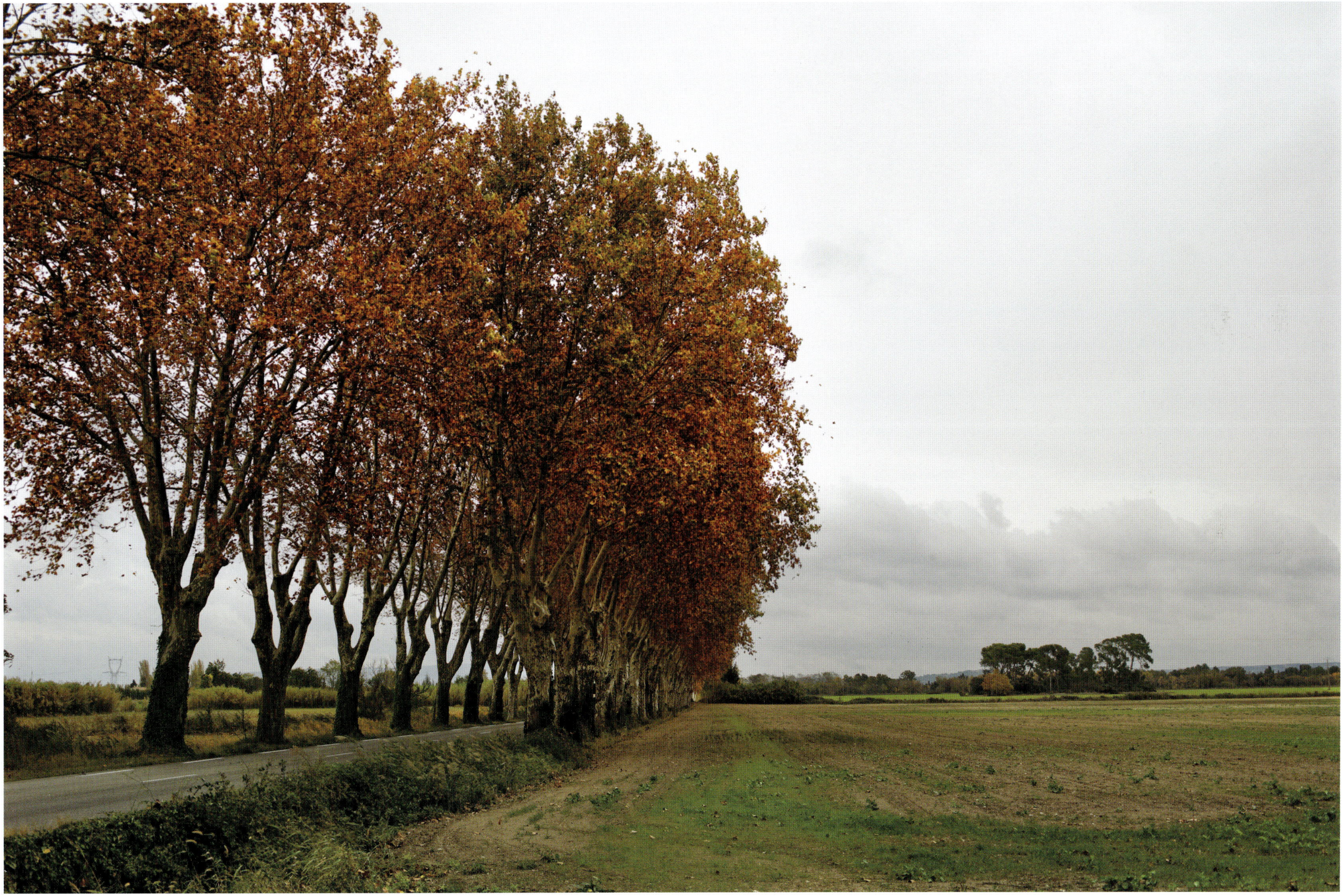

PLATE 116

PLATE 117

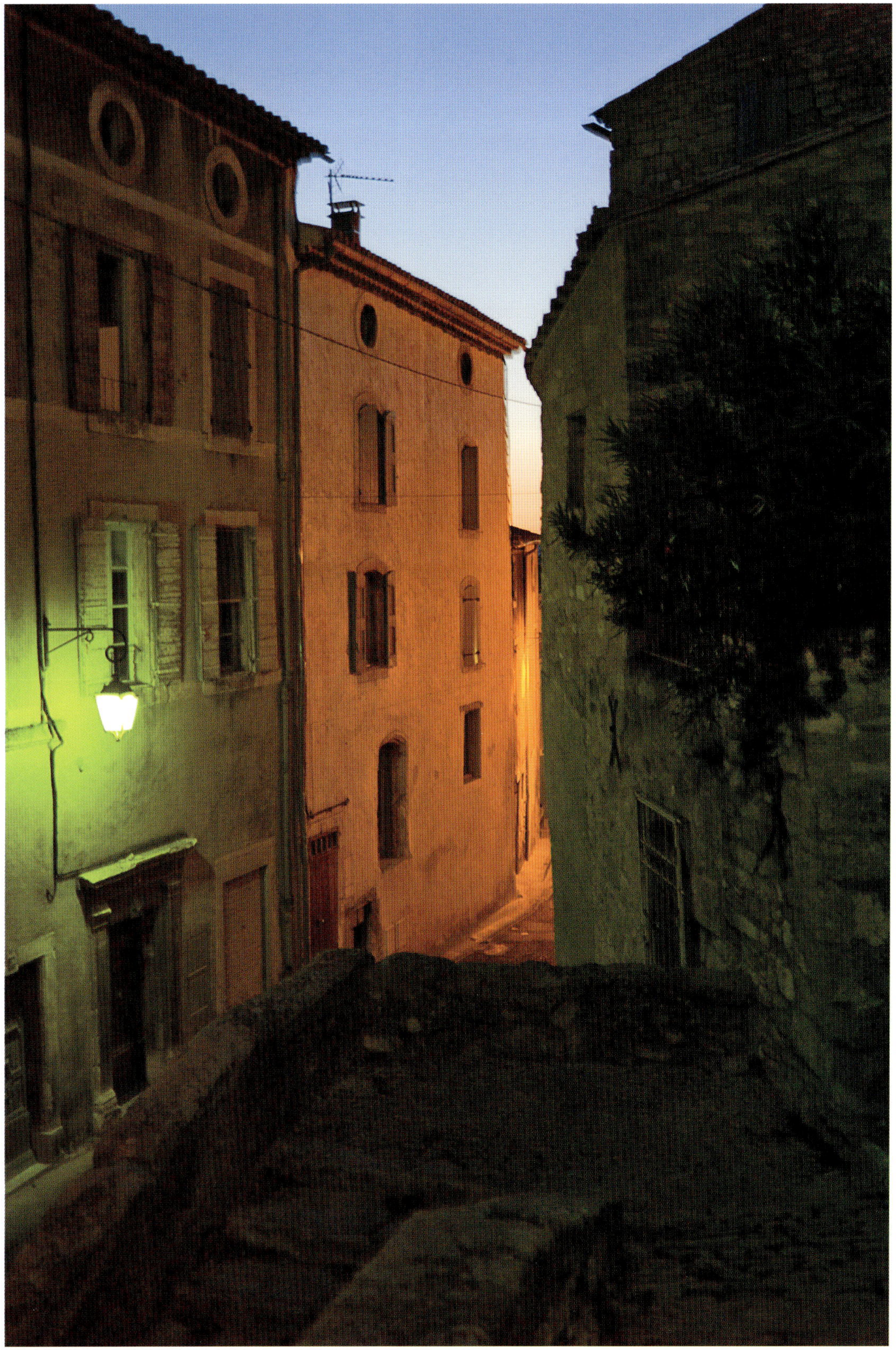

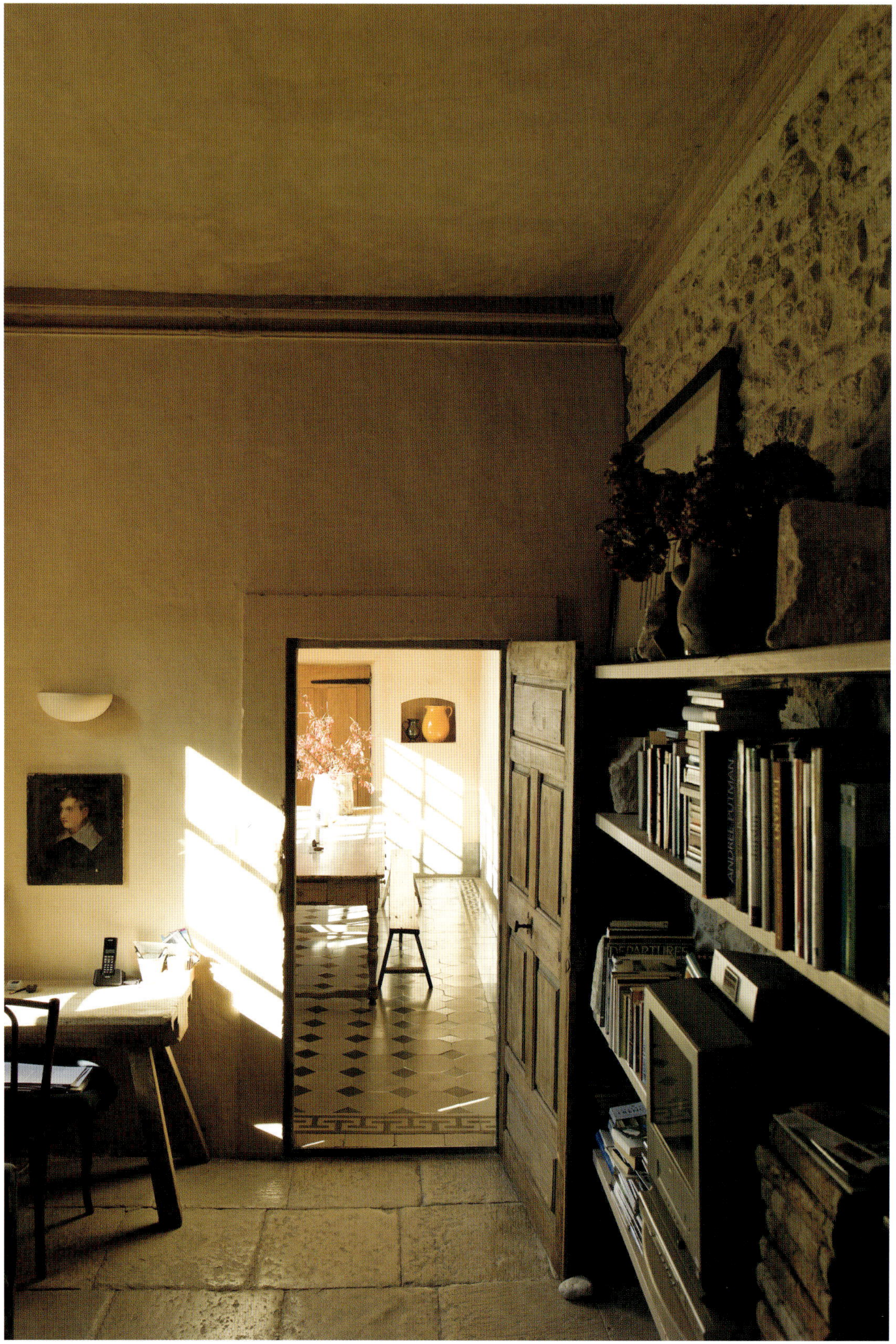

PLATE 118

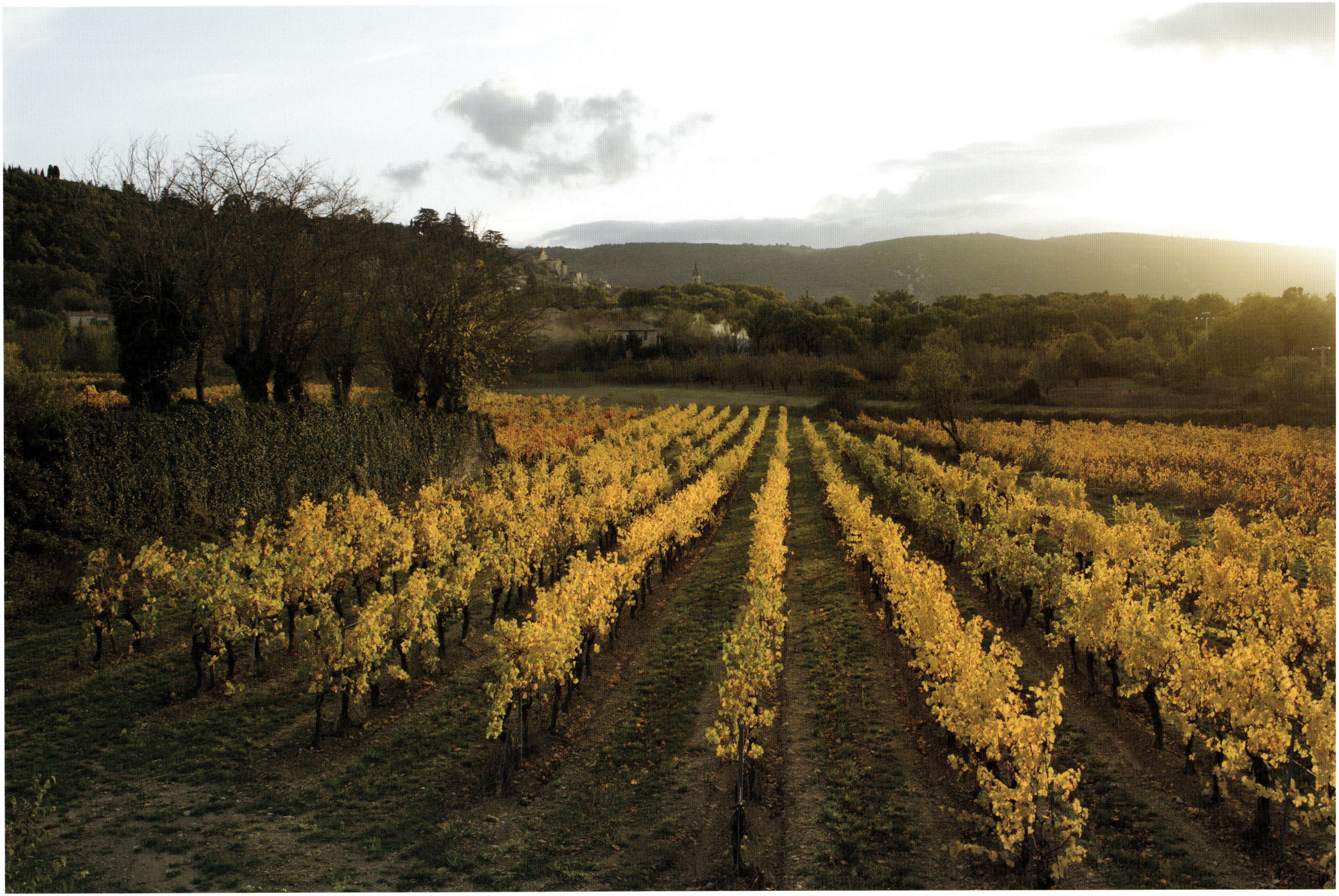

PLATE 119

PLATE 120 (OVERLEAF)

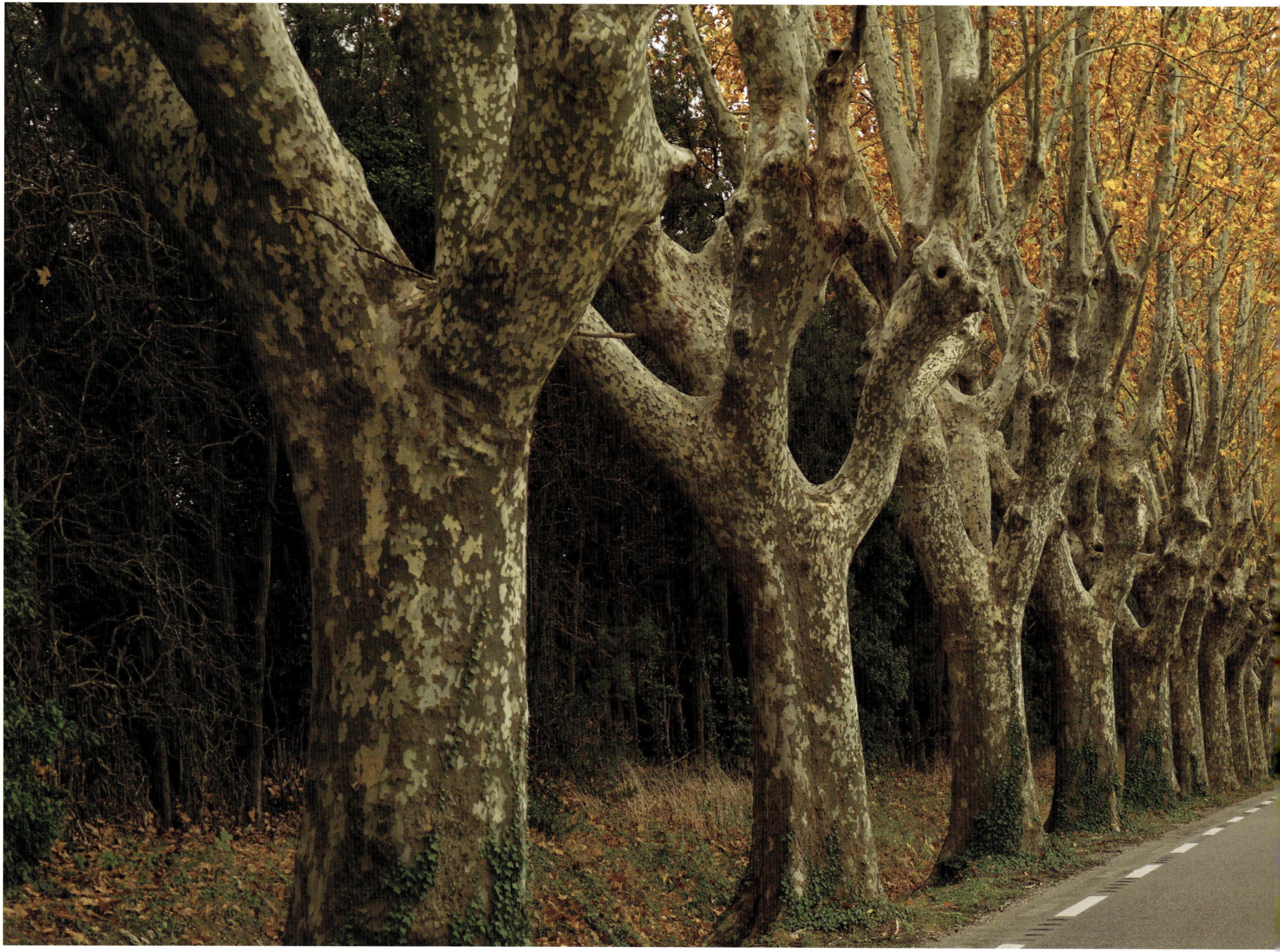

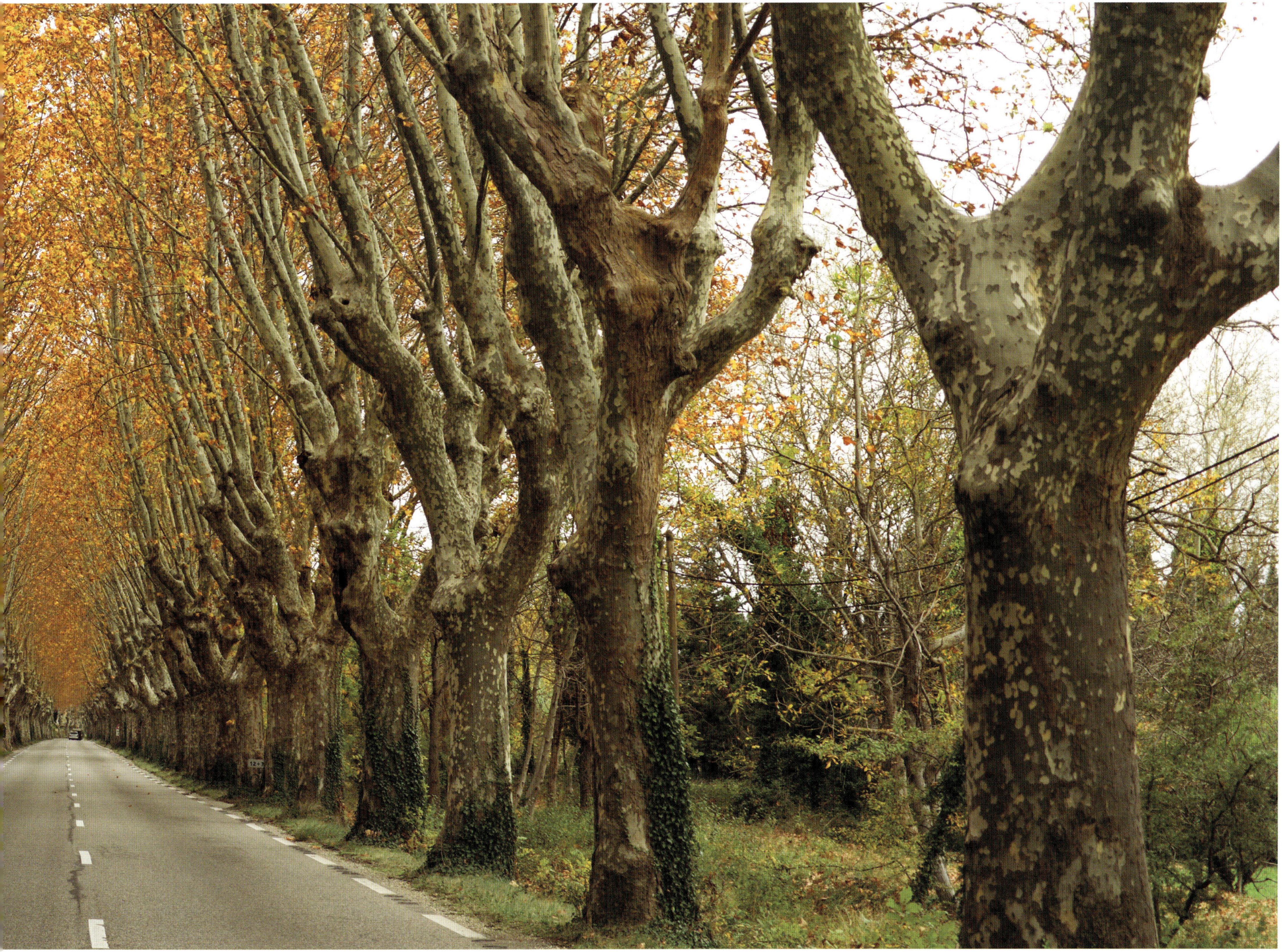

CODA

IT IS OUR LAST DAY HERE. WE GET OUR PACKING DONE EARLY SO WE CAN GO FOR OUR LAST MOSEY, STOPPING first at Les Trois Sources to say goodbye to Paul and Caro. Paul, great spirit that he is, and knowing Joel is in search of fire for his Elements series, has stacked a huge bonfire and with a single match sets it ablaze. In front of us the heat of the flames, behind us the heat of the sun. The air is still, the ground succulent from the rains. A persimmon tree, bare now of its leaves, stands almost comically laden with its satin orange fruit. I pick three juicy ones, which we will have for dessert with some *fromage*.

Then we drive over to Goult to see Patricia, our favorite goat-cheese lady. Her farm is out of a storybook: a stone farmhouse, chickens, two cats on a windowsill, two dogs all woof and wagging tails, and a horse just hanging out and munching grass, coming over for a nuzzle once in a while. We stand outside the cheese shed and watch Patricia's herd of goats being led by a neighboring lad across a field down to a stand of poplars to graze.

Patricia Mercier has been doing this for 25 years, 13 hours a day, with 10 days off a year to visit her children in Paris, from whence she originally hails. In peak season she makes two hundred artisanal cheeses a day, selling them each week at local farmer's markets and restaurants.

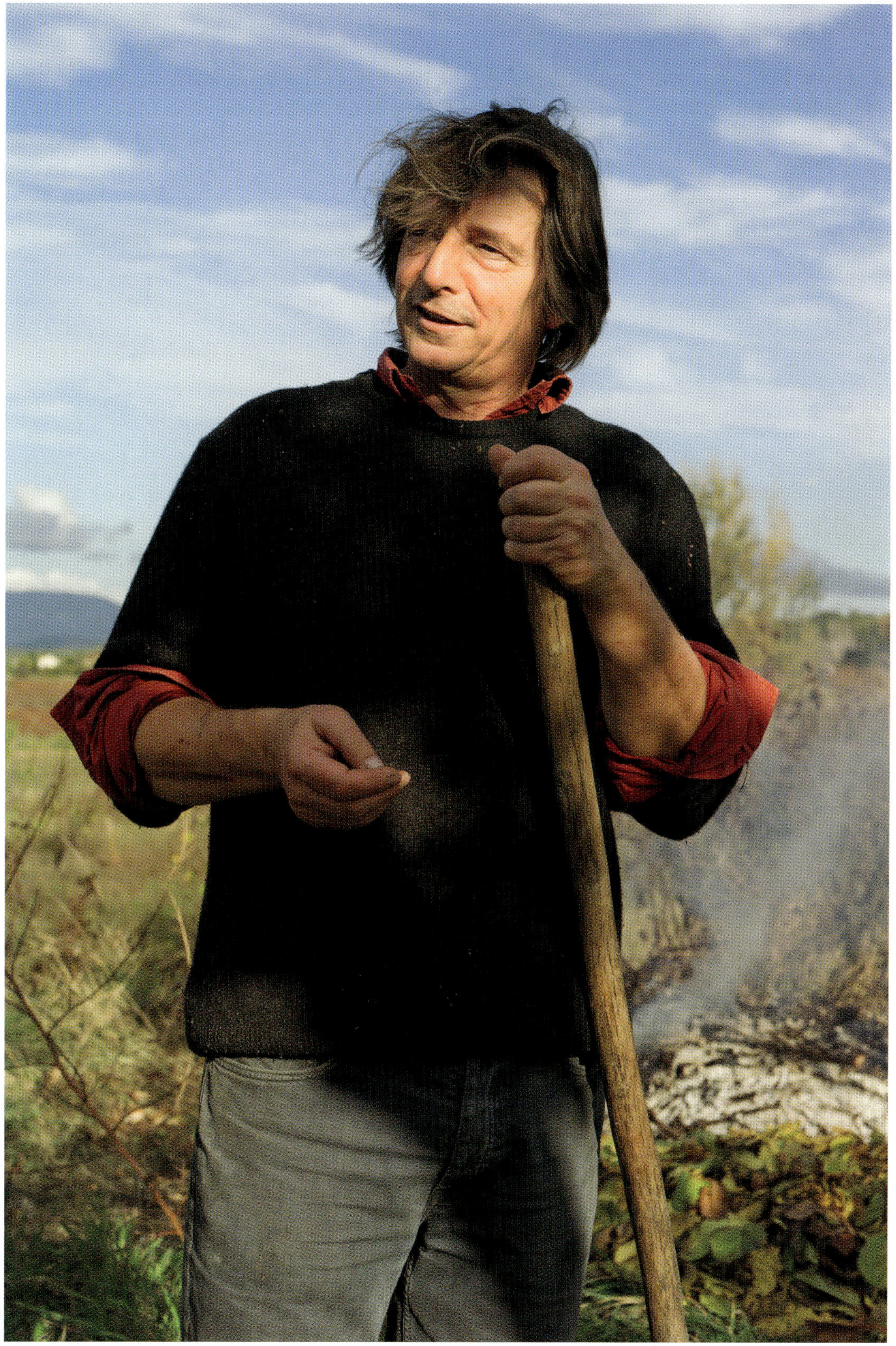

PLATE 121

PLATE 122

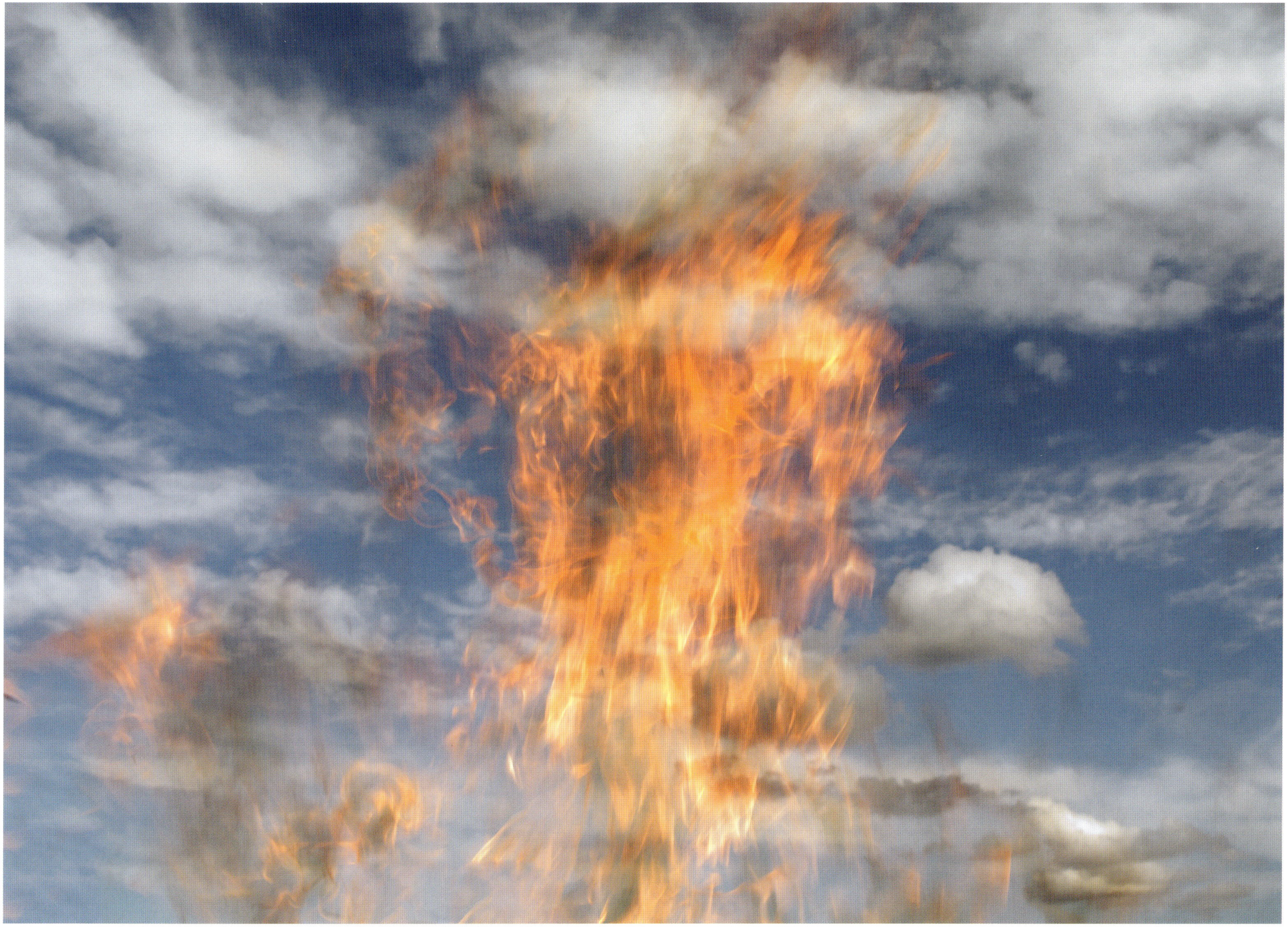

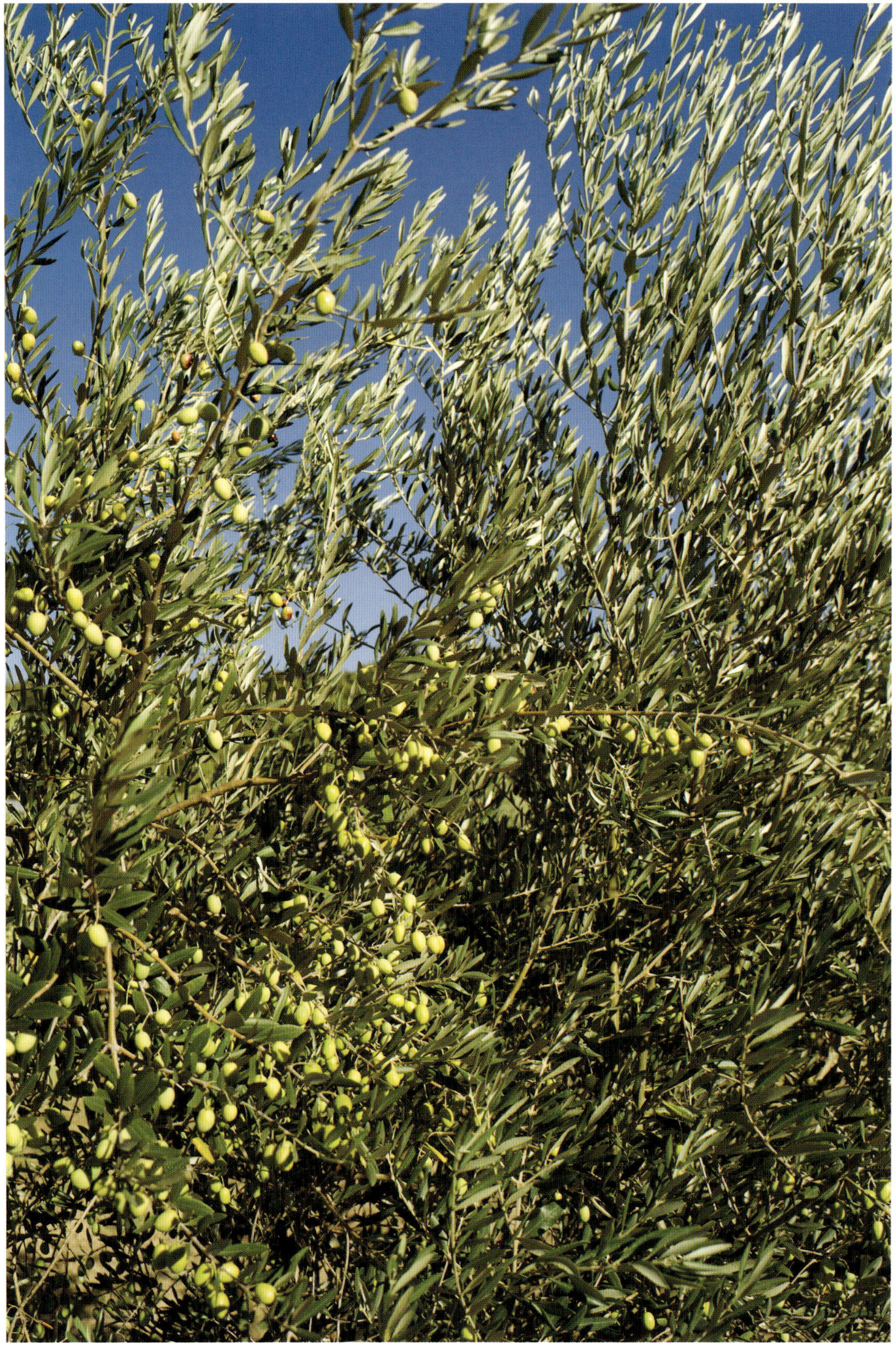

PLATE 123

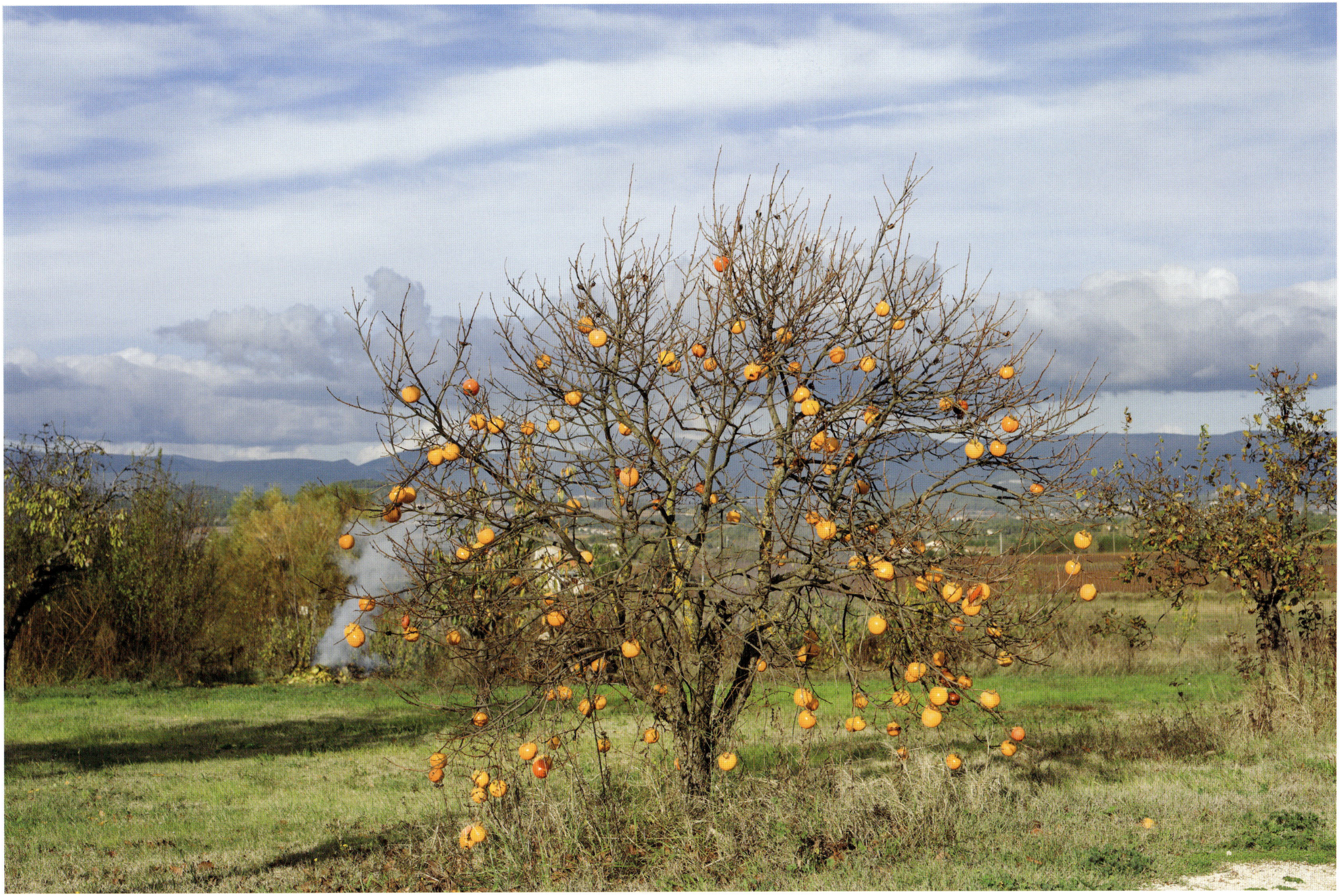

PLATE 124

PLATE 125 (OVERLEAF)

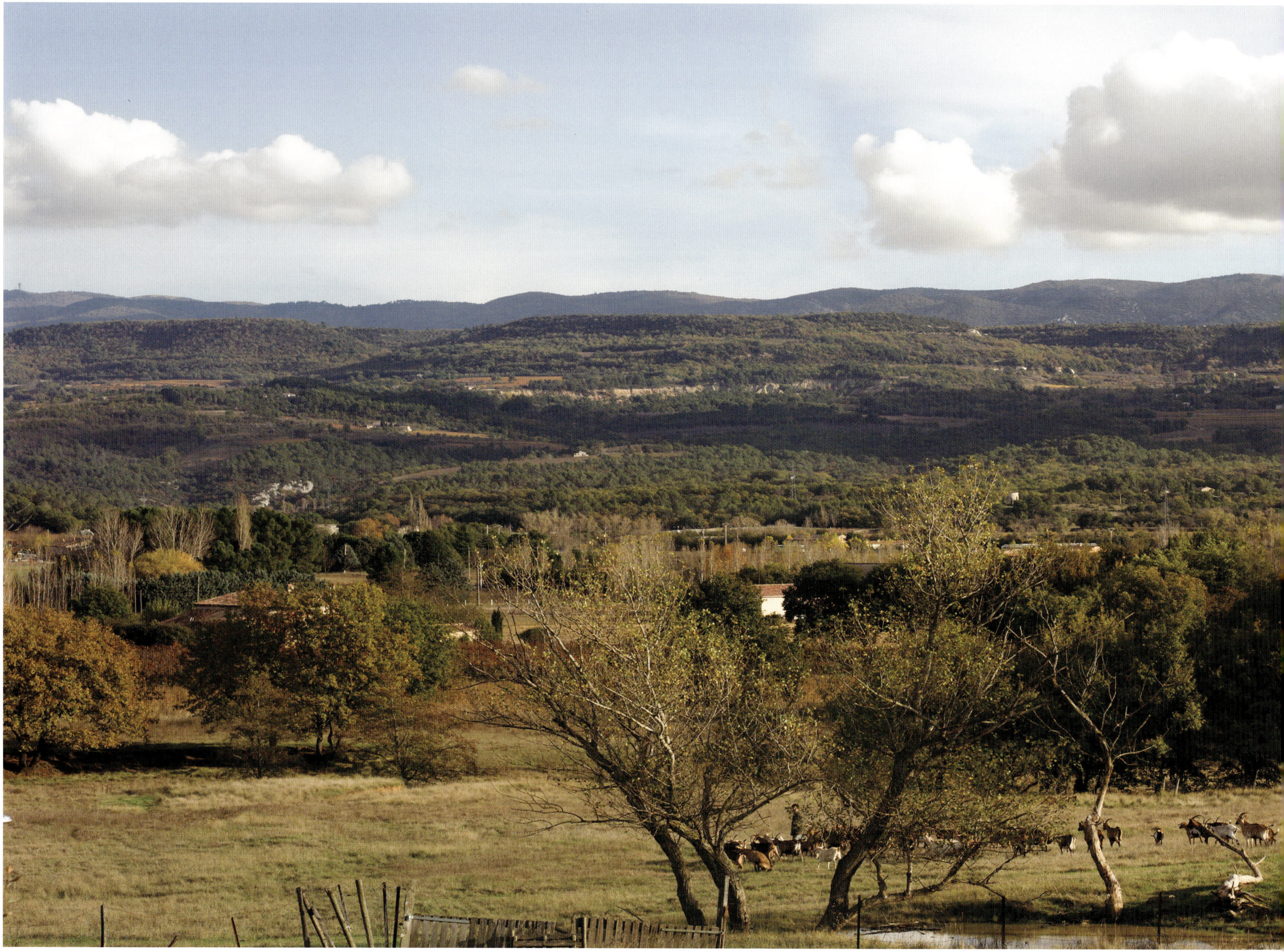

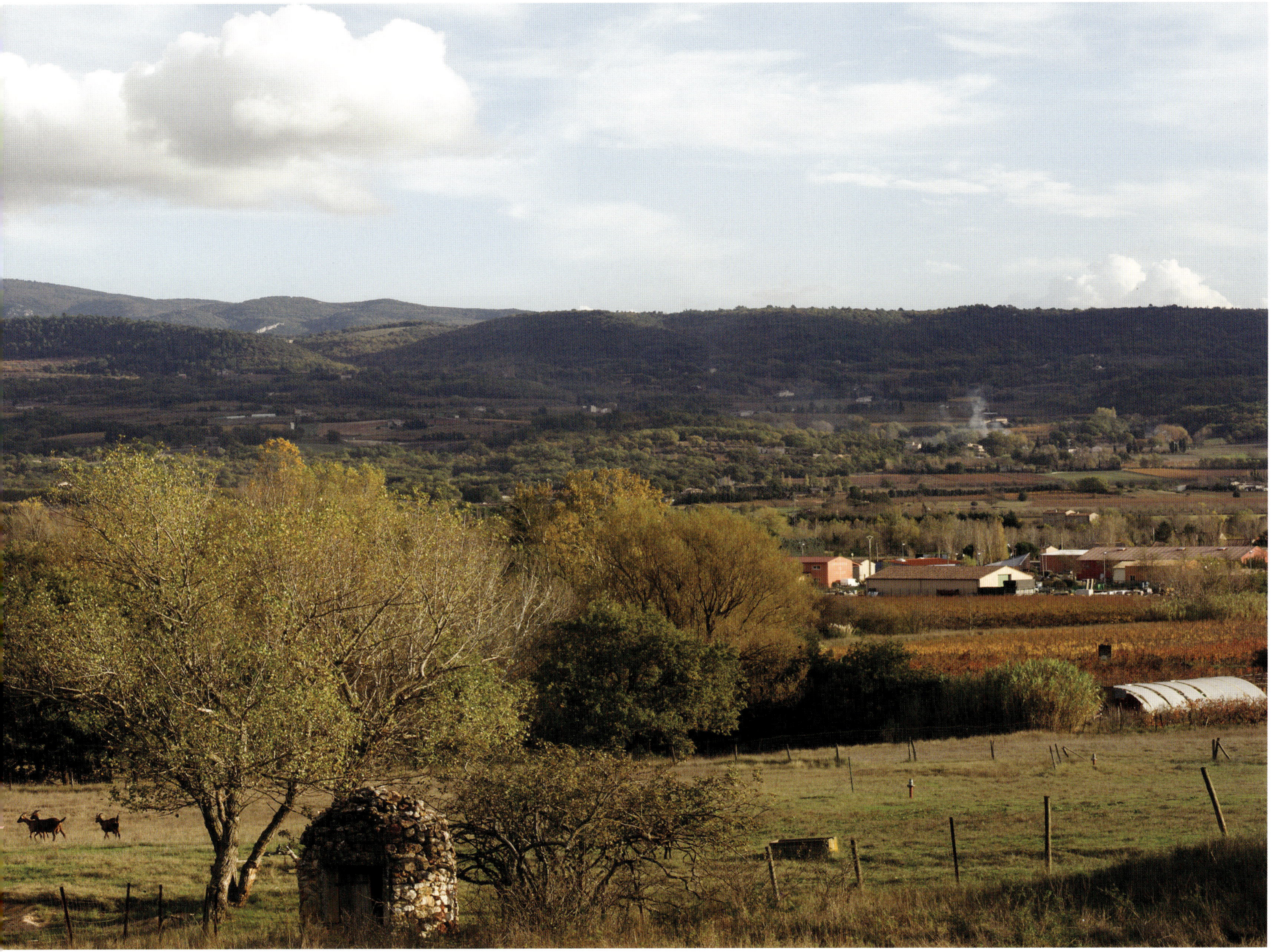

IT'S BEEN A BAD WEEK FOR CHEESE-MAKING. NUMEROUS DAYS OF RAIN, UNUSUAL FOR HERE, HAVE saturated the air with moisture, making her delicate cheese hard to set. We buy two lovely runny ones to accompany the persimmons and wistfully take our leave.

When it comes to the land here, we feel we've really taken it in. But now, just as we are leaving, we are being taken in by the people. We can imagine all the winter fireside meals we could have . . . but then, it's good to leave hungry for more.

The sun is going down now. This late autumn day, which had managed a couple of hours of summer warmth, is now turned toward the chill of a winter evening. The fields and vineyards sail by, bathing us one more time with their last hurrah of color. The sky, not to be outdone, has abandoned its blue tease and has gone to grays with hints of navy and lavender. Old houses, smoke curling from their chimneys, are almost too quaint to be real. It's true that other realities exist here, too. Down the road eight miles are the suburbs of Apt. Then again, once you've passed through them, you are in the medieval town.

And that's how it goes here, the ancient and the modern, the suburbs and the country. Yet the balance seems right. The Provençal people care too much about their hard-won culture, about their food, and about preservation, to let the scales tip in the wrong direction. You have to care this much to keep a good thing going, you have to love it and appreciate it enough to support each other in the endeavor to keep this way of life intact.

I don't see corporate greed steamrolling these people any time soon. After all, all they have to do is invite the suit in, sit him or her down at a table, and serve some good country food and wine—and watch Provence do its work.

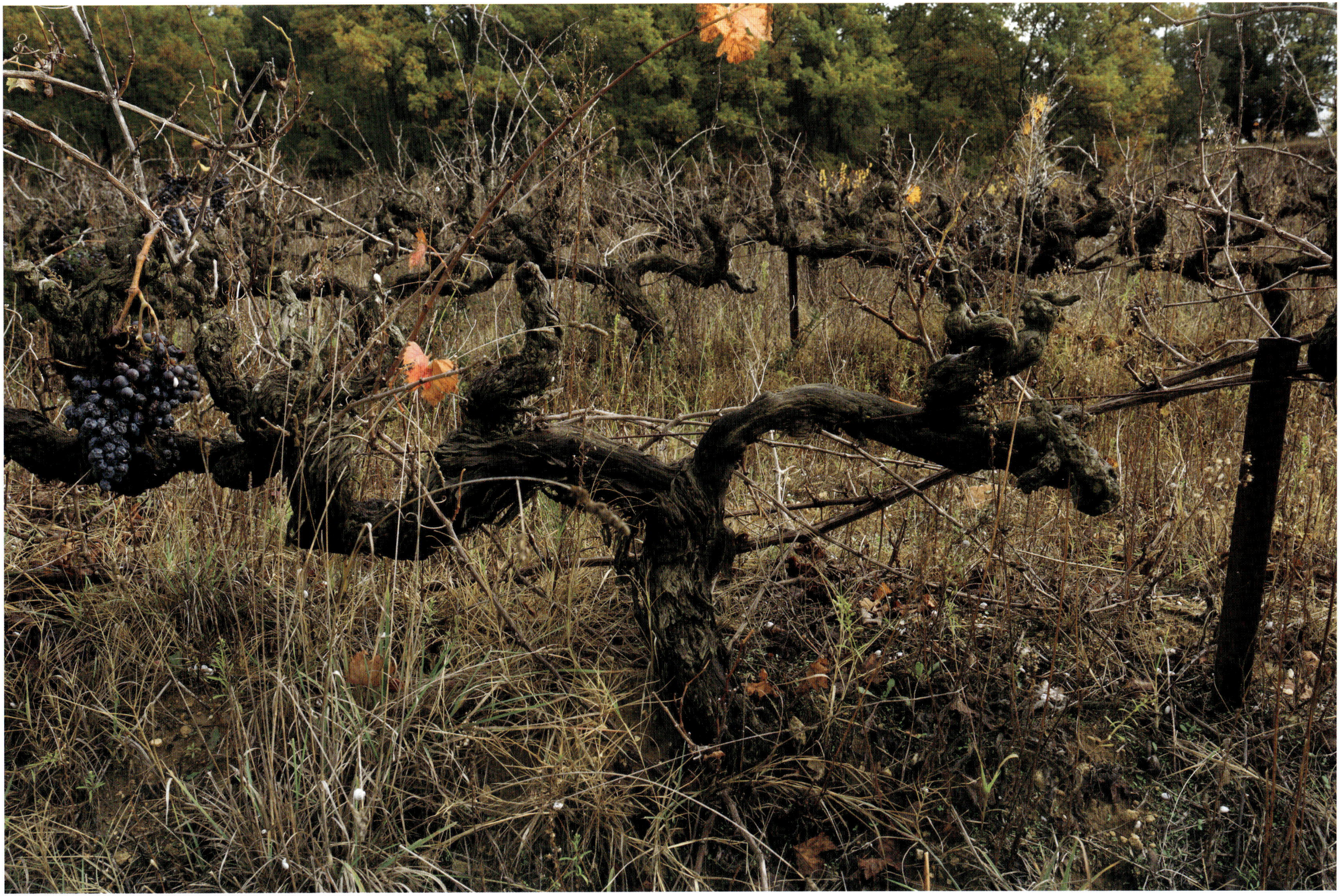

PLATE 126

PLATE 127

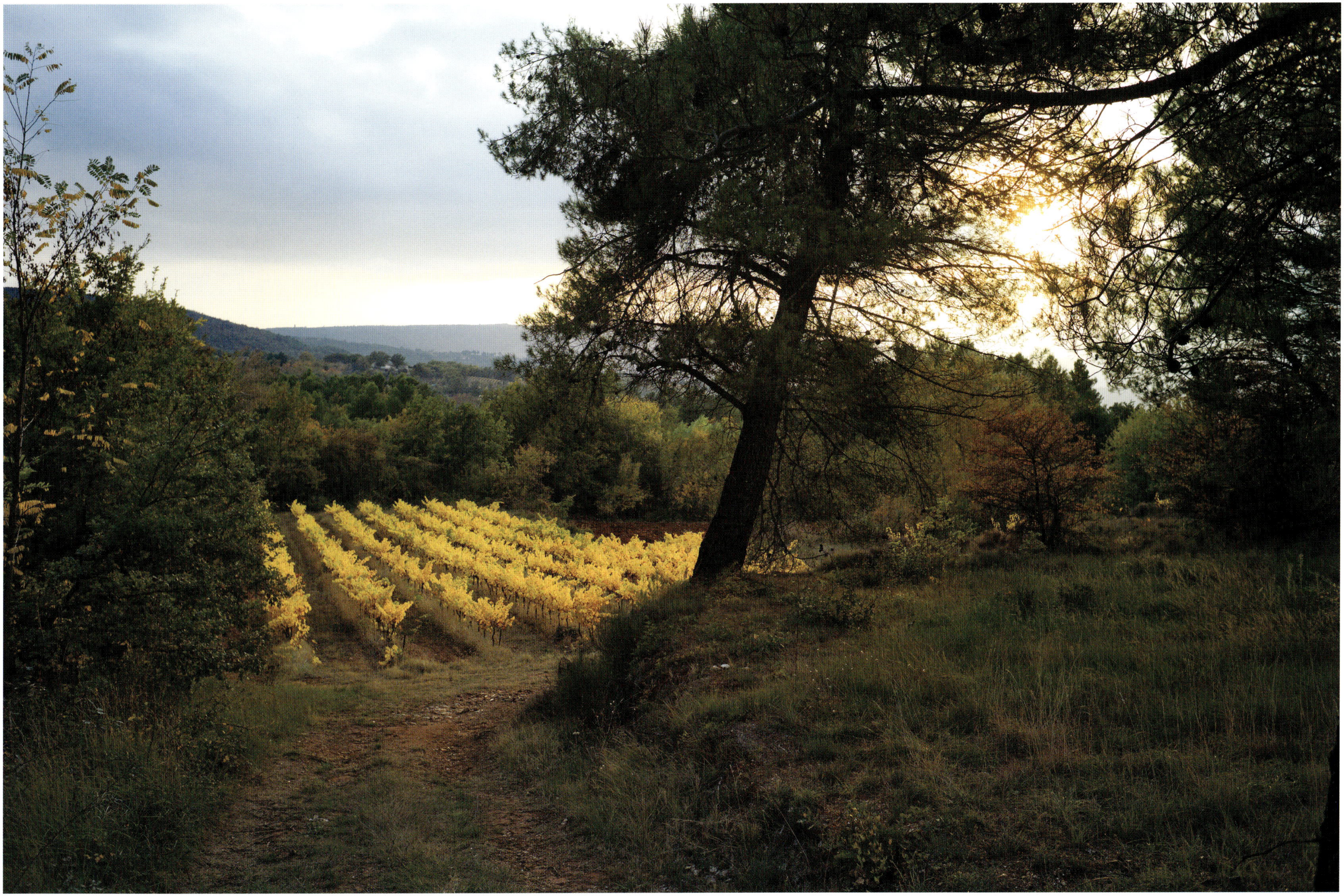

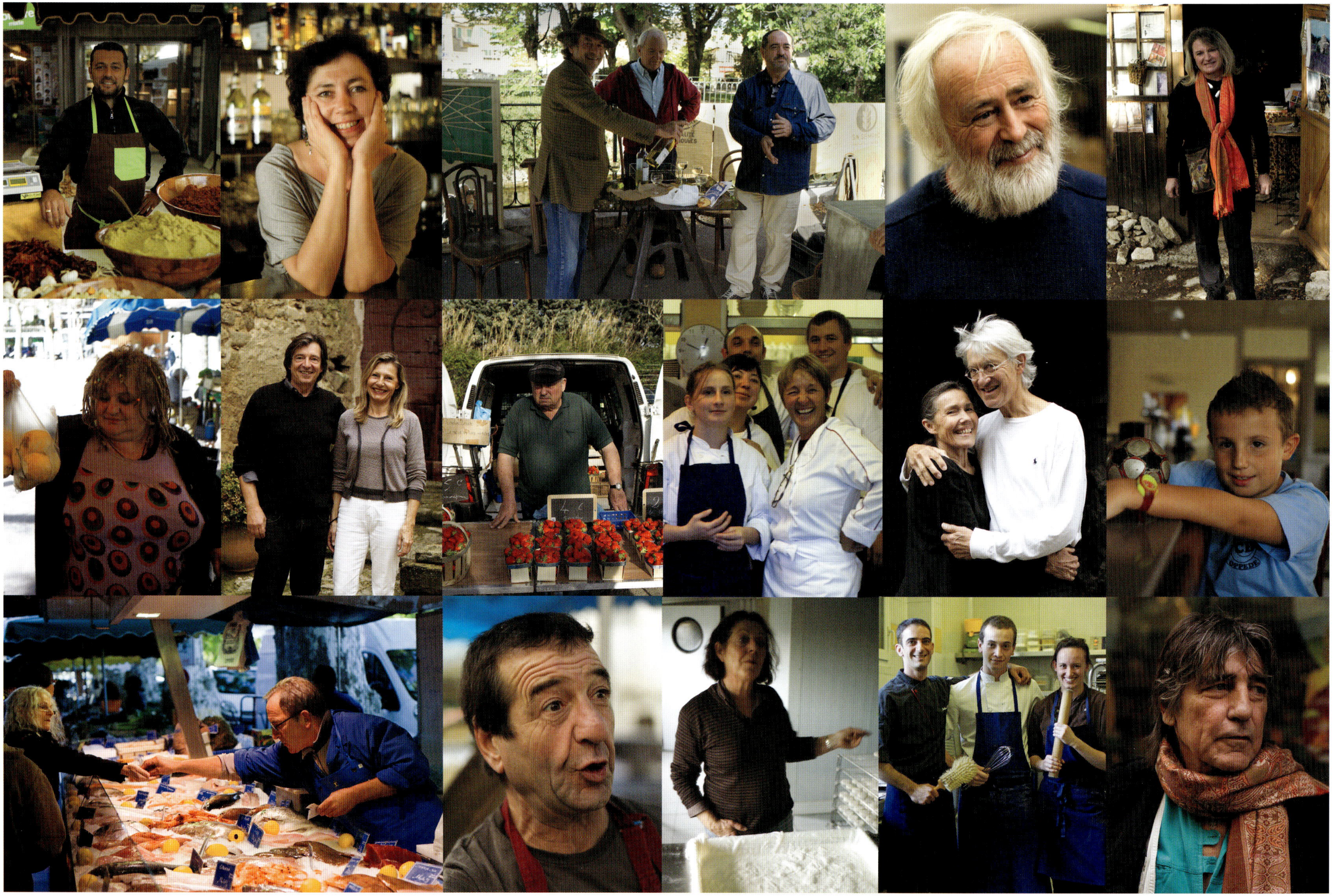

A LICENSE TO SEE

FOR FIFTY YEARS NOW, THE CAMERA HAS GIVEN ME A LICENSE TO SEE. I HAVE LEARNED TO ACCEPT THAT WHEREVER I FIND myself is an opportunity to be conscious and attentive, and the camera in my hand is the tool that connects me to what I see. So it was that in March of 2011 we arrived in Provence, sent there by Sterling Publishing to photograph and write about our experiences in a place unknown to both Maggie and me. It was daunting, at first, to think about the vast scale of Provence with its varied terrains, many cultures, and distinct regional character, and then to conceive of a method with which to approach this new and unfamiliar place.

But nature provides, in its own unpredictable way, a guide to being—if we just open ourselves to the suggestions it presents. That March, winter was drawing to a close and spring was already emerging from dormancy with the faintest traces of its green energy. Within a few days we both understood that we had an opportunity to live with, and watch, a season unfold. So simple an understanding! The kind of simplicity that makes one doubt one's reasoning. Was that it? Was this a method to trust enough to go forward on and make a book? I cannot now imagine a better way of being or beginning. To have the opportunity to simply watch a season unfold and take my cues from the smallest notes that the season plays is to engage in a dance with time, which is what we are all doing anyway.

From the perspective of a year later, I see that by slipping into the stream of the seasons we entered into a communion with what was there and thus witnessed the primeval powers of nature in Provence; we were shown the subtle differences—a matter of merely a degree or two on the globe—that makes one region distinctly different from another. I can say now that nature itself was alive to me during the seasons we spent there, and it made me see in a way that I never fully understood before—and has now directed me toward a simpler way of looking at the world.

As you can see from the photographs reproduced here, there is nothing grand or monumental: no cathedrals, palaces, or touristic showpieces, but rather the most ordinary turns in the road, street corners in twilight or rain, ancient dwellings, wild bits of nature tossed by the wind or lying in benign neglect, and always the light—seasonal sunlight picking its way through the undifferentiated density of nature or illuminating the ordered rows of a vineyard. In all cases, what I am saying is simply this: stop for a moment in your travels and take a good look at where you are, let it, this place you have been called to stop at, show you its mystery, its ordinary secret; and, by a steady accumulation of these moments, you will discover a deeper connection to yourself.

VERY SPECIAL THANKS NEED TO BE GIVEN HERE TO LEICA CAMERA. ALL THE WORK IN THE BOOK WAS MADE WITH THE NEW S2, medium-format, Digital Leica, which was loaned to me by Leica's managing director, Andreas Kaufmann, and supported by his New York team of Christian Erhardt, Jim Wagner, Kelsey Fain, and Justin Stailey. This remarkable new camera made the economics of doing the book possible, but more importantly the extraordinary quality and reliable function of the equipment were a measure of great security and freedom to me, and gave to this book that unmistakable Leica clarity.

—JOEL MEYEROWITZ

LIST OF PLATES

ACKNOWLEDGMENTS

This page is always one of our favorites in any book. It is a reminder that we all owe a part of any journey we undertake to those willing to offer assistance along the way. And so it is that friends and strangers alike helped make this journey and this book not only possible but richer. Our gratitude and thanks to Agathe Amzallag, who found us our first home in Provence, and to Josje Van Huffel for lending it to us. To Paula Rubenstein (Paula Rubenstein Ltd., NYC) who collects rare people as well as rare objects, our thanks for introducing us to Paul and Sharon (marstonhouse.com), new friends who fit like old slippers. To Paul and Sharon, for lending us their exquisite apartment in Bonnieux and for introducing us to Caroline and Paul, to whom we give thanks for their generosity and guidance—not to mention the pleasure of staying in their B&B, Les Trois Sources. To Ember Rilleau, director supreme of Joel's studio, without whose hard work and loyalty this book, and much else in our lives, would not have been possible. Our thanks also to our interns: Ilona Szwarc, Eli Durst, Mark Townsend, Jonny Abraham, and Frank Kearl. Thanks must be given to Stephen Briscoe of Seascape Realty in Provincetown, in whose loving and capable hands we placed the sale of our little cottage by the sea, making it possible to walk away and give ourselves over to the discovery of Provence. To designer Jeff Batzli, for his great eye and enthusiasm for the work. To Barbara Berger, Maggie's editor, for her light touch and exquisite suggestions. And finally, to Michael Fragnito and Barbara Berger of Sterling Publishing, for their vision and generosity in an era in publishing when these qualities are hard to find. You gave us the gift of a lifetime in a time in our lives when letting go of the known and leaping into the unknown deepened our creativity and our love.

Sterling Signature
NEW YORK

An Imprint of Sterling Publishing
387 Park Avenue South
New York, NY 10016

STERLING SIGNATURE and the distinctive Sterling Signature logo are registered trademarks of Sterling Publishing Co., Inc.

Design by Jeff Batzli

ISBN 978-1-4027-9024-9

Library of Congress Cataloging-in-Publication Data

Meyerowitz, Joel, 1938-
Provence : lasting impressions / photography by Joel Meyerowitz ; text by Maggie Barrett.
p. cm.
ISBN 978-1-4027-9024-9 (hardcover)
1. Provence (France)--Pictorial works. 2. Seasons--France--Provence--Pictorial works. 3. Provence (France)--Description and travel. I. Barrett, Maggie. II. Title.
DC611.P958M382 2012
914.490022'2--dc23
2012005756

Distributed in Canada by Sterling Publishing
c/o Canadian Manda Group, 165 Dufferin Street
Toronto, Ontario, Canada M6K 3H6
Distributed in the United Kingdom by GMC Distribution Services
Castle Place, 166 High Street, Lewes, East Sussex, England BN7 1XU
Distributed in Australia by Capricorn Link (Australia) Pty. Ltd.
P.O. Box 704, Windsor, NSW 2756, Australia

For information about custom editions, special sales, and premium and corporate purchases, please contact Sterling Special Sales at 800-805-5489 or specialsales@sterlingpublishing.com.

Manufactured in China

10 9 8 7 6 5 4 3 2 1

www.sterlingpublishing.com

A Note on the Fine Art Print

The vellum envelope at the back of Provence contains a fine art print of *Girl in the red dress, Saint-Jeannet*. The enclosed print is reproduced on 200 gsm Garda Pat 13 Kiara paper, and is printed stochastically by 1010 Printing International Ltd., in China. *Girl in the red dress, Saint-Jeannet* is also reproduced on Plate 54 of this book, in the Winter/Spring chapter.

A Note on the Production

Provence is composed largely in the font known as Frutiger, a Humanist sans serif designed by noted Swiss type designer Adrian Frutiger in 1975. He originally designed it for use in signage at Charles de Gaulle International Airport at Roissy, France. The Frutiger family was released publicly in 1976, by the Stempel type foundry, in conjunction with Linotype. Frutiger is known for its simple, clean lines, as well as its legibility, modernity, and approachability, making it popular in books, magazines, and advertising. *Provence* is printed on 157 gsm Lumi matte art paper. Printed and bound by 1010 Printing International Ltd., in China.